PENGUIN CANADA

IN DEFENSE OF ATHEISM

MICHEL ONFRAY was born in 1959. He is
the author of over thirty books. A high-
school philosophy teacher for twenty years,
he resigned from the state education sector
and in 2002 set up the Popular University
of Caen. He divides his time between
Normandy and Paris.

IN DEFENSE OF ATHEISM

The Case Against Christianity,
Judaism and Islam

Michel Onfray

Translated from the French by Jeremy Leggatt

PENGUIN
CANADA

PENGUIN CANADA

Published by the Penguin Group

Penguin Group (Canada), 90 Eglinton Avenue East, Suite 700, Toronto, Ontario, Canada M4P 2Y3
(a division of Pearson Canada Inc.)

Penguin Group (USA) Inc., 375 Hudson Street, New York, New York 10014, U.S.A.
Penguin Books Ltd, 80 Strand, London WC2R 0RL, England
Penguin Ireland, 25 St Stephen's Green, Dublin 2, Ireland (a division of Penguin Books Ltd)
Penguin Group (Australia), 250 Camberwell Road, Camberwell, Victoria 3124, Australia
(a division of Pearson Australia Group Pty Ltd)
Penguin Books India Pvt Ltd, 11 Community Centre, Panchsheel Park, New Delhi – 110 017, India
Penguin Group (NZ), 67 Apollo Drive, Rosedale, North Shore 0632, New Zealand
(a division of Pearson New Zealand Ltd)
Penguin Books (South Africa) (Pty) Ltd, 24 Sturdee Avenue, Rosebank, Johannesburg 2196,
South Africa

Penguin Books Ltd, Registered Offices: 80 Strand, London WC2R 0RL, England

First published in France in 2005 by Éditions Grasset & Fasquelle.
English-language translation published in Viking Canada hardcover by Penguin Group (Canada),
a division of Pearson Canada Inc., 2007. Simultaneously published in the U.S.A.
by Arcade Publishing, Inc., New York.
Published in this edition, 2008

1 2 3 4 5 6 7 8 9 10   (WEB)

Manufactured in Canada.

LIBRARY AND ARCHIVES CANADA CATALOGUING IN PUBLICATION

Onfray, Michel, 1959–
In defense of atheism : the case against Christianity, Judaism and Islam /
Michel Onfray ; translated from the French by Jeremy Leggatt.

Translation of: Traité d'athéologie.
Includes bibliographical references.
ISBN 978-0-14-305057-5

1. Atheism. 2. Religion—Controversial literature. 3. Monotheism—Controversial literature.
I. Leggatt, Jeremy II. Title.

BL2747.3.O5413 2008   211'.8   C2007-906619-4

ISBN-13: 978-0-14-305057-5
ISBN-10: 0-14-305057-5

Visit the Penguin Group (Canada) website at **www.penguin.ca**

Special and corporate bulk purchase rates available; please see
www.penguin.ca/corporatesales or call 1-800-810-3104, ext. 477 or 474

The concept of "God" invented as a counter-concept of life — everything harmful, poisonous, slanderous, the whole hostility unto death against life synthesized in this concept in a gruesome unity! The concept of the "beyond," the "true world" invented in order to devaluate the only world there is — in order to retain no goal, no reason, no task for our earthly reality! The concept of the "soul," the "spirit," finally even "immortal soul," invented in order to despise the body, to make it sick — "holy"; to oppose with a ghastly levity everything that deserves to be taken seriously in life, the questions of nourishment, abode, spiritual diet, treatment of the sick, cleanliness, and weather! In place of health, the "salvation of the soul" — that is, a *folie circulaire* [manic-depressive insanity] between penitential convulsions and hysteria about redemption! The concept of "sin" invented along with the torture instrument that belongs with it, the concept of "free will," in order to confuse the instincts, to make mistrust of the instincts second nature!

— Nietzsche, *Ecce Homo*

Contents

CONTENTS

Part Two: Monotheisms

Part Three: Christianity

CONTENTS

CONTENTS

Preface

1

Desert memory. After a few hours on the trail in the Mauritanian desert, I saw an old herdsman traveling with his family. His young wife and his mother-in-law rode camels; his sons and daughter were on donkeys. The group carried with them everything essential to survival — and therefore to life. The sight of them gave me the impression that I had encountered a contemporary of Muhammad. Burning white sky, scattered, scorched trees, uprooted thorn bushes blown by the desert wind across unending vistas of orange sand . . . the spectacle evoked the geographical and psychological background of the Koran, in the turbulent period of camel caravans, nomad encampments, and clashing desert tribes.

I thought of the lands of Israel, Judaea and Samaria, of Jerusalem and Bethlehem, of Nazareth and the Sea of Galilee. Places where the sun bakes men's heads, desiccates their bodies, afflicts their souls with thirst. Places that generate a yearning for oases where water flows cool, clear and free, where the air is balmy and fragrant, where food and drink are abundant. The afterlife suddenly struck me as a counterworld invented by men exhausted and parched by their ceaseless wanderings across the dunes or up and down rocky trails baked to white heat. Monotheism was born of the sand.

It was nighttime at Ouedane, east of Chinguetti, where I had traveled to see the Islamic libraries long buried in the sand. Even today, sand dunes are patiently but inexorably swallowing up whole villages. Abduramane, our driver, unrolled his prayer mat under the stars in the courtyard of the house where we were staying. I was quartered in a small room with a makeshift mattress. As the full moon shone on Abduramane's black skin, the blue-gray light caused his flesh to appear purple. Slowly, as though impelled by the ancestral movements of the planet, he knelt, lowered his forehead to the ground, and prayed. Light from dead stars reached down to us in the hot desert night. I felt that I was witnessing a primitive ritual, similar to humankind's earliest act of worship. As we continued our journey next day, I talked with Abduramane about his religion. Surprised that a westerner, a white man, was interested in Islam, he challenged every assertion I made. I had just read the Koran, pen in hand, and I had memorized several passages word for word. But his unquestioning faith led him to deny that any verses in his holy book were contrary to basic Islamic principles of goodness, tolerance, generosity, and peace. Holy war? Proclamation of jihad against unbelievers? A fatwa issued for the execution of an author? State-of-the-art terrorism? Madmen did those things, certainly not Muslims . . .

Abduramane did not like it. There I was, a non-Muslim, reading the Koran and pointing out that, despite the many chapters that comforted him and supported his beliefs, there were just as many verses in the same book that justified armed fighters wearing the green banner of martyrdom, Hezbollah terrorists wrapped with explosives, the Ayatollah Khomeini condemning Salman Rushdie to death, the kamikaze attackers flying commercial aircraft into Manhattan's towers, and bin Laden's disciples beheading civilian hostages. I was skirting blasphemy. We lapsed into silence in that landscape devastated by the sun's fire.

2

Ontological jackal. After hours of silence and the same un-changing desert scenery, I returned to the Koran and the prospect of paradise. Did Abdou believe that the Koran's fantas-tic description of paradise was meant to be taken literally or as a symbol? Rivers of milk and wine, beautiful virgins, beds of silk and brocade, celestial music, magnificent gardens? Yes, he said, adding: *That is what it is like* . . . And hell? *Just as the Koran says it is* . . . What of Abduramane himself, a man of near-saintly ways— considerate, tactful, willing to share, ever mindful of others, gen-tle and calm, at peace with himself, with others, and with the world—would he one day experience those delights? *Yes, I hope so* . . . I wished it for him with all my heart. But deep down, I knew that he was wrong, that he was deceived.

After another silence, he went on to say that before enter-ing paradise he would have accounts to settle. He was worried that his whole life as a pious believer would probably not be enough to make up for a certain error that he had committed, one that might well cost him peace and life everlasting . . . What crime? A murder? A mortal sin, as Christians say? Yes, in a way: once, in his car, he ran over a jackal. Abdou was driving too fast that night, over the speed limit. But it was a desert trail, and ap-proaching headlights were visible from miles away. The road was clear, he saw nothing ahead . . . when suddenly a jackal leaped out of the shadows, and two seconds later it was dying under the wheels of his car.

Had he obeyed the rules of the road, he would not have committed that act of sacrilege—killing an animal when he had no need to eat it. Apart from the fact that the Koran makes no such stipulation, surely we cannot be held responsible for every-thing that happens to us! But Abduramane believed that we are. Allah is behind even the smallest of incidents. Allah used this event to demonstrate the necessity of submission — to the law, to rules, to order, because even the most trifling transgression brings us closer to hell. It can even lead us there directly.

The jackal long haunted his nights, keeping him from falling asleep, and he often saw it in his dreams, barring the road to paradise. As he spoke of it, his emotions resurfaced. His father, a wise old man in his nineties who had fought in World War I, was uncompromising: clearly, Abdou had failed to respect the law, and would have to account for his crime on the day he died. In the meantime, he must strive in his smallest actions to atone as best he could. The jackal would be waiting at the gates of paradise. I would have given anything for the animal to disappear and liberate the soul of this honest man.

It may seem truly remarkable that this good man with his humble aspirations should share the same faith as the September 11 pilots. One bore the burden of a jackal inopportunely thrown to the dogs, the others rejoiced in their annihilation of the greatest possible number of innocent people. Abdou believed that paradise might deny him entrance because he had turned a carrion-eater into carrion; the 9/11 terrorists believed they had earned eternal bliss by consigning the lives of thousands — including fellow Muslims — to ashes. Yet the same book inspired both types of men operating at opposite ends of the human spectrum, one aspiring to saintliness, the others carrying out an act of inhuman cruelty.

3

Mystical postcards. I have often seen *God* in the course of my life. There, in the Mauritanian desert, under a moon that repainted the night in blue and violet. In the cool mosques of

Benghazi or Tripoli, in Libya. On my trip to Cyrene, the home of Aristippus. Not far from Port-Louis on Mauritius, in a shrine dedicated to Ganesh, the colorful elephant-headed Hindu god. In a synagogue in Venice, with a yarmulke on my head. Hearing the choir of Orthodox churches in Moscow. Waiting at the entrance to the Novodevichy Monastery, while inside priests with magnificent voices, gold-robed and swathed in incense, prayed with grieving family and friends over an open coffin. In Seville, standing before the Virgin de la Macarena, among women in tears and men with ecstatic faces. In Naples, in the Church of San Gennaro, god of the city built at the foot of the volcano, whose dried blood is said to liquefy at set times. At the Capuchin convent in Palermo, filing past eight thousand skeletons of Christians all dressed up in their most splendid clothes. At Tbilisi in Georgia, where passersby are invited to share boiled, bloody mutton under trees fluttering with small votive handkerchiefs hung there by devout Christians. On Saint Peter's Square one day when I had neglected to check the calendar: I was there to revisit the Sistine Chapel, but it was Easter Sunday and John Paul II was projected on a giant screen. His miter had slipped on his head, and he might have been speaking in tongues as he mumbled his divine message into the microphone.

I have seen God elsewhere too, and in other forms. In the icy waters of the Arctic during the landing of a salmon caught by a shaman, damaged by the net and ritually returned to the cosmos from which it had been extracted. In a back kitchen in Havana, where a Santeria priest performed a ceremony that involved a crucified, smoked agouti and a handful of volcanic rocks and seashells. In a voodoo temple deep in the Haitian wilderness, among basins stained by red liquids, the air filled with the acrid smells of herbs and extracts, the walls decorated with drawings to gain the favor of the Loa. In Azerbaijan, at Surakhany near Baku, in a Zoroastrian fire worshippers' temple. In Kyoto in Zen gardens — excellent exercises in negative theology.

I have also seen dead gods, fossil gods, gods as old as time itself. At Lascaux, I was stunned by the cave paintings in that earthly womb where the soul ebbs and flows under vast layers of time. At Luxor, in the royal burial chambers, located deep underground, watched over by men with dogs' heads, by scarabs and inscrutable cats. In Rome in the temple of Mithras, who slew the cosmic bull and whose cult might have transformed the world had it possessed its own Emperor Constantine. In Athens, climbing the steps of the Acropolis on my way to the Parthenon, as my mind dwelled on the city below where Plato had met Socrates . . .

In none of those places did I feel superior to those who believed in spirits, in the immortal soul, in the breath of the gods, the presence of angels, the power of prayer, the effectiveness of ritual, the validity of incantations, communion with voodoo spirits, hemoglobin-based miracles, the Virgin's tears, the resurrection of a crucified man, the magical properties of cowrie shells, the value of animal sacrifices, the transcendent effects of Egyptian saltpeter, or prayer wheels. Never. But everywhere I saw how readily men construct fables in order to avoid looking reality in the face. The invention of an afterlife would not matter so much were it not purchased at so high a price: disregard of the real, hence willful neglect of the only world there is. While religion is often at variance with immanence, with man's inherent nature, atheism is in harmony with the earth — life's other name.

IN DEFENSE OF ATHEISM

Introduction

1

Keeping company with Madame Bovary. In Flaubert's novel, Madame Bovary relieved her despair by pretending. Many people do the same. Without romantic daydreams, their lives would be utterly desolate. A man can certainly avoid facing tragic reality by imagining himself as somehow different from the being he truly is — but only at the cost of turning himself into something unrecognizable. I do not despise believers. I find them neither ridiculous nor pathetic, but I lose all hope when I see that they prefer the comforting fairy tales of children to the cruel hard facts of adults. Better the faith that brings peace of mind than the rationality that brings worry — even at the price of perpetual mental infantilism. What a demonstration of metaphysical sleight of hand — and what a monstrous price!

Having realized all this, I experience the feeling that always arises deep within me when I am confronted with the symptoms of indoctrination and deception: compassion for the sufferer, coupled with burning anger toward those who perpetuate the deception. No hatred for the man on his knees, but a fierce resolve never to collude with those who urge him to adopt this humiliating posture and keep him there. Who would not sympathize with the victims of fraud? And who would not approve of battling the perpetrators?

Spiritual poverty engenders self-renunciation; it is just as significant as other deficiencies, whether sexual, mental, political, or intellectual. How ironic that other people's credulity should bring a smile to the face of the man who is supremely unaware of his own! The Catholic who eats fish on Friday derides the Muslim who refuses pork — who in turn scoffs at the Jew for refusing shellfish. The Lubavitcher swaying at the Wailing Wall looks askance at the Christian kneeling on a prayer stool and at the Muslim laying out his prayer mat in the direction of Mecca. Yet none concludes that the mote in his neighbor's eye might be smaller than the beam in his own. No one reaches the opinion that the critical mind, so relevant and always so welcome when applied to others, would be put to good use in a scrutiny of one's own beliefs.

Human credulity is beyond imagining. Man's refusal to see the obvious, his longing for a better deal even if it is based on pure fiction, his determination to remain blind have no limits. Far better to swallow fables, fictions, myths, or fairy tales than to see reality in all its naked cruelty, forcing him to accept the obvious tragedy of existence. *Homo sapiens* wards off death by abolishing it. To avoid solving the problem, he wishes it away. Only mortals have to worry about death's inevitability. The naïve and foolish believer *knows* that he is immortal, that he will survive the carnage of Judgment Day.

2

Profiteers waiting to pounce. I cannot fault those who need a metaphysical crutch in order to bear their lot. On the other hand, I am diametrically opposed to those who preach the ascetic ideal — and who also care for themselves in so doing. We are on opposite sides of the existential barricade. The traffic in afterlives benefits the men who engage in it by providing them the means to bolster their faith, for they find in it the material essential for reinforcing their own need for mental help. Just as psychoanalysts often treat others in order to avoid questioning themselves too closely about their own weaknesses, so the vicars of monotheist gods foist their vision of the world on the faithful — and day by day their own convictions become more secure.

Masking one's own spiritual poverty while exaggerating the same weakness in others, avoiding the display of one's own shortcomings by dramatizing those of the world at large, are tactics crying out to be denounced. No one is faulting the believer. But with the man who claims to be his shepherd, the case is different. As long as religion remains a purely private matter, we contend simply with neuroses, psychoses, and other personal factors. We deal with what aberrations we can, provided they do not threaten or endanger the lives of others . . .

My atheism leaps to life when private belief becomes a public matter, when in the name of a personal mental pathology we organize a world for others. For between personal existential anguish and management of the body and soul of our fellow human beings, there exists a whole world in which those who profit from human anguish lurk in concealment. Redirecting their own death fixation toward the world at large neither saves sufferers nor alleviates their suffering — but it contaminates the universe. The attempt to avoid negativity merely spreads negativity around like manure — ushering in a wholesale mental pandemic.

In the name of Yahweh, God, Jesus, and Allah — those convenient excuses — Moses, Paul of Tarsus, Constantine, and Muhammad exploit the dark forces that penetrate them, that work so powerfully within them. By projecting their somber visions on the world they blacken it still further — and with impunity. The pathological grip of the death fixation does not heal

itself through chaotic and magical muckspreading but by philosophical work upon oneself. Well-conducted introspection dis-
pels the dreams and delirium on which gods feed. Atheism is not
therapy but restored mental health.

3

Rekindling the Enlightenment. This work on oneself requires philosophy. Not faith, belief, fables, but reason and properly
directed thought. We must fight against obscurantism, that fertile
loam of all religions, with the weapons of the Western rationalist
tradition. Sound use of our understanding, rational ordering of
our minds, implementation of a true critical will, general mobilization of our intelligence, the desire to evolve while standing on
our own feet — all these are strategies for dispelling phantoms. In
other words, we need a return to the spirit of Light, of Enlightenment, that gave its name to the eighteenth century.

There is certainly much to be said on the historiography of
that luminous century. With the French Revolution fixed firmly
in their memories, and writing in its wake, the historians of the
following century gave retrospective preference to whatever
seemed to have contributed to that still recent event. They invoked the ironic deconstructions by Voltaire, by Montesquieu
with his separation of the Three Powers, by the Rousseau of the
Social Contract, by Kant and the cult of reason, by d'Alembert the
master builder of the *Encyclopédie*, etc. But these dazzling Enlightenment figures — respectable, indeed politically correct — are
the boldest that nineteenth-century historians could stomach.

I prefer sharper, more direct, and much bolder shafts of light.
For behind their seeming diversity, all the revered figures mentioned above were united in deism. They strenuously rejected
atheism. And they added an equal and sovereign contempt for

materialism and the sensual. In other words, contempt for a host of alternative philosophical options that effectively constituted a "left wing" of the Enlightenment, a pole of radicalism that was soon forgotten but which might be usefully invoked today.

Kant is a monument of timid audacity. The six hundred pages of his *Critique of Pure Reason* contain the ingredients for blowing Western metaphysics sky-high, but the philosopher ultimately shrinks from the task. His separation of faith and reason, of presiding deities and concrete phenomena, is a step in the right direction. A little more effort would have obtained for one of these two world — reason — the right to claim precedence over the other — faith. It would also have made possible an unsparing analysis of the whole question of belief. But Kant stops short. In declaring the two spheres separate, he allows reason to abdicate its powers: he lets faith go scot-free, and religion is saved. Kant can then *postulate* (why did he need so many pages in order merely to postulate . . .) God, the soul's immortality, and the existence of free will, three pillars (along with the death drive) of all religion.

4

Once again, what was the Enlightenment? We know that Kant wrote a 1784 essay entitled *What Is Enlightenment?* Is it still readable over two centuries later? Yes. We can and we must subscribe to the Enlightenment project, which remains as viable as ever. It aims to lift man out of his infantile condition and set his feet on the path to adulthood; to remind him of his own responsibility for his infantile state; to inspire him with the courage to use his intelligence; to give himself and others the capacity to attain self-mastery; to make public and communal use of his reason in every field, with no exception; and not to accept as revealed truth what emanates from public authority. A magnificent project . . .

Why then did Kant have to be so un-Kantian? For how can we permit the attainment of adulthood and at the same time prohibit the use of reason in the religious sphere, which prefers the faithful to have the minds of children? We may of course think, says Kant; we must have the courage to ask questions, including of the teacher and the priest. Why then should we stop there, having reached such an encouraging point? Full steam ahead, surely! Let's postulate the nonexistence of God, the death of the soul, the nonexistence of free will!

So a final push is needed to rekindle the flames of Enlightenment. A little more Enlightenment, more and more Enlightenment! Let's be Kantian in opposition to Kant, let us pick up the gauntlet of boldness he throws down — without daring to act boldly himself. His mother, an austere and rigorous pietist if ever there was one, must have been holding her son's hand when he finished his *Critique of Pure Reason*. It must have been Frau Kant who helped defuse the unparalleled explosive potential of Kant's argument.

5

Atheology's dazzling light. The luminaries who succeeded Kant are well-known: among others, Ludwig Feuerbach, Nietzsche, Marx, and Freud. The "age of suspicion" gave the twentieth century a genuine decoupling of reason and faith, and then redirected the weapons of rationality against the fictions of belief. At last the battlefield was cleared and a new space set free. On this virgin metaphysical terrain an untested discipline saw the light of day. It is time to introduce *atheology*.

The term is to be found as early as March 29, 1950, in a letter from Georges Bataille to Raymond Queneau. In it, Bataille wrote that he would like to see a new edition of his books, previously published by Gallimard. For the three-volume collection, he proposed the overall title *Summa Atheologica*. In 1954, Bataille embarked on another project involving several texts announced four years earlier but not yet written, others still in the outline stage, and the internal integrity of the whole in constant flux. A fourth volume was announced, *Pure Happiness*, and then a fifth, *The Unfinished System of Nonknowledge*. None would see the light of day in the form envisioned. These works exist today only as a collection of incidental writings and selections from his notebooks.

The unfinished state of this important body of work, the abundance of plans and projects, the obvious equivocations in Bataille's correspondence on architectonics, his fierce insistence that he really did not want to be a philosopher—all this is evidence of an abandoned construction site. Above all, he gave up the project—founding a new religion—that had inspired his early reading, thinking, and writings. Atheology was left an orphan. Yet it is a brilliant concept.

Gilles Deleuze and Michel Foucault understood concepts as instruments in a toolbox at the disposal of anyone aspiring to philosophical work. That being so, I am adopting Bataille's term "atheology" for my own use. I am not, however, advocating Bataille's version of atheology—especially since it would require a tremendous amount of painstaking research and would likely yield only unsatisfying results. I am proposing the concept of atheology as a countercurrent to theology, a channel to carry us past discourse on God and flow upstream to the source, where we may examine the mechanisms of theology up close. On a world stage saturated with monotheism, it is high time to expose the back side of the theological scenery. This is an opportunity for philosophical deconstruction.

Beyond this preliminary *In Defense of Atheism*, then, the effort requires a mobilization of multiple disciplines. *Psychology* and *psychoanalysis*: consideration of the mechanisms of the fable-generating function. *Metaphysics*: plotting the genealogy of transcendence. *Archaeology*: giving a voice to the substrata beneath the surface geography of religions. *Paleography*: establishing archival texts. *History*, of course: acquainting ourselves with the epistemologies and their development in the areas where religions were born. *Comparative psychology*: establishing fundamental principles of thinking, learning, and behavior in various time periods and widely separated regions. *Mythology*: research into the details of poetic rationality. *Hermeneutics, linguistics, languages*: stressing local idiom. *Aesthetics*: tracing the iconic propagation of beliefs. And then of course *philosophy*: for philosophy seems best fitted to preside over the organization of all these disciplines. And the stakes? A physics of metaphysics, a true theory of man's inherent nature (immanence), a materialist ontology.

PART ONE

ATHEOLOGY

I

Odyssey of the Freethinkers

1

God is still breathing. Is he dead or not? The question is still undecided. However, such glad tidings would surely have generated cosmic events — which haven't yet transpired. Instead of the fertile field such a death would have opened up, we seem confronted today by nihilism, the cult of nothingness, the passion for nonbeing, a morbid relish for the twilight of waning civilizations, a fascination with the abyss and with bottomless pits where we lose our souls, our bodies, our identity, our being, and all interest in anything whatsoever. A lugubrious picture, a depressing apocalypse . . .

God's death was an ontological gimmick, a conjuror's trick. It was consubstantial with a twentieth century that saw death everywhere — the death of art, of philosophy, of metaphysics, of the novel, of music, of politics. So let's announce the death of all these fictional deaths! Tongue-in-cheek obituaries that once served certain thinkers — before they turned their metaphysical coats — as a dramatic setting for the paradoxes they uncovered. The death of philosophy engendered works of philosophy, the death of the novel generated novels, the death of art produced works of art, etc. As for God's death, it has released an outpouring of the sacred, the divine, the religious. Today we swim in these purgative waters.

Clearly, the announcement of God's death was as world-shaking as it was false—trumpets blaring, news bellowed from the rooftops, drums thundering in an orgy of premature rejoicing. Our era staggers under the weight of revelations solemnly hailed as the authorized utterances of new oracles. Abundance holds sway, to the detriment of quality and truth: never have so many false tidings been celebrated as so many revealed truths. For God's death to be certified, irrefutable facts, clues, and courtroom exhibits should have been produced. Yet none has emerged.

Who has seen the corpse? Apart from Nietzsche (and even then . . .). Like that of the corpus delicti in Ionesco's *Rhinoceros*, we should have felt its presence, its dominion, it would have been all-pervading, defiling, malodorous, it would have fallen apart little by little, day by day, and we would have witnessed a process of real decomposition—in the philosophical as well as the physical sense of the term. Instead of which God, invisible while alive, has remained invisible even when dead. And we are still without proof of his death. But who could furnish it? What new lunatic for this impossible task?

For, *pace* Nietzsche and Heine, God is neither dead nor dying because he is not mortal. A fiction does not die, an illusion never passes away, a fairy tale does not refute itself. Neither hippogriff nor centaur is bound by the laws governing mammals. A wildebeest or a horse, yes; an animal from the mythological bestiary, no. And God too (listed somewhere between "Gnome" and "Golem") is of that mythological bestiary, like the thousands of other creatures enumerated in dictionaries with numberless entries. The oppressed creature's sigh will endure for as long as the creature itself, in other words forever.

Besides, where would he have died? In Nietzsche's *The Gay Science*? Murdered at Nietzsche's summer home in Sils-Maria by an inspired philosopher—tragic and sublime, haunted and haggard—in the second half of the nineteenth century? And what was the weapon? A book, books, a life's work? Imprecations, analyses, proofs, refutations (the cold steel of writers)? Was the killer alone? Did he lurk in ambush? Or was he one of a group, along with the Abbé Meslier and the Marquis de Sade as guardian forebears? If he existed, would God's murderer not himself have been a superior God? And doesn't this noncrime mask an Oedipal urge, an impossible desire, an irrepressible ambition powerless to carry through a task essential to the creation of freedom, of identity, and of meaning?

You cannot kill a breeze, a wind, a fragrance, you cannot kill a dream or an ambition. God, manufactured by mortals in their own quintessential image, exists only to make daily life bearable despite the path that every one of us treads toward extinction. As long as men are obliged to die, some of them, unable to endure the prospect, will concoct fond illusions. We cannot assassinate or kill an illusion. In fact, illusion is more likely to kill us—for God puts to death everything that stands up to him, beginning with reason, intelligence, and the critical mind. All the rest follows in a chain reaction.

The last god will expire with the last man. And with him fear, terror, anguish, those devices designed to create divinities. They include horror of death's void, the inability to integrate death as a natural process with which we must come to terms, in whose presence intelligence alone can have any effect. And there is denial, the absence of any meaning beyond what we ourselves have to offer, with absurdity as a starting point. These are the genetic bloodlines of the divine. A dead God would imply a vanquished void. We are light-years away from such ontological progress . . .

2

Seeking a name for freethinkers. Thus, God will endure for as long as the reasons that brought him into being; and so will those who deny him . . . All attempts at establishing a family tree are a sham: God has no date of birth. Nor does practical atheism (atheism in the abstract is another matter). The first man (yet another fiction) to affirm belief in God must simultaneously, or successively and alternately, not have believed in him. Doubt is coeval with belief. The religious impulse, along with uncertainty or denial, have probably coexisted in one and the same individual from the beginning. Affirming and denying, knowing and not knowing: a time for kneeling, a time for rebellion, depending on the need either to create or immolate a divinity.

God thus seems immortal. On this point his standard-bearers prevail. But not for the reasons they imagine, for the neurosis that impels men to forge gods results from the usual workings of the psyche and the subconscious. Creation of the divine coexists with terror of the void in a life that must end. God is born of the rigor, rigidity, and stillness of dead members of the tribe. At the sight of a corpse, the dreams and smoke clouds that nourish gods take on more solid substance. When a soul collapses before the cold body of a loved one, denial takes over and transforms this ending into a beginning. The completion of the cycle becomes instead the start of a new adventure. God, heaven, and spirits come forth to dispel the pain and violence of death.

And what of the atheist? Denial of God and of afterlives probably shared the stage with faith in the soul of the first believer. Revolt, rebellion, refusal of the evidence, rejection of the decrees of fate and of necessity: the genealogy of atheism seems just as simple as that of belief. Afterlives and denial of God no doubt shared space in the mind of the first believer. Even as he rejected the evidence and refused to accept the dictates of fate and necessity, the seeds of doubt were sprouting and rebellion was brewing: the development of atheism was simultaneous with that of belief. Satan, Lucifer the light-bearer (that emblematic philosopher of the Enlightenment), the one who says no and refuses to submit to God's law, was created in the same gestational period as God. The devil and God were opposite sides of the same coin, like atheism and theism.

Atheism rejects the existence of God as a fiction devised by men desperate to keep on living in spite of the inevitability of death. The word "atheist" entered the French and English languages in the sixteenth century. Thus the word itself and the position it came to stand for arrived late in the West. But the idea of "godlessness" is old. The Bible alludes to atheists: Psalm 10:4, Psalm 10:13, and Jeremiah 5:12 speak of the wicked who will not seek after God, who despise God, who belie the Lord. The Greek term "atheos" dates from the seventh century BCE, was later incorporated into Latin, and thus was in use throughout Greek and Roman antiquity. It was an expression of severe censure and moral condemnation. Sometimes, indeed often, "wrong belief" was equated with "unbelief." The accusation of atheist could be leveled not only at the man who did not believe in God, but at the man who did not worship the dominant deities of the moment, the local, socially prescribed forms of divinity. Even a person deeply committed to a god—if it was a foreign, unorthodox god—might find himself condemned as an atheist. The word described not the individual who emptied heaven of its inhabitants, but one who peopled it with his own fabrications.

Throughout history, the authorities of a particular time and place have pledged allegiance to God or gods in the interest of consolidating their power. "Atheism" has served politically to thrust aside, label, or castigate individuals who believe differently. God himself is invisible, inaccessible, and therefore silent about what he can be made to say or endorse, but he makes no objection when people claim to be vested by him with the right to speak, ordain, and act (for better or worse) in his name. God's silence enables his ministers to exploit and abuse that title. Whoever does not believe in their god, and therefore in them, automatically becomes an atheist. The worst of men: immoral, loathsome, unclean, the incarnation of evil. Someone to be locked up on sight or tortured or put to death.

It is dangerous in such circumstances to proclaim oneself an atheist . . . But others say it, and always from the deprecatory standpoint of an authority bent on condemnation. The word's very structure makes this clear: a-theist. An exclusionary prefix, implying a negation, a lack, a void, an antagonistic stance. We possess no positive term to describe the man who does not worship phantoms of the imagination. All we have is this linguistic construction suggestive of amputation: so we have a-theist, but also mis-creant, a-gnostic (but no a-dieu!), un-believer, ir-religious, in-credulous, a-religious, im-pious, and all the words that flow from them: irreligion, unbelief, impiety, etc. Nothing that conveys the solar, affirmative, positive, free, and healthy aspects of the individual standing beyond magical thinking and fables.

"Atheism" is thus the product of a verbal creation by the manufacturers of gods. The word does not flow from the deliberate and sovereign decision of a person who defines himself historically by this term. "Atheist" describes the Other, the man who spurns the local god when everyone else, or almost everyone, believes in him. (And is well-advised to do so — for theology exercised behind closed doors is always buttressed by armed militias, existential police, and ontological soldiers who exempt us from thinking and instead demand the swiftest possible transition to belief and very often to conversion.)

Baal and Yahweh, Zeus and Allah, Ra and Odin — but also Gitche Manitou, the Great Spirit of the Algonquin tribes — owe their names to geography and history. In accordance with the metaphysics that made their existence possible they simply assume different names for one and the same fantasized reality. Yet none of them is truer than another. They all live in a pantheon of fictitious revelers where Ulysses and Zarathustra, Dionysus and Don Quixote, Tristan and Lancelot of the Lake — so many magical figures, just like the Fox of the Dogon or the Loa of voodoo — sit down to feast together.

3

The fruits of antiphilosophy. Lacking the perfect word to express the inexpressible, to name the unnamable — the madman with the audacity not to believe in God — we must therefore make do with *atheist*. There are of course roundabout ways of referring to nonbelievers without using the word, but it was Christians who invented such circumlocutions, introducing them to the intellectual marketplace with the same disparaging intent. After Pascal's death a Memorial he had written was discovered sewn into the lining of his coat. It spoke of the "God of Abraham, God of Isaac, God of Jacob, not of the philosophers and scholars . . ." In that context, Pascal used the word "philosophers" to mean *deists*. Terms then used in place of nonbeliever included *freethinker* and *libertine*, not in the sense of one leading a dissolute life but rather in the sense of one who doubts or denies religious dogma. Today, Belgian authors have coined the phrase "partisans of free examination."

Antiphilosophy — that eighteenth-century school of thought located on the dark side of the Enlightenment medal — is a current we wrongly neglect, but one on which we should train the light of current experience. For it demonstrates how far the Christian community will go in deploying means (including the most morally indefensible) to discredit the thinking of independent temperaments not blessed with belief in its fables. Indeed, antiphilosophy fights with unthinkable violence against freedom of thought and against all thinking that deviates from the path of Christian dogma.

Witness, for example, the work of Father François Garasse, the Jesuit who invented modern propaganda in the seventeenth century. His *Curious Doctrine of the Beaux-Esprits* [figures rightly or wrongly celebrated for their wit and learning] *of Our Times, or Those who Claim to be Such* (1623) is an overstuffed volume of more than a thousand pages. In it he heaps abuse on the lives of independent philosophers, depicting them as debauchees, sodomites, drunkards, fornicators, gluttons, pedophiles (poor Pierre Charron, Montaigne's friend), and other satanic labels in order to dissuade people from looking into their progressive works. The next year that same Jesuit propaganda minister published a *Justification for His Book against the Atheists and Libertines of Our Times*. In it, Garasse adds another layer along the same lines, equally full of lies, calumny, villainy, and ad hominem attacks. Love of one's neighbor knows no limits.

Garasse used character assassination to undermine the influence of freethinkers. His tactics were not new. In the fourth century BCE, Epicurus was vilified by bigots and by the great and powerful. Today, the same tactics are still being used against any philosopher who (often without rejecting Christianity) does not think the Bible represents the ultimate truth — God's word, wholly inspired and infallible. Certain philosophers attacked by Garasse have yet to recover: they languish in obscurity. Some have undeserved reputations as immoralists and social outcasts, and those labels also stick to their works. For centuries, atheist thought was not presented in a fair light, and atheists were prevented from making their mark on the world. In philosophy, the term *libertine* still carries derogatory and polemical implications and libertine works encounter closed minds.

Because of the dominance of antiphilosophy in the official historiography of thought, a vast number of philosophical works remain unknown even to professional philosophers (apart from a handful of specialists). Many of these works are vigorous, powerful, and compelling, but they remain unread simply because their authors were anti-Christian, irreverent, or outside the mainstream belief system. Who for example, in the case of the century of France's Sun King, has read Pierre Gassendi? Or La Mothe Le Vayer? Or Cyrano de Bergerac — the philosopher, not the fictional character? So few . . . Yet an understanding of Pascal, Descartes, Malebranche, and other practitioners of the official philosophy is inconceivable without some familiarity with these philosophers, who strove for the autonomy of philosophy in relation to theology — to the Judeo-Christian religion, as it happens.

4

Theology and its fetishes. This dearth of positive terms to describe atheism, and the refusal to consider possible substitutions, goes hand in hand with the wealth of the vocabulary surrounding believers. There is not a single variation on this theme lacking its descriptive epithet: theist, deist, pantheist, monotheist, polytheist, to which we might add animist, totemist, fetishist, and even, in the case of historically established forms, Catholics and Protestants, Evangelicals and Lutherans, Calvinists and Buddhists, Shintoists and Muslims, Shiite and Sunni of course, Jews and Jehovah's Witnesses, Orthodox and Anglicans, Methodists and Presbyterians — the catalog is endless.

Some worship stones — from the most primitive tribes to today's Muslims walking around the Black Stone in the eastern corner of the Kaaba. Others venerate the moon or the sun, some an invisible god who cannot be represented on pain of idolatry, or else an anthropomorphic figure — white, female or male, Aryan of course. Another, a thoroughgoing pantheist, will see God everywhere, while another, an adept of negative theology, nowhere. By some he is worshipped covered in blood, crowned with thorns, a corpse; by others in a blade of grass, Eastern Shinto fashion. There is no man-made foolery that has not been dragooned into the ranks of putative divinities.

For those who still doubt the possible excesses of religions on the question of support media, let us consider the urine dance of New Mexico's Zuni, the manufacture of amulets of excrement of the Great Lama of Tibet, the cow dung and urine used for ritual ablution among Hindus, the Roman cults of Stercorius, Crepitus, and Cloacinus — respectively the divinities of filth, farts, and sewers — offerings of manure to the Assyrian goddess Siva, the consumption of her own excrement by Sushiquecal, the Mexican goddess and mother of gods, Ezekiel's divinely ordained recipe for the use of human fecal matter to cook food, and so many other impenetrable pathways or singular means of maintaining a relationship with the divine and the holy.

Faced with these multiple names, these endlessly varying practices, the immense vocabulary available for describing the unbelievable passion of believers, the atheist must be content with this single weak epithet, tailored to discredit him! Those who worship anything and nothing (the very ones who, in the name of their fetishes, justify intolerant violence and unending war against the godless) are thus the ones who reduce the freethinker to the etymological condition of an incomplete being, truncated, fragmented, mutilated, an entity without God and therefore without real existence.

God's soldiers have even developed a whole discipline entirely devoted to the examination of his names, his deeds and gestures, his memorable sayings, his thoughts, his words — for God speaks! — and his actions. It is the discipline of discourse on God, the province of loyal (and salaried) thinkers, his professionals, his lawyers, his spear-carriers, his contract killers, his dialecticians, his rhetoricians, his philosophers (yes, even those!), his henchmen, his servants, his representatives on earth and their institutions, his ideas, his diktats, and other nonsense — in other words, theology. The discipline of discourse on God.

The rare moments in Western history when Christianity has been manhandled — 1793 for example — yielded a few new philosophical activities and therefore a handful of new terms (which were quickly consigned to oblivion). Admittedly, people still speak of *de-Christianization*, but they do so only as historians to identify that phase of the French Revolution in which citizens turned churches into hospitals, schools, orphanages, when revolutionaries replaced roof crosses with tricolor flags and crucifixes of dead wood with living, healthy trees. The *atheist* in Montaigne's *Essays*, the *attayists* of Monluc's *Letters* (chapter 137), and Voltaire's *atheistic* quickly disappeared. So did the *atheist* of the French Revolution.

5

Naming infamy. The poverty of the atheist vocabulary is rooted in the unshakable historical domination of God's liegemen. For more than fifteen centuries they have enjoyed undisputed political authority. Tolerance is the least of their virtues, and they use every weapon in their arsenal to make the phenomenon, and therefore the word, impossible. The word "atheism" dates from the middle of the sixteenth century. But "atheist" existed in the second century of the common era among Christians who denounced and stigmatized the *atheos*—those who did not believe in a god raised from the dead on the third day. It was but a short step to conclude from their indifference to children's fables that they worshipped no god at all. Thus pagans—who, as their name tells us, worship the gods of the countryside—were seen as defying the gods and therefore God. No god, the wrong god, too many gods . . . to early Christians, it made no difference. The Jesuit Garasse stamped Luther as an atheist (!), and the poet Pierre de Ronsard reserved the same treatment for France's Huguenots.

The word stands as an absolute insult: the atheist is the immoralist, the amoral, the unclean, further consideration of whose life and books becomes a crime once the epithet has been uttered. The word is enough to block access to the works. It functions as a cog in the war machine launched against everything that does not move in the purest register of Catholic, Apostolic, and Roman orthodoxy. Atheist and heretic: in the last analysis they are the same. Which amounts in the end to a great many people!

Epicurus was forced very early to face charges of atheism. Yet neither he nor the Epicureans denied the gods' existence. The gods of Epicurus and of his disciples were creatures made of subtle matter. They were numerous, they inhabited between-worlds, they were imperturbable, indifferent to men's and the world's fate, true embodiments of freedom from care. They well and truly existed . . . But they were not like those of the Greek *polis*, who through the mediation of their priests demanded compliance with communal and social norms. That was their only fault: their antisocial nature.

The historiography of atheism—rare, skimpy, and generally of poor quality—is thus wrong to date the phenomenon from the earliest days of humankind. Social crystallizations require transcendence — order and hierarchy (etymologically, the power of the sacred) . . . Politics and the *polis* can the more easily function by invoking the vengeful might of the gods, officially represented on earth by the powerful (who happen most opportunely to wield the levers of political control).

Commandeered into an exercise designed to justify secular power, the gods — or God — are seen as privileged interlocutors of tribal chieftains, of kings, of princes. Those terrestrial figures professed to hold their power from the gods, who confirmed this through signs decoded by the priestly caste, itself equally interested in the benefits of exercising a power for which it claimed legal sanction. Thereafter, "atheism" became a useful weapon for consigning this one or that one — providing that he resisted or protested a little — to jails, solitary confinement, even to the stake.

Atheism does not begin with those condemned and identified as such by official historiography. The name of Socrates cannot be decently included in a history of atheism. Neither can Epicurus and his disciples, any more than Protagoras, the first and most famous of the Greek Sophists, who contents himself in his *Concerning the Gods* with saying that he can conclude nothing about them — neither their existence nor their nonexistence. Which at the very least identifies a kind of agnosticism, an uncertainty, even a skepticism — but assuredly not atheism, which implies a frank assertion of the nonexistence of gods.

The God of philosophers often enters into conflict with the God of Abraham, Jesus, and Muhammad. First because the former proceeds from intelligence, reason, deduction, argument, and second because the latter proposes instead dogma, revelation, and obedience — the fruit of collusion between spiritual and temporal powers. The God of Abraham tends to define the God of Constantine, and then the God of not very Christian popes and warrior princes. That God had little in common with the extravagant constructions cobbled together out of causes lacking causality, out of motionless prime movers, innate ideas, preestablished harmonies and other cosmological, ontological or psychotheological proofs.

Any philosophical attempt to think about God outside the dominant political framework is usually reduced to atheism. Thus when the church cut out the tongue of the priest Giulio Cesare Vanini, hanged him, then burned him at the stake at Toulouse on February 19, 1619, it was murdering the author of a work entitled *Amphitheatre of the Eternal Divino-Magical, Christiano-Physical and Nonetheless Astrologico-Catholic Providence against the Philosophers, Atheists, Epicureans, Peripatetics, and Stoics* (1615).

Unless we choose to consider the above title meaningless, we must acknowledge that Vanini's oxymoronic wording rejects neither Providence, Christianity, nor Catholicism — but firmly opposes atheism, Epicureanism, and other pagan philosophical schools. Yet none of that makes an atheist (a man liable to the death penalty). He is more probably a kind of eclectic pantheist. But in any case, he is a heretic because he is unorthodox.

Spinoza, himself a pantheist — and of unequaled intelligence — was also condemned for atheism, or rather for insufficiently rigid Jewish orthodoxy. On July 27, 1656, the *parnassim* in session at the *mahamad* — the Jewish authorities of Amsterdam — read out in Hebrew, before the ark of the Houtgracht synagogue, a text of appalling violence. They charged him with horrible heresies, monstrous deeds, dangerous opinions, and evil conduct, with the result that a *harem* was pronounced against him — and never rescinded!

The community used language of extreme brutality: excluded, hounded out, execrated, cursed day and night, sleeping and waking, leaving home or returning ... The men of God invoked the wrath of their fiction and his explicit anathema in time and space. To round out this gift, the *parnassim* asked that Spinoza's name be erased forever from the surface of the planet. The request was never granted, as we know.

Whereupon the rabbis, theoretical supporters of brotherly love, added to this excommunication a ban on any contact, verbal or written, with the philosopher. No one could help him, approach within six feet of him, or be under the same roof with him. It was of course forbidden to read his writings: Spinoza at that time was twenty-three, and had published nothing. His *Ethics* appeared posthumously twenty-one years later, in 1677. Today he is read all over the world.

Where is Spinoza's atheism? Nowhere. We could scour his life's work in vain for one sentence asserting the nonexistence of God. Admittedly, he denies the soul's immortality and asserts the impossibility of posthumous punishment or reward. He advances the notion that the Bible is a work composed by diverse authors and a work of historical — and therefore not "revealed" — facts. He refuses to subscribe to the theory of a chosen people, and proclaims this clearly in his *Tractatus Theologico-Politicus* (*A Theologico-Political Treatise*). He taught a hedonist morality of joy beyond good and evil; he held no brief for Judeo-Christian hatred of self, the world, or the body. Although a Jew, he discerned philosophical qualities in Jesus. But none of all that made him a denier of God, an atheist.

The list of wretches put to death for atheism in the history of the planet — priests, practicing believers sincerely convinced of the existence of a one God, Catholic, Apostolic, and Roman — is endless. So also is the roster of supporters of the God of Abraham or of Allah, they too executed in unbelievable numbers for failing to profess a faith bound by the accepted norms. The list of anonymous people who did not even rebel against the powers identifying themselves with monotheism, people who were neither refractory nor fractious — all these macabre numbers bear witness. Well before it was used to describe the God-denier, the word "atheist" served to condemn the thinking of the man even marginally liberated from authority and social supervision in questions of thought and reflection. The atheist was a man free in God's eyes—and ultimately free to deny God's existence.

II

Atheism and the Escape from Nihilism

1

The invention of atheism. The Epicurean Christianity of Erasmus or Montaigne, that of Gassendi, canon of Digne, the Pyrrhonian Christianity of Pierre Charron, theologian of Condom, accredited teacher of theology at Bordeaux, the deism of the Protestant Pierre Bayles or the Anglican John Hobbes sometimes exposed them to charges of impiety, of atheism. Here again, the term does not fit. Unorthodox believers, freethinkers beyond a doubt, but Christians, philosophers set free yet Christian by tradition, this wide spectrum permits belief in God without the constraints of an orthodoxy supported by army, police, and established power. Montaigne an atheist? What of his pilgrimage to Our Lady of Loreto, his professions of Catholic belief in his masterwork, his private chapel, his death in the presence of a priest at the moment (or so it is said) of the Elevation? No. All these fine, respectable philosophers believed in God.

What we need is a missing link, a precursor, an inventor, a proper name, a milestone from which we may proclaim: this was the first atheist, the one who denied the existence of God, the philosopher who thought it and wrote it clearly, precisely, without embellishment and without a wealth of innuendo, of prudence, and of endless contortions. A radical atheist, outspoken, widely known! Even proud. A man whose credo — if I may be allowed the term — does not have to be inferred, is not a matter of speculation, does not proceed from the convoluted hypotheses of readers in search of documentary proof.

The precursor we seek might well have been Cristovão Ferreira, a Portuguese and former Jesuit who renounced his faith under Japanese torture in 1614. (Ferreira's faith must have been feeble indeed, to judge by the relevance of arguments that must have occurred to him well before he was forced to recant.) In 1636, the year Descartes was writing his *Discourse on Method*, Ferreira wrote a small, explosive, radical book entitled *The Deception Revealed*.

In just thirty pages, he asserted that God did not create the world and that moreover the world had never been created. Neither hell, paradise, nor predestination existed; stillborn children were innocent of original sin (which in any case did not exist); Christianity was an invention. The Ten Commandments were impracticable lunacy; the pope was immoral and dangerous; payment for masses and indulgences, excommunication, dietary laws, Mary's virginity, the Three Kings, were all so much twaddle. The Resurrection was a tale bereft of reason, ludicrous, scandalous, a hoax; the sacraments and confessions were nonsense; the Eucharist a metaphor; the Last Judgment an unbelievable delusion.

Could there be a more violent assault, a more concentrated barrage? And the Jesuit had not finished. Religion? An invention by men to ensure power over their brethren. Reason? The instrument permitting men to fight against such rubbish. Cristovão Ferreira dismantled all these crude inventions. Was he an atheist then? No, for at no point did he say, write, assert, or think that God did not exist. And then, as if to confirm that he was a spiritualist but nonetheless a believer, he abandoned the Christian religion — but converted to Zen Buddhism . . . So he will not be our first atheist. But we are no longer far short of our goal.

The miracle occurred shortly after Ferreira, in the person of another priest, Jean Meslier — at last an identifiable saint, hero, and martyr of the atheist cause! The parish priest of Etrépigny in the Ardennes, the soul of discretion (apart from a clash with the village seigneur) through the whole span of his ministry, the Abbé Meslier (1664–1729) has left us a voluminous testament. It is a scathing attack on the church, religion, Jesus, God, but also on the aristocracy, the monarchy, and the ancien régime. He violently denounces social injustice, idealist thinking, and the dolorist brand of Christianity that promulgates the value of suffering. At the same time he professes an anarchistic communalism, an authentic and brand-new materialist philosophy, and a surprisingly modern hedonistic atheism.

For the first time (but how long will it take us to acknowledge this?) in the history of ideas, a philosopher had dedicated a whole book to the question of atheism. He professed it, demonstrated it, arguing and quoting, sharing his reading and his reflections, and seeking confirmation from his own observations of the everyday world. His title sets it out clearly: *Memoir of the Thoughts and Feelings of Jean Meslier*, and so does his subtitle: *Clear and Evident Demonstrations of the Vanity and Falsity of All the Religions of the World*. The book appeared in 1729, after his death. Meslier had spent the greater part of his life working on it. The history of true atheism had begun.

2

Planned obscurity. The dominant historiography hides atheism from our sight. The Abbé Meslier is largely forgotten. Occasionally he is alluded to as a curiosity, a scholastic incongruity, a miscreant priest! Whenever he is honored with a passing mention, we look in vain for references to other authors worthy of being cited. The materialist philosophers come to mind. One was Julien de La Mettrie, who asserted in his *Natural History of the Soul* (1745) that psychic phenomena were due to organic changes in the brain. Or Nicolas Deschamps, a Jesuit also known as Dom Deschamps, whose work *Les Sociétés Secrètes* was published after his death, or the Baron d'Holbach, born Paul Heinrich Dietrich, who caustically derided religion in his book *The System of Nature*. Then there was Claude-Adrien Helvétius, who placed hedonistic emphasis on physical sensation and whose book *On the Mind* attacked all forms of morality based on religion. There was Sylvain Maréchal and his *Atheist Dictionary*. The ideologues of the French Revolution, such as Cabanis, Volney, and Destutt de Tracy, are also habitually ignored. By contrast, the bibliography of German idealism overflows with titles, works, and research.

Thus the work of Baron d'Holbach cannot be found in the university: no scholarly or scientific edition by any philosophical publisher worthy of the name; no works, theses, or ongoing research; no paperback edition, of course (whereas editions of Rousseau, Voltaire, Kant, or Montesquieu abound); no classes or seminars devoted to analytic examination and propagation of his thinking; not one biography . . . Painful!

The university harps on the same old themes, invariably returning to the so-called century of Enlightenment: Rousseau's social contract, Voltaire's tolerance, Kant's critiques, or the separation of powers dear to the thinker of Brède — so many musical saws, so many pious philosophical icons. And nothing on d'Holbach's atheism, on his caustic readings of biblical texts; nothing on his critique of Christian theocracy, of the collusion of state and church, on the need for separation of the two; nothing on the equal and separate status of the ethical and the religious; nothing on the dismantling of Catholic fables; nothing on comparative study of religions. There is likewise nothing on the critiques of his work by Rousseau, Diderot, Voltaire, and the supposedly enlightened deist clique; nothing on his concept of a post-Christian morality; nothing on the uses of practical knowledge in combating belief; nothing on the innate intolerance of Christian monotheism; nothing on the necessary submission of the political to the ethical; nothing on his call to use part of the church's wealth for the benefit of the poor; nothing on feminism and his assault on Catholic misogyny — all of them Holbachian theses of surprising contemporary relevance.

Silence on Meslier the wielder of *curses* (*Testament*, 1729), silence on d'Holbach the *demystifier* (his *Contagion Sacrée* dates from 1768). Silence too on Feuerbach the *deconstructionist* — (*The Essence of Christianity*, 1841) — that third great moment of Western atheism, a substantial pillar of an atheology deserving of the name. For Ludwig Andreas Feuerbach proposes an explanation of what God is. He does not deny his existence, he simply dissects the chimera. No assertion that *God does not exist*, but a question: *Who is this God in whom the majority of men believe?* His answer: a fabrication, a creation by men, a fiction that obeys particular laws — in this case projection and hypostasis. Men create God in their own inverted image.

Mortal, finite, limited, suffering from all these constraints, haunted by the desire for completeness, human beings invent a power endowed with precisely the opposite characteristics. With their faults turned inside out, like the fingers of a pair of gloves, they manufacture characteristics at whose feet they kneel and finally prostrate themselves. I am mortal, but God is immortal. I am finite, but God is infinite. I am limited, but God knows no limits. I do not know everything, but God is omniscient. I cannot do everything, but God is omnipotent. I am not blessed with the gift of ubiquity, but God is omnipresent. I was created, but

God is uncreated. I am weak, but God is the Almighty. I dwell on earth, but God is in heaven. I am imperfect, but God is perfect. I am nothing, but God is everything. And so on.

Religion thus becomes the exploitation par excellence of man's vulnerability to deception. It asserts man's separation from himself and proposes the creation of an imaginary world falsely invested with truth. Theology, says Feuerbach, is a "psychic pathology," against which he opposes his own brand of anthropology. Not without humor, he invites us to engage in "pneumatic water therapy" — using the cold water of natural reason against religious, and particularly Christian, hot water and steam.

Despite his immense philosophical undertaking, Feuerbach remains a forgotten figure in a history written by the dominant philosophy. His name does come up. It resurfaced notably in the 1960s, the glory days of philosopher-teacher Louis Althusser, the "Crocodile" of France's Ecole Normale Supérieure. Althusser credits Feuerbach with influencing the ideas of young Marx (as opposed to mature Marx). Feuerbach's influence is evident in Karl Marx's early works, *Economic and Philosophical Manuscripts of 1844* and *The German Ideology* (1845). Althusser saw a profound difference between Marx's early views and his later opinions, which he characterized as an "epistemological break." He used Feuerbach as a tool to help sell his theory, and Feuerbach's own genius disappeared beneath the great Althusser's utilitarian concerns. Sometimes total obscurity is preferable to a lasting misunderstanding or false interpretation.

3

Philosophical earthquake. And then came Nietzsche . . . First, the priest Meslier with his imprecations. Next, demythologization by the chemist (d'Holbach was a distinguished geologist and scientist). Eventually, deconstruction by the businessman. (Feuerbach was not a professional philosopher: the university blocked him from academic advancement after he published *Thoughts on Death and Immortality* [1830], an attack on the concept of personal immortality. But thanks to his marriage, he ended up the left-wing owner of a porcelain factory, beloved by his workers.) And now enter Nietzsche! At last the dominant thinking — idealist, spiritualist, Judeo-Christian, dualist — had good reason to be worried. Nietzsche's Dionysian monism, his logic of forces, his genealogy of morals, and his atheist ethic made it possible to envisage an exit from Christianity. For the first time, radical and well-thought-out post-Christian thinking appeared on the Western landscape.

Nietzsche was being facetious (or was he?) when he wrote in *Ecce Homo* that he was splitting history in two in the manner of Christ, with one half before and one half after him. The philosopher of Sils-Maria (the Swiss village where he spent many summers) had no Paul or Constantine to call on, no hysterical traveling salesman and no emperor to expand his personal epiphany into conversion of the entire world. Historically speaking, it is just as well that he didn't. The explosive nature of his thought represents too great a danger for the earthbound clods who play the leading roles in real-life history.

But on philosophical terrain, the father of Zarathustra was right. After *Beyond Good and Evil* and *The Antichrist*, it was no longer the same ideological world. Nietzsche had breached the Judeo-Christian edifice. Although he did not achieve the whole atheological task, he did make it possible. Hence the advantage of being Nietzschean. Definition? It is absurd to think that "being Nietzschean" means "being the same as Nietzsche." It does not entail subscribing to his major themes: resentment, eternal return, the superman, will to power, physiology of art, or any other aspect of his philosophical system. No need. What good would it do? To take oneself for Nietzsche, to don his mantle, adopt his ideas wholesale, and assume his thinking . . . that is not Nietzschean, and only small minds could think it was.

Being Nietzschean requires one to think apart from him, starting from the spot where the "work in progress" that is philosophy was transformed by his passage. He called for unfaithful disciples who, by their betrayal, would prove their loyalty. He wanted people to obey him by following themselves and no one else, not even him. Particularly not him. In *Thus Spake Zarathustra*, the parable of "The Three Metamorphoses" tells how the spirit becomes first a camel, then a lion, and finally a child. This and other of his works teach a dialectic and theory of aesthetics that we can put to practical use. We must honor Nietzsche but go past him. Certainly we remember his work, but above all we lean on it the way one leans one's weight on a huge lever in order to move philosophical mountains.

Nietzsche launched a new building project that represents an advance for atheism. Meslier denied all divinity, Holbach dismantled Christianity, Feuerbach deconstructed God. Then Nietzsche introduced transvaluation: atheism is not an end in itself. Do away with God, yes, but then what? Another morality, a new ethic, values never before thought of because unthinkable, this innovation is what makes it possible to arrive at atheism and to surpass it. A formidable task, and one still to be brought to fruition.

The Antichrist narrates European nihilism — which is still with us — and proposes a pharmacopoeia for that metaphysical and ontological disease of our civilization. Nietzsche's solutions are known to us. They register more than a century of life and of misunderstandings. Being Nietzschean means proposing alternative hypotheses, fresh, new, post-Nietzschean, but assimilating his struggle on the mountain peaks. The various forms of contemporary nihilism call more than ever for a transvaluation that finally leaves behind it the religious and secular hypotheses born of the monotheisms. Zarathustra must return to the conflict: atheism alone makes an exit from nihilism possible.

4

Teaching the case for atheism. While September 11, 2001, as seen by the United States and therefore by the West, calls upon everyone to choose sides in the religious war that supposedly pits Judeo-Christianity against Islam, we might prefer to avoid choosing either side and opt instead for a Nietzschean position. That position would be neither Judeo-Christian nor Muslim, for the very good reason that these belligerents are continuing the religious war that began with the Torah bidding the Jews to do battle with their enemies. The book of Numbers, chapter 21, verse 14, refers to the "book of the wars of the Lord." The justification for bloody battle against one's enemies is an important part of the Torah. And the Koran is infused with recurrent variations on the same theme: slaughter of the enemy. In other words, nearly twenty-five centuries of calls *by both sides* to acts of crime! Nietzsche's lesson: we can choose not to choose. And a decision not to side with Israel and the United States does not automatically mean that one is a fellow traveler of the Taliban.

Talmud and Torah, Bible and New Testament, Koran and the Hadith offer insufficient grounds for the philosopher to choose between Jewish, Christian, or Muslim misogyny. Or to opt against pork and alcohol but in favor of the veil or the burka, to attend the synagogue, the temple, the church, or the mosque, all places where intelligence is ailing and where, for centuries, the faithful have practiced obedience to dogma and submission to the Law — and therefore obedience and submission to those who claim to be the elect, the envoys and the word of God.

At a time when the West is debating the teaching of religion in schools on the pretext of manufacturing social solidarity, of reuniting a community slipping out of its grasp (precisely, let us remember, because of a liberalism that daily generates negativity), of inspiring a new form of social contract, of rediscovering common sources (which all happen to be monotheistic), it seems to me that we might prefer the teaching of atheism. The *Genealogy of Morals* (1887) rather than the epistles to the Corinthians.

Today we are witnessing efforts to smuggle the Bible and other monotheistic bric-a-brac back through the window into the house after centuries of philosophical struggle to eject them through the front door. The struggle was led by the Enlightenment and the French Revolution, socialism and the Paris Commune, the left and the Popular Front, the libertarian spirit and May 1968, but also by Freud and Marx, the Frankfurt School, and the French left's mistrust of the Nietzscheans. This itch to restore the trappings of religiosity arises strictly and etymologically from willingness to accept reactionary thinking. Not in the manner of Joseph Le Maistre, Louis de Bonald, or Blanc de Saint-Bonnet but in the Gramscian manner of a return to the diluted, deceptive, travestied, and hypocritically reactivated ideals of Judeo-Christianity.

These days, it is true that no one openly vaunts the merits of theocracy or advocates doing away with rule by the people (the ideals of 1789). No one has written a book entitled *On the Pope*, extolling the supreme pontiff's political power. But we do denounce the individual, deny him rights, and heap him with duties by the shovelful. We celebrate collectivity over the singular, plead for transcendence, exempt the state and its parasites from explaining their actions on the grounds of their ontological extraterritoriality. We ignore the people and brand as populists and demagogues those who care about them. We despise the intellectuals and philosophers who go against the tide. The list could go on forever.

Never more than today has there been such evidence of vitality in what the eighteenth century called "antiphilosophy": the return of religious thinking, proof that God is not dead but that he was merely and briefly dozing, and that his awakening foretells great disenchantment. The trend has escalated to such an extent that we are now obliged to take up old defensive positions. We used to think that progress had rendered those positions out of date. But no. Atheism is forced to step into the breach once more. Religious instruction has put the fox back among the chickens. If professors cannot teach religion openly, they do it on the sly, claiming that the stories of the Old Testament, New Testament, Koran, and Hadith give students a greater appreciation and understanding of Marc Chagall, the *Divine Comedy*, the Sistine Chapel, and Ziryab's music.

But religions should be taught as a part of the existing curriculum — philosophy, history, literature, plastic arts, languages, etc. — the way the proto-sciences are taught: for example alchemy within chemistry courses, phytognomonics and phrenology within the natural sciences, totemism and magical thinking as a part of philosophy, Euclidean geometry within mathematics, mythology within history. Or in order to explain etymologically how myth, fable, fiction, and folly preceded reason, deduction, and debate. Religion proceeds from a primitive, genealogical, and outdated mode of rationality. Reactivating this prehistoric history means delaying and even missing altogether the history of today and tomorrow.

Presenting the case for atheism requires delving into the religious impulse. It stems from fear, misgiving, unease, inability to look death in the face, the feeling that something is lacking, and distress at the realization that human life is finite: the primary components of existential angst. Religion is a fabric woven with fictions and metaphysical placebos. It calls for a systematic un-raveling—just as in philosophy one investigates the occult and the borderline of insanity during the search for the essential nature of reason.

5

Plate tectonics. We are still in a theological or religious stage of civilization. But there are signs of movement, comparable to the types of motion in plate tectonics: convergence, divergence, sliding, collision, subduction, overriding, fracture. The *pre-Christian era* is clearly demarcated: from pre-Socratic mythology to Roman Empire Stoicism; i.e., from Parmenides to Epictetus. Next came a turbulent transition period, as early-stage Christianity overlapped late-stage paganism. The *Christian era* is easily defined: it started with the church fathers, was spread in the second century by millenarian prophets (proclaiming that God is about to destroy the world and only true believers will be saved), and continued to the eighteenth century with the secular deism of the Enlightenment. The beheading of Louis XVI in January 1793 marked the end of theocracy in France. Christianity, of course, persisted.

We are now living in a new transitional phase, heading toward a third era, the *post-Christian era*. In some ways, our current period is curiously similar to the transitional stage between the pagan and Christian eras. Thus, the end of the pre-Christian and the beginning of the post-Christian both exhibit the same nihilism, the same anxieties, the same dynamic interplay between progressive and reactionary trends. Today we have conservatism, reaction, yearning for the past, and rigid religion vying with liberalism, progressivism, social reform, and movements dedicated to building a better future. Religion is anchored in tradition and cashes in on nostalgia. Philosophy looks to the future.

The forces in play are clearly identifiable. It is not Western, progressive, enlightened, democratic Judeo-Christianity pitted against Eastern, backward-looking, obscurantist Islam. Rather, it is yesterday's monotheisms pitted against the atheism of tomorrow. Not Bush versus bin Laden. Instead, it is Moses, Jesus, Muhammad, and their religions of the book versus Baron d'Holbach, Ludwig Feuerbach, Friedrich Nietzsche, and their philosophical formulae of radical deconstruction of myths and fables.

Historically speaking, the post-Christian era will deploy its forces the same way the Christian era did: the monotheist empire can be toppled. The religion of an only God cannot become the fixed horizon of philosophy and of history itself—as communism once was for some people or as free-market liberalism is for others today. A Christian era once replaced a pagan era, and it will inevitably be replaced by a post-Christian phase. The turbulent period we live in suggests that change is at hand and the time has come for a new order. Hence the importance of an atheological project.

III

Toward an Atheology

1

Spectrum of nihilism. The age we live in seems atheistic, but only to Christians or believers. In fact, it is nihilistic. The true believers of yesterday and the day before have every interest in characterizing the worst and most negative aspects of contemporary life as products of atheism. The old idea of the immoral, amoral atheist, with neither faith nor ethical rules, dies hard. The phrase "if God does not exist, then everything is permitted" — a refrain picked up from Dostoyevsky's *The Brothers Karamazov* — continues to resonate, and people in fact associate death, hatred, and poverty with individuals who supposedly seek justification for their misdeeds in the nonexistence of God. This misguided notion needs to be thoroughly demolished. For the opposite seems to me to be true: "because God exists, everything is permitted." Let me explain. Thirty centuries, from the earliest texts of the Old Testament to the present day, teach us that the assertion of one God, violent, jealous, quarrelsome, intolerant, and bellicose, has generated more hate, bloodshed, deaths, and brutality than it has peace . . . There is the Jewish fantasy of a chosen people, which vindicates colonialism, expropriation, hatred, animosity between peoples, and finally an authoritarian and armed theocracy . . . There is the Christian image of the Temple moneylenders, or of a Pauline Jesus claiming to have come bearing a sword. This justifies the Crusades, the Inquisition, the French Religious Wars, the Saint Bartholomew's Day massacre of Paris's Protestants, the stake, the *Index*, but also worldwide colonialism, North American ethnocides, support for twentieth-century fascist movements, and the centuries-long temporal hold of the Vatican over the smallest details of daily life . . . And there is the clear exhortation on almost every page of the Koran to destroy unbelievers — but also the Jews and Christians of the book — their religion, their culture, their civilization, all in the name of a merciful God! So many pathways to entrench the idea that precisely because of God's existence everything is permitted — in him, through him, and in his name, without the slightest objection by believers, clergy, the masses, or the ruling spheres.

If the existence of God, independently of its Jewish, Christian, or Muslim form, had given us at least a little forewarning against hatred, lies, rape, pillage, immorality, embezzlement, perjury, violence, contempt, swindling, false witness, depravity, pedophilia, infanticide, drunkenness, and perversion, we might have seen not atheists (since they are intrinsically creatures of vice) but rabbis, priests, imams, and with them their faithful, all their faithful (which amounts to a great many) doing good, excelling in virtue, setting an example, and proving to the godless and perverse that morality is on their side. Let their flocks scrupulously respect the Commandments and obey the dictates of the relevant suras, and thus neither lie nor pillage, neither rob nor rape, neither bear false witness nor murder — and still less plot terrorist attacks in Manhattan, launch punitive raids into the Gaza Strip, or cover up the deeds of their pedophile priests. Then we would see the faithful converting their neighbors right, left, and center through the example of their shining conduct. But instead . . .

So let us have an end to this linkage of the world's woes to atheism! God's existence, it seems to me, has historically generated in his name more battles, massacres, conflicts, and wars than peace, serenity, brotherly love, forgiveness of sins, and tolerance. To my knowledge, no popes, princes, kings, caliphs, or emirs have excelled in the practice of virtue, so outstandingly did Moses, Paul, and Muhammad excel in murder, torture, and orgies of plunder—I call the biographies to witness. So many variations on the theme of loving one's neighbor.

The history of the human race unquestionably teaches the rewards of vice and the disappointments of virtue . . . There is no transcendent justice any more than there is an immanent justice. Whether God is or is not, he has never made anyone pay for insulting, neglecting, despising, forgetting, or crossing him! Theists indulge in every kind of metaphysical contortion to justify evil in the world, while simultaneously affirming the existence of a God whom nothing escapes! Deists seem less blind, atheists more lucid.

2

A Judeo-Christian epistemology. So the times we live in are no longer atheist. Nor do they yet seem post-Christian, or barely. On the other hand, they are still Christian, much more so than first appears. Nihilism stems from the turbulence of this transit zone between still very present Judeo-Christianity and timidly blooming post-Christianity. The background is an atmosphere where the presence or absence of gods, their proliferation, their fantastic multiplicity, and their extravagances intersect. Heaven is not empty but on the contrary full of divinities manufactured from one day to the next. And the nihilism coexists with a flagging Judeo-Christianity and a post-Christian era still relegated to the sidelines.

While waiting for an outspokenly atheistic era, we must

plan for and be content with a Judeo-Christian epistemology pregnant with significance. Precisely because the institutions and the contract killers who have embodied and transmitted it for centuries no longer possess a readily identifiable style and visibility. The waning of religious practice, the apparent autonomy of ethics in relation to religion, the perceived public indifference at the prospect of a papal visit, churches empty on Sundays—but not for weddings and still less for funerals—the separation of church and state . . . all these give the impression of a period indifferent to religion.

But let's remain on our guard . . . Never before, perhaps, has this apparent eclipse so effectively hidden the strong, powerful, and decisive presence of Judeo-Christianity. The disaffection of the faithful does not mean a retreat from belief. To see a correlation between the two is to misinterpret the situation. We might even argue that the end of the official church monopoly over religious issues has liberated the irrational, generating a greater profusion than ever of the sacred, of religiosity, and of widespread acquiescence in religious folly.

The retreat of Judeo-Christian forces has not undermined their strength or their control over territories conquered, held, and administered by them for nearly two thousand years—testimony to their long-standing ideological, mental, conceptual, and spiritual control. Even after their physical departure the conquerors are still there, because they have subdued the bodies, souls, minds, and flesh of the majority. Their strategic withdrawal does not mean the end of their effective rule. Judeo-Christianity has left an epistemology, a platform on which all mental and symbolic exchanges still take place. Even without the priest, without the religious and their incense-bearers, their former subjects remain submissive, manufactured, formatted by two millennia of history and ideological domination. Hence the permanence and the current relevance of the struggle against this renascent force, all the more dangerous because it wrongly appears to be obsolete.

Of course, not many people still believe in transubstantiation, in Mary's virginity, the Immaculate Conception, papal infallibility, and other dogma of the Catholic, Apostolic, and Roman Church. The real, not symbolic, presence of Christ's body in the Host or the wine? The existence of hell, paradise, and purgatory, with their associated geography and their own logic? The existence of a limbo in which the souls of infants dead before baptism stagnate? No one still subscribes to such twaddle, even (and especially) those many Catholics who fervently attend Sunday Mass.

Where then does the Catholic substratum survive? And where the Judeo-Christian epistemology? Simply in the notion that matter, the real, and the world are not all there is. That *something* remains outside all the explanatory apparatus: a force, a power, an energy, a determinism, a will, a desire. And after death? Well, certainly not nothing. *Something* ... And how can it be explained? By a series of causes, of rational and deducible linkages? Not altogether: *something* escapes the logical sequence. And the world—is it absurd, irrational, illogical, monstrous, senseless? Assuredly not ... *Something* must exist to justify, legitimize, make sense. Otherwise ...

This belief in *something* gives rise to a vigorous superstition suggesting that if all else fails the believer will still subscribe to the dominant religion—of his king and of his nanny, as Descartes put it—of the country where he sees the light of day. Montaigne maintains that one is a Christian the way one is Breton or a native of Picardy! And many individuals who consider themselves atheists profess—without noticing it—an ethic, a way of thinking, a vision of the world saturated in Judeo-Christianity. Between a sincere priest's homily on the excellence of Jesus and the praise of Christ offered by the anarchist Peter

Kropotkin in *Ethics*, we look in vain for a gulf, or even a small ditch.

Atheism implies the banishing of transcendence. With no exceptions. It also demands the transcending of Christian gains. Or at least it demands the right to take stock of them, to examine virtues presented as such and vices equally summarily asserted. A secular and philosophical reevaluation, from the ground up, of the Bible's values and the question of their preservation and their use, is not enough to produce a post-Christian ethic.

In *Religion within the Limits of Reason Alone* (1793), Kant proposes a secular ethic. Reading this book, of major historical importance in the construction of a Western secular morality, we again encounter the philosophical formulations of a seemingly inexhaustible Judeo-Christian spring. The book's revolutionary implications are evident in the form, style, vocabulary. But at what point do the Christian ethic and Kant's differ? Nowhere . . . The Kantian mountain gives birth to a Christian mouse.

People laugh at the pope's words on the need to ban contraceptives. But a lot of people still get married in church — to please their families and in-laws, according to some. They smile when reading the *Catechism* — that is, if they even have the curiosity to consult it. But the number of registered civil funerals is tiny. They mock priests and their beliefs. But they seek them out for blessings, those updated indulgences that reconcile the pious hypocrisies of both sides: the consumers come to a compromise with their churchgoing peers, and by the same token, the providers find customers.

3

Vestiges of empire. Michel Foucault characterized epistemology as a device invisible but effective in discourse, in the envisioning of things and the world, in representations of the real. A device that locks in, crystallizes, and hardens an era in frozen postures. From the hysteria of Paul of Tarsus on the road to Damascus to the globally televised utterances of John Paul II on Saint Peter's Square, Judeo-Christian epistemology identifies a conceptual and mental empire pervading every component of civilization and culture. Two examples among a multitude of possibilities: the body, and law.

The Western body (including that of atheists, Muslims, deists, and agnostics raised in the geographic and ideological Judeo-Christian zone) is Christian. Two thousand years of Christian discourse — anatomy, medicine, physiology, of course, but also philosophy, theology, and aesthetics — have fashioned the body we inhabit. And along with that discourse we have inherited Platonic-Christian models that mediate our perception of the body, the symbolic value of the body's organs, and their hierarchically ordered functions. We accept the nobility of heart and mind, the triviality of viscera and sex (the neurosurgeon versus the proctologist). We accept the spiritualization and dematerialization of the soul, the interaction of sin-prone matter and of luminous mind, the ontological connotation of these two artificially opposed entities, the disturbing forces of a morally reprehensible libidinal humanity . . . All have contributed to Christianity's sculpting of the flesh.

Our image of ourselves, the scrutiny of the doctor or the radiologist, the whole philosophy of sickness and health — none of this could exist in the absence of the above-mentioned discourse. Nor could our conception of suffering, the role we allot to pain and therefore our relationship with pharmacology, substances, and drugs. Nor could the special language of practitioner to patient, the relationship of self to self, reconciliation of one's image of oneself with an ideal of the physiological, anatomical, and psychological self. So that surgery and pharmacology, homeopathic medicine and palliative treatments, gynecology and thanatology, emergency medicine and oncology, psychiatry and clinical work all obey Judeo-Christian law without any particularly clear understanding of the symptoms of this ontological contamination.

The current hypersensitivity on the subject of bioethics proceeds from this invisible influence. Secular political decisions on this major issue more or less correspond to the positions formulated by the church. This should be no surprise, for the ethos of bioethics remains fundamentally Judeo-Christian. Apart from legislation on abortion and artificial contraception, apart from these two forward steps toward a post-Christian body — what I have elsewhere called a *Faustian body* — Western medicine sticks very closely to the church's injunctions.

The *Health Professionals' Charter* elaborated by the Vatican condemns sex-change operations, experiments on the embryo, in vitro fertilization and transfer, surrogate motherhood, medical assistance with reproduction, but also therapeutic cloning, analgesic cocktails that suspend consciousness as life comes to an end, therapeutic use of cannabis, and euthanasia. On the other hand, the charter praises palliative care and insists on *the salutary role of pain*. These are all positions unanimously echoed by ethical committees calling themselves secular and believing themselves independent of religious authority.

Naturally, when practitioners in the West are confronted with a sick body, they are generally unaware that they think, act, and diagnose in the way they have been trained, that is, in the Judeo-Christian tradition. The conscience is not involved but rather a series of deeper, more ancient determinisms referring back to the hours that have gone into developing a temperament, a character, and a conscience. The therapist's and the patient's subconscious emerge from one and the same metaphysical bath. Atheism demands a study of these formattings, no longer visible but meaningful in the details of daily bodily living: a detailed analysis of the sexed, sexual body and related interactions would take up a whole book.

4

Garden-grown torture. Second example: the law. Our courthouses forbid the open display of religious symbols. A judicial decision cannot be handed down beneath a crucifix displayed on its walls, much less beneath a verse from the Torah or a sura from the Koran. The civil and penal codes supposedly assert the law independently of religion and the church. Yet there is nothing in French jurisprudence that fundamentally contradicts the prescriptions of the Catholic, Apostolic, and Roman Church. The absence of a cross in the courtroom does not guarantee a judiciary that is independent with respect to the dominant religion.

For the very foundations of judicial logic proceed from chapter 3 of Genesis. Hence a Jewish (the Pentateuch) and a Christian (the Bible) ancestry for the French Civil Code. The apparatus, the technique, and the metaphysics of the law flow in a direct line from what is taught in the fable of the original Garden—the story of a man who is free, and therefore responsible for his acts, and therefore potentially guilty. Because he is endowed with freedom, the individual may choose and prefer one option over another in his spectrum of possible choices. Every action thus proceeds from a free choice, a free will, informed and manifest.

The premise that human beings have free will is the key to the cause-and-effect relationship between crime and punishment. For eating the forbidden fruit, disobedience—the error perpetrated in the Garden of Earthly Delights—flow from an act of the will, and therefore from an act that can be reproved and punished. Adam and Eve could have refrained from sinning, for they had been created free, but they chose vice over virtue. So they can be called to account for their action. They can even be punished. And on that score, God in the Garden of Eden did not hesitate. He sentenced them and their descendants to perpetual shame, to guilt, to toil, pain in childbirth, suffering, aging, woman's subjection to man, the near impossibility of any sexual intersubjectivity. From then on, based on this model and in virtue of this principle laid down in the first moments of scripture, a judge could play at being God on earth.

When a court functions without religious symbols, it nevertheless operates in accordance with this biblical metaphysics. The child-rapist is free: he has the choice of engaging in a normal sexual relationship with a consenting partner or of inflicting horrifying violence on a victim he destroys forever. In his soul and conscience, endowed with a free will permitting him to prefer one option over another, he chooses violence — when he could have decided otherwise! So that he can be required to account for himself in court, listened to with half an ear or not even heard, and sent to spend years in prison. There he will probably be raped in a gesture of welcome before rotting in a cell from which he will be released after failing to confront the disease he suffers from.

Who would ever countenance a hospital locking up a man or a woman diagnosed with a brain tumor — no more of a free choice than a pedophiliac fixation — in a cell, exposing him to the repressive violence of a handful of cellmates imbued with the savagery of confinement before abandoning him, after a quarter of his life span, to the ravages of cancer, without care or concern, without treatment? Who? Answer: all those who set the machinery of justice in motion and operate it like a device found outside the gates of the Garden of Eden, without ever wondering what it is, why it has been left there, how it works.

That same machine, present in Kafka's penal colony, daily produces the same results in Western courts and their adjacent prisons. This collusion between the principle of free will and the voluntary choice of evil over good — which legitimizes the notion of responsibility, and therefore guilt, and therefore punishment — requires the workings of magical thinking. There is no place here for what Freud's post-Christian project illuminates through psychoanalysis, or the work of other philosophers who highlight the power of subconscious, psychological, cultural, social, familial, and ethological causes.

Body and law, even (and especially) when they think, believe, and call themselves secular, proceed from Judeo-Christian epistemology. So do analyses of teaching, aesthetics, philosophy, politics — all of these areas are influenced by biblical religious doctrine. Yet another push is needed before we can call ourselves truly republican.

5

On Christian ignorance. Our failure to recognize the workings of this logic of penetration can be explained if we stress that much of it takes place in the subconscious register, concealed from informed and lucid consciousness. Christian ideology is transmitted insidiously, without the medium of language or overt assertions. Apart from the case of self-acknowledged theocracies — political regimes openly inspired by one of the three books — the Judeo-Christian roots of secular practices go unnoticed by most people, including the practitioners, actors, and individuals concerned.

The invisibility of this process is not simply the result of its subconscious mode of propagation. It is also attributable to gnorance of Judeo-Christian teaching. This includes believers and churchgoers, often undereducated, informed only by the crumbs of information they are fed by the clergy. Sunday Mass has never glittered as a place for reflection, analysis, culture, or the spread and exchange of knowledge; nor has the *Catechism*; and the same could be said of their counterparts in the other monotheist religions.

Thus, no learning occurs while standing at the Wailing Wall or while the Muslim is performing his five daily prayers. He prays, he recites the responses, he exercises his memory but not his intelligence. For Christian Frenchmen, Bossuet's sermons constitute an exception in a twenty-century sea of platitudes . . . And for every Averroës and Avicenna, how many hyper-mnemonic but intellectually challenged imams?

Knowledge of their religion's structure, understanding of its disputes and controversies, injunctions to reflect and criticize, the clash of contradictory information and polemical debate are all resoundingly absent. The community is marked rather by the triumph of parrotlike repetition and the recycling of fables, with the help of well-oiled machinery that repeats but never innovates, which solicits not the intelligence but the memory. Chanting psalms, reciting, and repeating are not thinking. Nor is praying. Far from it.

Believers listen to a text by Saint Paul for the umpteenth time but have never even heard the name of Gregory of Nazianze. They set up the Infant's crèche each year but know nothing of the founding quarrels of Arianism or the Council on iconophilia. They commune with an unleavened Host but are ignorant of the existence of the dogma of papal infallibility . . . Nor is this all. Believers attend Christmas Mass but are unaware that the church picked this date in order to coincide with the winter solstice, when pagans honored *Sol Invictus*, the Unconquered Sun. They attend church christenings, weddings, and funerals but have never heard of the existence of the apocryphal angels. They remove their hats before a crucifix but have never learned that death by stoning and not by crucifixion was the standard punishment for the crime with which Jesus was charged . . . and so many other cultural blind alleys resulting from the fetishization of rites and practices. The prospects for enlightened exercise of one's religion are dim.

It all began with that ancient lesson from Genesis: man is forbidden to seek awareness; he should be content to believe and obey. He must choose faith over knowledge, suppress all interest in science, and instead prize submission and obedience. None of this helps raise the level of debate. The etymology of "Muslim," which according to the dictionary means *submissive* toward God and Muhammad, the impossibility of thinking or acting outside the Torah, which has laws regulating every tiniest detail of daily life — all these things militate against reason and in favor of submission . . . It's almost as if religion needs innocence, lack of education, and ignorance in order to thrive!

There exist, of course, men of the cloth who are highly educated in religion, history, and science. But they are dedicated to proving the validity of religious dogma; thus, they only add to a church arsenal already brimming with specious arguments. Centuries of rhetoric, a millennium of theological sophistry, whole libraries of scholastic nitpicking have promoted the use of knowledge as a weapon designed less for honest argument than for apologia. This was an art that Tertullian exercised brilliantly on behalf of Christianity, an art that required manipulating history to support the ideological agenda of the polemicist. (After all, the term "Jesuit" is also virtually synonymous with casuistry . . .)

Point out to a Christian that ever since the conversion of Constantine the church has chosen the camp of the powerful and neglected the weak and the poor. He replies triumphantly, "What about liberation theology?" — forgetting at the same time that liberation theology was condemned by John Paul II, leader and guide of the church. Suggest the obvious fact that Pauline Christianity, the official model, decries the pleasures of the flesh and despises women. He might retort, "'Mystical ecstasy' is on a higher plane than carnal ecstasy." There have been many cases of men seemingly possessed by the Holy Ghost who fall to the ground, flailing about in an orgasm of religious fervor. (Women too; notably Saint Teresa of Ávila.) But the speaker does not realize that in most cases the carnally inclined mystic was discredited during his lifetime (although after his death he may be welcomed back into the bosom of the faithful via beatification, canonization, and other ceremonies dedicated to the redemption of yesterday's lost sheep). Mention the massacres of the New World Indians perpetrated in the name of the most Catholic religion, the Spanish colonizers' denial of the soul and humanity of the Indians. The believer will laugh and say, "You're forgetting Bartolomé de Las Casas." But does he realize that Las Casas, theoretical defender of the Indians though he may have been, consigned every book written by the ancient Guatemalans to the flames? And that Las Casas (who believed that African blacks, soon to be swallowed up in the transatlantic slave trade, were endowed like the Amerindians with human souls) did not reveal his belief until after his death . . . in his will?

The same logic drives the interpreters — ayatollahs and mullahs — of Koranic law. They strive to give meaning and coherence to the contradictory texts in their holy book, juggling suras, verses, and thousands of hadith or fine-tuning abrogatory and abrogated verses! Should we point out to them the instances of hatred of Jews and non-Muslims that stuff the pages of the Koran? They would point to the practice of *dhimma*, theoretically intended to assure non-Muslim people of the book of their right to exist and be protected. But they would be careful not to add that this protection exists only after payment of a staggering tax, the *gizya*. Which aligns the professed Muslim tolerance with the Mafia's "protection" of an individual forced to finance the organization that persecutes him . . . Another variant on the revolutionary tax!

These oversights, this defective information, this reliance on obedience rather than intelligence empties religion of its authentic contents, leaving only a pallid echo of the original, more or less compatible with every kind of metaphysical and sociological flavoring. Like Marxists who consider themselves Marxists yet deny the class struggle and reject the dictatorship of the proletariat, many Jews, Christians, and Muslims construct for themselves a made-to-measure morality. This implies selective borrowings (tailored to fit their needs) from their holy books in order to establish rules of play and participation by the community — to the detriment of all the other tenets of their faith. Hence a disappearance of outward religious practices alongside a strengthening of the dominant epistemology. Which brings us to Christian atheism.

6

Christian atheism. For too long, and on every point, the atheist has seen himself as the reverse of the priestly coin. Fascinated by his enemy, the God-denier has all too frequently borrowed a great many of his endearing idiosyncrasies. But this "clerical" atheism offers us nothing of interest. Chapels of free thinking and rationalist unions are just as bent on conversion as the clergy, while Masonic lodges modeled on those of France's Third Republic barely merit attention. Henceforth, we must aim for what Gilles Deleuze calls a *quiet atheism* — less a static concern with negating or fighting God than a dynamic method designed for postconflict reconstruction. Negation of God is not an end in itself, but a means of working toward a post-Christian or frankly secular ethic.

To draw the outlines of post-Christian atheism, let us stop for a moment at this obstacle we still have to cross: *atheist Christianity* — or Christianity without God. Yet another curious creature! The phenomenon exists: it characterizes one who denies God but at the same time asserts the excellence of Christian values and the incomparable virtue of evangelical morality. Its operation implies the disassociation of morality and transcendence: good has no need of God, of heaven, or of any intelligible anchorage. It is sufficient unto itself and arises from an immanent necessity — proposing a set of rules, a code of conduct among men.

Theology ceases to be the foster parent of morality, and philosophy takes over. Where a Judeo-Christian reading implies a vertical logic — from the low of human beings to the high of values — the Christian atheist hypothesis proposes a horizontal layout: nothing outside what can be rationally deduced, no design on any terrain but that of the real, tangible world. God does not exist, virtues do not flow from a revelation: they do not descend from heaven but proceed from a utilitarian and pragmatic viewpoint. Men give themselves laws and have no need to call on an extraterrestrial power to provide them.

The immanent ordering of the world distinguishes the Christian atheist from the Christian believer. But not their values, which remain identical. All operate on common ground — Priest and philosopher, Vatican and Kant, the Gospels and the *Critique of Practical Reason*, Mother Teresa and Paul Ricoeur, Catholic love of one's neighbor and the transcendental humanism of Luc Ferry as set out in *Man Made God: The Meaning of Life*, the Christian ethic and the great virtues of André Comte-

Sponville. Their concerns are charity, temperance, compassion, mercy, and humility, but also love of one's neighbor and the forgiveness of offenses, the injunction to turn the other cheek, indifference to the goods of this world, the ethical asceticism that rejects power, honors, and wealth as so many false values leading away from true wisdom. Those are the *theoretically* professed options.

Most of the time, this Christian atheism dismisses the Pauline hatred of the body, its rejection of desires, pleasures, drives, and passions. More in step with their period on questions of sexual morality than Christians on God, these advocates of a return to the Gospels—under cover of a return to Kant, even to Spinoza—consider that the cure for the nihilism of our period does not require a post-Christian effort but a secular and immanent rereading of the message left by Christ. Jewish philosophers provide some of the models for this Judeo-Christianity without God: Vladimir Jankélévitch (see *Treatise on the Virtues*), Emmanuel Levinas (read his *The Humanism of the Other* and *Totality and Infinity*), Bernard-Henri Lévy (*The Testament of God*), or Alain Finkielkraut (*The Wisdom of Love*).

7

A postmodern atheism. If we could get past Christian atheism, we might arrive at a true *atheistic atheism* (no redundancy implied). The term encompasses more than negation of God and of a part of the values derived from him. It calls for a different *episteme*, a Greek word used in philosophy to indicate the set of ideas, the science, the body of knowledge that makes it possible to separate the true from the false. *Atheistic atheism* would place morality and politics on a new base, one that is not nihilist but post-Christian. Its aim is neither to reconstruct churches nor to destroy them, but to build elsewhere and in a different way, to build something else for those no longer willing to dwell intellectually in places that have already done long service.

Postmodern atheism divests itself of its theological and scientific trappings in order to construct a moral system. Neither God nor science, neither intelligible heaven nor the operation of mathematical propositions, neither Thomas Aquinas nor Auguste Comte nor Marx. But philosophy, reason, utility, pragmatism, individual and social hedonism — these constitute so many invitations to maneuver on the terrain of pure immanence, in the interests of men, by themselves and for themselves, and not by God and for God.

Historically, two Englishmen were among the first to go outside the religious and geometric mold: Jeremy Bentham and his disciple John Stuart Mill. Bentham's *Deontology* merits reading over and over again. Both men turned their intellects to projects meant to serve society in the here and now. If German idealism envisioned immense cathedrals, beautiful but unlivable, Bentham and Mill built modest structures, practical and beneficial to the common man.

Good and evil continue to matter not because they coincide with religious concepts of belief and nonbelief, but simply as factors in the struggle to ensure the greatest possible happiness of the greatest number. The hedonist contract — nothing could be more immanent — legitimizes all intersubjectivity, conditions all thought and action, dispenses utterly with God, religion, and priests. With it, there is no need to brandish the threat of hell or dangle the glittering bauble of paradise, no point in establishing an ontology of posthumous reward and punishment to elicit good, just, and honest action. It is an ethic without transcendent obligations or sanctions.

8

In Defense of Atheism **takes on three challenges**. The book sets out to accomplish three objectives: deconstruction of the three monotheisms, deconstruction of Christianity in particular, and deconstruction of theocracy. Part two undertakes the first task: to analyze the three monotheisms and demonstrate how they are alike. Despite their historical and geographical divergences, despite centuries of the mutual hatred that has inflamed their supporters, despite the apparent irreconcilability of Mosaic law, Jesus's teachings, and the Prophet's words, the fundamentals remain the same. To adopt a musical metaphor, these three movements (elaborated over more than a thousand years) have different backgrounds and are played at different tempos, but they are variations on one and the same theme. Variations of degree, not of kind.

But what exactly are these shared fundamentals? First, a sequence of waves of hatred set in violent motion throughout history by men claiming to be the repositories and interpreters of God's word—the priestly castes. Second, hatred of intelligence, which monotheists reject in favor of submission and obedience; hatred of life coupled with a passionate and unshakable obsession with death; hatred of the here and now, consistently undervalued in favor of a beyond, the only possible reservoir of sense, truth, certainty, and bliss; hatred of the corruptible body, disparaged in every aspect, while the soul—eternal, immortal, divine—is invested with all the higher qualities and all the virtues; and finally, hatred of women, condemnation of liberated sexuality and sex for pleasure. Religion sets up the Angel, a bodiless archetype, in preference to real women. Chastity is a virtue common to all three religions.

All three monotheisms have a negative attitude toward the

joy of life and even toward some of the basic human drives. Once that has been established, this book will focus on one religion in particular. Christianity grew on the fertile soil of collective hysteria: a psychological term for the fears and volatile emotional state of the masses. It rooted itself in fallacious principles; it put forward lies, fiction, and myths, and then conferred on them the stamp of authenticity. The repetition of a sum of errors by the greatest number eventually becomes a corpus of truths that is sacrosanct. Questioning those truths could be dangerous for freethinkers — from the Christian bonfires of the day before yesterday to the Muslim fatwas of today.

To illustrate how a mythology is constructed, part three of this text offers a *deconstruction of Christianity*. We can pinpoint the moment in history when Jesus was forged; construction of his image proceeded over the next one or two hundred years. First-century Palestine under Roman occupation was a theater of unrest. A suffering, oppressed people needed a savior who could perform miracles. Jesus — a conceptual and in no way historical character — embodied the millenarian, prophetic, and apocalyptic aspirations of the times. His life, death, and message were embellished and promoted by Paul of Tarsus, who believed he had a mandate from God — when, in actuality, he was driven by a host of psychological problems. Paul converted his self-loathing into hatred of the world. His impotence and resentment took the form of revenge: the revenge of a weakling. Paul became the driving force behind a messianic cult that spread throughout the Mediterranean basin. This was one man's experience of masochism extended to the dimension of a sect. Furthermore, his was just one among thousands of sects active in that turbulent epoch. All of this becomes evident if we think about it just a little. It will require us to set aside obedience and submission in matters of religion and to reactivate an ancient taboo: tasting the fruit of the Tree of Knowledge.

Deconstructing Christianity entails an analysis of how the myth was fabricated and how Paul's neurosis was a contributing factor. But that is only the beginning. Promulgation of the myth had worldwide repercussions. We shall reflect on the historical implications of the emperor Constantine's conversion to the sectarian religion, motivated by pure political opportunism. In consequence of that conversion, the beliefs and practices formerly limited to a handful of visionaries expanded to encompass an empire. From a persecuted minority, the Christians became a persecuting majority, thanks to the intervention of an emperor who had become one of their own.

The thirteenth apostle, as Constantine proclaimed himself in the course of one church council, installed a totalitarian regime that enacted harsh laws against non-Christians and set out to systematically eradicate the ancient culture. It was an era of book burnings and autos-da-fé, physical persecution, confiscation of goods, forced exiles, assassinations, demolition of pagan buildings, desecration of shrines and objects of worship, library burnings, and architectural recycling: turning ancient temples into Christian churches or else using their rubble to build roads, etc.

Following several centuries of such unchecked power, the spiritual became confused with the temporal . . . Hence, part four: a *deconstruction of theocracies.* These forms of government exert a practical and political claim to power supposedly emanating from God. He himself does not speak (for good reason), but his priests and clergy lend him a voice. In the name of God, but through the agency of God's self-styled servants, heaven ordains what must be done, thought, experienced, and practiced on earth in order to please him! And the same people who purport to be bearers of his word also assert their ability to interpret what he thinks of the actions carried out in his name.

Theocracy's cure lies in democracy: the power of the

people, the immanent sovereignty of the citizens against the supposed dominance of God—or rather, the dominance of those
claiming to speak in his name . . . In the name of God, as centuries of history attest, the three monotheisms have caused unbelievable rivers of blood to flow! Wars, punitive operations,
massacres, murders, colonialism, the elimination of entire cultures, genocides, crusades, inquisitions, and today's global terrorism.

Deconstructing the monotheisms, demythologizing Judeo-
Christianity and Islam, deconstruction of theocracy: these are
three initial tasks for atheology. The next step is to formulate a
new ethic and produce the conditions for a true post-Christian
morality in the West—a morality in which the body is not a
punishment; the earth ceases to be a vale of tears; this life is no
longer a tragedy; pleasure stops being a sin; women, a curse; intelligence, a sign of arrogance; physical pleasure, a passport to
hell.

With that behind us, we might then point to the advantages
of a guiding principle less obsessed with the death wish than
with love of life. The Other would no longer be considered an
enemy, a "difference" to be suppressed, reduced, and dominated.
Meeting the Other would be an opportunity to build interper-
sonal relationships here and now, not under the gaze of God or
gods, but under the eyes of the protagonists only, a meeting of
their minds and their inherent natures. In that event, paradise
might function less as a fiction having to do with Heaven and
more as a rational ideal here below. We can dream, can't we?

PART TWO
MONOTHEISMS

I

The Tyranny of Afterlives

1

Monotheism's somber vision. Animals, as we know, are un-contaminated by God. Excused from religion, they know nothing of incense and the Host, genuflections and prayers. We do not see them in ecstasy over celestial bodies or priests, they build neither cathedrals nor temples, and they are never caught praying to fictions. Like Spinoza, we imagine that if they created a god for themselves they would create him in their own image: long ears for donkeys, a trunk for elephants, a sting for bees. Just as men — when they take it into their heads to give birth to one God — do so in their own violent, jealous, vengeful, misogynistic, aggressive, tyrannical, intolerant image. In short, they sculpt their own death instinct, their own dark side, and make of it a machine hurled at breakneck speed against themselves.

For only men invent afterlives, gods, or a single God. Only men prostrate themselves, humble themselves, abase themselves, weave fables, and believe unquestioningly in the tales they have so painstakingly concocted in order to avoid looking their fate in the face. Only men extract from this fiction a delirium that draws in its train a welter of dangerous nonsense and of new ways out. They alone work passionately to bring about what they nevertheless hope more than anything else to avoid: death.

Does life, with death as its inevitable ending, seem unlivable to them? Swift to respond, they arrange matters so that the enemy governs their lives. They set out to die little by little, systematically, day by day, so that when the hour strikes death will seem less difficult. The three monotheistic religions call on their faithful to renounce life in the here and now because they will one day be forced to accept its loss. Their glorification of a (fictional) beyond prevents full enjoyment of the (real) here below. And what motivates them? The death instinct and unceasing variations on that theme.

An extraordinary paradox! Religion is a response to the ontological void apparent to everyone who learns that he will one day die, that his sojourn on earth is finite, that each life constitutes a brief interlude between the nothingness that came before it and the nothingness that comes after it. Fables only accelerate the process. They establish death on earth for the sake of eternity in heaven. In so doing, they spoil the only gift we possess: the living matter of a potential existence killed in the egg just because its life is finite! Fleeing life in order not to have to die is not a good bargain. It pays death twice, when once is enough.

Religion proceeds from the death wish. That strange dark force in the depths of our being works toward the destruction of what is. Wherever life begins to move, expand, vibrate, a countercurrent sets in, tending to arrest the newborn movement and immobilize its ebb and flow. As soon as life fights its way out of the tunnel, death is there, ready to start the clock ticking — that is its function, its modus operandi — and to collapse all life's hopes and plans. Being born starts the process of dying. Living for death means counting off one by one the days of our life while waiting to die. Religion alone seems to halt the mechanism. But in fact it speeds it up.

Turned against ourselves, the fixation with death generates every kind of risky behavior, suicidal impulse, and self-destruc-

tive conduct. Directed against others, it triggers aggression, violence, crimes, murders. The religion of the one God espouses
these impulses. It seeks to promote self-hatred to the detriment
of the body, to discredit the intelligence, to despise the flesh, and
to prize everything that stands in the way of a gratified subjec-
tivity. Launched against others, it foments contempt, wickedness,
the forms of intolerance that produce racism, xenophobia, colonialism, wars, social injustice. A glance at history is enough to
confirm the misery and the rivers of blood shed in the name of
the one God.

Fired by the same inborn death drive, the three monotheisms share a series of identical forms of aversion: hatred of
reason and intelligence; hatred of freedom; hatred of all books in
the name of one book alone; hatred of sexuality, women, and
pleasure; hatred of the feminine; hatred of the body, of desires, of
drives. Instead Judaism, Christianity, and Islam extol faith and
belief, obedience and submission, taste for death and longing for
the beyond, the asexual angel and chastity, virginity and monog-
amous love, wife and mother, soul and spirit. In other words, life
crucified and nothingness exalted.

2

Down with intelligence! Monotheism loathes intelligence,
that sublime gift defined as the art of connecting what at first
and for most people seems unconnected. Intelligence reveals
unexpected but undeniable causalities; it produces rational, convincing explanations based on reasoning; it rejects every manufactured fiction. With its help, we can spurn myths and fairy tales.
We need no posthumous paradise, no salvation or redemption of
the soul, no all-knowing, all-seeing God. Properly and rationally
directed, intelligence wards off all magical thinking.

The advocates of Mosaic law, Christian tale-spinning, and their Koranic clones share the same fable on the origins of negativity in the world. In Genesis 3:6—common to the Torah and to the Old Testament of the Christian Bible—and in the Koran (2:29) we find the same story of Adam and Eve in a paradise where a God forbids them to approach a tree while a demon urges disobedience. In this monotheistic version of the Greek Pandora fable, a woman (of course) commits the irreparable, and her act spreads evil all over the world.

This story, in normal circumstances just good enough to earn a place in the roster of fairy tales or cautionary fables, has had incalculable consequences for human civilizations! Loathing of women and the flesh, guilt and desire for atonement, the quest for an impossible amends and submission to necessity, fascination with death and passion for suffering—all so many occasions for activating the death instinct.

What do the files on this story tell us? We find a God who orders the primal couple not to eat the fruit of the tree of knowledge. Clearly we are in the presence of metaphor. It took the church fathers to sexualize the story, for the text is clear: eating this fruit removes the scales from our eyes and allows us to distinguish between good and evil, and thus to resemble God. One verse (Genesis 3:6) mentions *a tree to be desired to make one wise.* Defying God's prohibition meant preferring knowledge to obedience, seeking to know rather than submitting. Or in different terms: opting for philosophy against religion.

What does this ban on intelligence mean? You can do anything in this magnificent Garden, except become intelligent—the Tree of Knowledge—or immortal—the Tree of Life. What a fate God has in store for men: stupidity and mortality! A God who offers such a gift to his creatures must be perverse . . . Let us then praise Eve who opted for intelligence at risk of death, whereas Adam did not realize right away what was at stake. The bliss of ignorance!

What do the poor wretches learn, once the lady tastes the sublime fruit? They see reality. Reality and nothing else. Nudity, their natural state. And with their freshly acquired knowledge, they discover their cultural allotment: the choice of fig leaves (rather than grape leaves) to cover their nakedness was symbolic of a future cultural heritage. Worse: they discover the hardship of daily life, the sorrow in every destiny, the battle between the sexes, the gulf forever separating man and woman, the inevitability of backbreaking toil, the pain of childbirth, and the sovereignty of death. Once liberated from their state of ignorance, they avoid the additional transgression that would have given them eternal life (the Tree of Life grew next to the Tree of Knowledge), for the one true God — decidedly gentle, good, loving, generous — spared them that fate by expelling Adam and Eve from paradise. And we have remained outside ever since.

Lesson number one: if we lose the illusion of faith, the consolation of God, and the fables of religion, if we prefer seeking knowledge and intelligence, then reality appears to us as it is, tragic. But which is better? A truth that removes all hope of immortality yet saves us from losing our life altogether by living it only half alive? Or a story that briefly consoles us but makes us waste the only thing we really possess: life here and now?

3

Litany of taboos. God was not content with that one prohibition on the forbidden fruit. Ever since, he has revealed himself to us only through taboos. The monotheist religions live exclusively by prescriptions and constraints: things to do and things not to do to, say and not to say, think and not to think, perform and not to perform. Forbidden and authorized, licit and illicit, agreed and not agreed: the religious texts abound in existential, dietary, behavioral, ritual, and other codifications.

For obedience can be measured only by proscriptions. The greater their number, the greater our chances of falling into error, the fewer our chances of attaining perfection, the deeper our guilt. And it's a good thing for God — or at least for the clergy who identify with him — to be able to manipulate this powerful psychological tool. Everyone must at all times know that he must always obey, must conform, must do as he should and as religion demands. Not to behave like Eve but, like Adam, to submit to the will of the only God.

Etymology teaches us that *islam* means *submission* . . . And what surer way of renouncing intelligence than by submitting to the taboos of men! For we hear the voice of God only with difficulty, infrequently or not at all! How can he make plain his dietary laws, his dress codes, and his ritual preferences other than through a clergy that imposes bans and decides in his name between the licit and the illicit? Obeying these laws and rules may be submission to God, but it is much more certainly submission to the one who speaks in his name: the priest.

In the Garden of Eden, that blessed time of communication between God and his creatures, God spoke to Adam and Eve . . . But contact is broken after the expulsion from paradise. Hence the widespread belief that God sends us signs of his presence. He is manifest in every minor detail of daily life, in the most trivial act. God is not only up in heaven: he is everywhere, watching us and warning us. That means the devil, too, is lurking in his shadow.

Since God is in the details, the details acquire vital importance. For example, Jews do not allow themselves to eat shellfish because God recoils from aquatic creatures lacking fins or scales and wearing their skeletons outside their bodies. Catholics likewise abstain from meat on Good Friday — a day presumably notorious for its excessive levels of hemoglobin, And Muslims forgo the pleasures of pork sausage. All three are occasions, among many others, for displaying faith, belief, piety, and devotion to God.

The permitted and the forbidden play a leading role in the Torah and Talmud, are somewhat less important in the Koran, but are especially prominent in the Muslim Hadith. Christianity — all praise (for once) to Saint Paul! — does not weigh itself down with the whole list of major taboos that Leviticus and Deuteronomy invoke in order to coerce, forbid, and constrain in every field: table and bedroom behavior, harvesting, textures and colors of the wardrobe, the hourly employment of time, etc.

The Gospels forbid neither wine nor swine nor any other food, any more than they insist on particular garments. Membership in the Christian community requires adhesion to the Christian message, not to the details of lunatic taboos. It would never occur to a Christian to deny access to the priesthood to a deformed, blind, lame, disfigured, misshapen, hunchbacked, sickly individual, as Yahweh demands of Moses when he is selecting a candidate for the profession (Leviticus 21:16). On the other hand, Paul remains a stickler for the licit/illicit rule in the sexual domain. On this point, the Acts of the Apostles testify to an intimate link between Old Testament and New.

Jews and Muslims demand that we think of God in every waking second. From dawn to dusk, sleeping to waking, no aspect of behavior, even in principle the most trivial, is exempt from interpretation: observing the ritual prayer hours, what to eat and not to eat, how to dress. No personal judgment or individual choice is involved, just obedience and submission, denial of all freedom of action, insistence on the rule of necessity. The licit/illicit logic locks the believer into a prison where abdication of will signifies an act of allegiance and a proof of pious behavior. It is an investment repaid a thousandfold — but later, in paradise.

4

Obsession with purity. The marriage of licit and illicit works in parallel with the coupling of pure and impure. What is pure? Or impure? Who is? Who is not? Which individual decides these questions? Who authorizes and validates the decision? "Pure" designates the unmixed. Its opposite is the alloy. On the side of the pure are the one, God, paradise, mind, spirit. On the other side of the barricade are the impure: the diverse, the multiple, the world, the real, matter, body, flesh. The three monotheisms share this vision of an ideal world, and hold the physical world in low esteem.

Clearly, a series of impurities identified by the Talmud can proceed from practical wisdom. There is no question that a dead body, a rotting cadaver, the leaking of bodily fluids, leprosy all signify impurity. Common sense associates decomposition, putrescence, and disease with risks and dangers to individuals and the community. Catching fever, contracting an illness, causing an epidemic or pandemic, spreading sexually transmittable diseases, all these justify concern with prevention and an effective public-health response. Not allowing evil to take us by surprise is the first duty of virtue.

Impurity contaminates: place, location, life inside the tent, contact with other people of course, but also close personal proximity, uncovered vessels in the household, all may be implicated in contamination. The infected person in turn contaminates everything he approaches or touches until purification and ablution put an end to this state of collective danger. The health professional rightly sees such measures as steps designed to avoid the propagation of impurity. But for other kinds of impurity, the prophylactic argument does not answer. What do we risk in approaching a menstruating woman? Or one who has just given birth? Both are impure. Just as we may understand fear of abnormal flows that might point to hemorrhage, gonorrhea, or syphilis, so we must question ourselves about this horror of menstrual blood or of the woman who has recently given birth. Unless we advance the theory that in both these cases the woman is not fertile, and that she may therefore freely dispose of her body and her sexuality without risking pregnancy — a condition ontologically unacceptable to the rabbis, proponents of the ascetic ideal and of demographic expansion.

Muslims share many concepts with Jews, and in particular this fixation on purity. In a general sense, the body is impure from the simple fact of being. Hence a sustained and permanent effort to keep it pure through a series of precise steps: circumcision, cleaning and trimming the beard, mustache, and hair, paring nails, forbidding the ingestion of food not ritually prepared, proscription of all contact with dogs, naturally an absolute prohibition on pork and alcohol, and radical avoidance of all bodily matter — urine, blood, sweat, saliva, sperm, feces.

Once again, of course, all this can be justified rationally as prophylaxis, hygiene, cleanliness — but with never a hint of why pork rather than camel meat must be avoided. Some suggest that the pig is an animal emblematic of certain Roman legions, an unpleasant localized memory. Others point to the omnivorous nature of the animal, a consumer of public refuse . . . Hatred of the dog may hark back to risks of bites and rabies; the ban on alcohol to the fact that hot countries seem favorable to indolence, siestas, and the urge to reckless slaking of thirst, in which case water or tea in quantity are preferable to alcohol because of its known effects. All this can be rationally explained.

But why not be content with a secular rationale? Why transform these sound, legitimate prohibitions into grounds for strict rules and inflexible laws, and then make eternal salvation or damnation dependent on their observance? No one questions the need for clean latrines, particularly in periods or places where sewage facilities, running water, flush toilets, septic tanks, and disinfectant products do not exist.

In the Hadith, there are detailed instructions regarding anal cleansing: no fewer than three stones to be used, no recourse to garbage (!) or to bones (!), and no urination in the direction of Mecca. There are also rules on one's state of preparation before prayer: no previous emission of seminal fluid, of gas, urine, feces, menstrual blood of course, but also — and this leads to a break in the link with Islam — no sexual relations during one's partner's menstruation nor anal penetration (here again because it means sex divorced from procreation) . . . It is hard to see the rational, reasonable connection.

5

Respecting the body. All the Jewish and Muslim taboos — so similar to each other — are due to associating the body with impurity. The body is dirty, unclean, infected, composed of vile materials. There are all sorts of bodies: libidinous, malodorous, sodomite, filled with nasty fluids and secretions. Some are infected, sick, bleeding. There are cadavers, bodies of dogs and women, made of garbage, made of filth. Stinking bodies, sterile bodies, barren bodies, loathsome bodies.

One hadith preaches the need to purify the body through the practice of ablution (ritual washing). It states that the more often ablution is performed, the greater one's chance of reaching heaven with a glorious (in the Christian sense) body. On Resurrection Day, the body is reborn, radiating light from the points where it contacted the prayer mat. A physical body of dark, black flesh is contrasted with a spiritual body, white and incandescent. Who among simple folk could love an earthly, sinful body when a beautiful, perfect, celestial one is guaranteed to every believer who abides by the licit/illicit rules in accordance with the pure/impure principle?

The purification ritual also furnishes an opportunity to treat the body with respect, as if it were not our own flesh but an entity unto itself. Every organ has its place in a process of organized, meticulously ordained prayer. Nothing escapes Allah's eye. He is concerned with: suitability of the materials utilized (water, stones, sand, soil), numbering the viscera, systematizing the steps of the ritual, the order of passing from one part of the anatomy to another during ablutions, choreography of the repetition of gestures. Fingers, the right wrist, forearms, elbows, do it three times, etc. Don't forget the heel; if you do, that omission leads to hell.

We can dispense with the notion that these rites are based solely on the desire for cleanliness. Some of the rules do promote cleanliness. For example, take care not to soil your garment with urine. In the toilet, do not wipe with the hand you eat with. But the argument does not hold up when we examine the hadith that authorizes *masah 'alal khuffain* (wiping wet hands over the tops of one's leather slippers) as a valid substitute for washing the feet. Some imams also permit performing *masah* on cloth socks, provided the cloth is very thick and sturdy. Either way, the feet get purified *without* getting washed! Can God's reasons be purely hygienic?

Training the body in the practice of purification goes hand in hand with training in the proper practice of prayer — the five daily prayers, all announced by the muezzin from the heights of his minaret. Organizing our time and even our bodies to suit our own needs is out of the question. Getting up and going to bed both depend on the muezzin's call, as does one's progress through the day, for everything comes to a halt for prayer. The schedule is rigid: it signifies order (the oldest go first), organization, and communal harmony. Prostration follows a very strict code: seven bones must be in contact with the ground—forehead, both hands, both knees, the extremities of each foot. (We will not quibble with the imam, but a single foot has five toes, two feet have ten, and, with a little help from chiropody, we have overshot the theoretical seven bones by a wide margin . . .)

Certain postures are prohibited because they do not conform to the rules. Certain ways of inclining the body or of prostration are also taboo: they too must be performed according to the rules. It is out of the question for the body to move with joyful spontaneity, for it must demonstrate its submission and obedience. One cannot be a Muslim without a zealous display of one's pleasure in observing the details. For Allah himself resides in the details. (One final word: the angels like neither garlic nor shallots. We therefore refrain from strolling in the vicinity of the mosque with those cloves in the folds of our djellabas, and even more from entering the sacred precincts with a burnoose redolent of garlic!)

II

Bonfires of the Intelligence

1

Producing the holy books. Hatred of intelligence and knowledge, the requirement to obey rather than think, the role of the licit/illicit–pure/impure coupling in eliciting obedience and submission rather than thinking for ourselves — all this is codified in the books. The three monotheisms are seen as the religions of the book — but their three books seem far from mutually supportive. Paulines have little liking for the Torah, Muslims do not really treasure the Talmud or the Gospels, upholders of the Pentateuch see the New Testament or the Koran as so much fraud . . . Naturally, they all teach brotherly love. Thus from the very start it seems difficult to appear beyond reproach to our brethren of the Abrahamic religions!

The creation of these so-called holy books proceeded in accordance with the most elementary historical laws. We should approach the whole corpus from a philological, historical, philosophical, symbolic, allegorical (and every other qualifier) standpoint hostile to the belief that these texts were inspired and dictated by God. None of them is a work of revelation. Who would have done the revealing? Their pages no more descend from heaven than those of Persian fables or Icelandic sagas.

The Torah is not as old as tradition claims; Moses is improbable. Yahweh dictated nothing — and in any case, Moses could not have written down what Yahweh said unless he wrote in hieroglyphics, since the Hebrew script did not exist in the time of Moses! None of the evangelists personally knew the famous Jesus. The testamental canon arose from later political decisions, particularly those reached when Eusebius of Caesarea, mandated by the emperor Constantine, assembled a corpus stitched together from twenty-seven versions of the New Testament in the first half of the fourth century. The apocryphal writings are more numerous than those that constitute the New Testament proper. Muhammad did not write the Koran. Indeed, that book did not exist as such until twenty-five years after his death. The second source for Muslim authority, the Hadith, saw the light of day in the ninth century, two centuries after the Prophet's death. Hence we must infer the very active presence of men in the shadows of these three Gods.

2

The book's bias against books. To establish the authority of the definitive version of the Koran, the political authorities — notably Marwan, governor of Medina — began by collecting and then burning and destroying all existing versions in order to avoid historical confrontation and chancing upon vestiges of human, too human, manufacture. (One version indeed escaped from this auto-da-fé of the seven earlier versions, and still holds sway in certain African countries.) Marwan's act was a precursor of the many book burnings kindled in the name of the one book. Each of these three books claims to be "the only book that matters." Each of the three main religions claims that it alone possesses the one true holy book, which contains the whole of what needs to be learned and known. Like encyclopedia compilers, they have gathered the essentials, rendering it unnecessary to look in other books (pagan, secular, heretical) for wisdom that is already found.

The Christians set the tone with Paul of Tarsus, who called for the burning of dangerous books (Acts 19:19). The demand did not fall on deaf ears: Constantine and most subsequent Christian emperors sent philosophers into exile and persecuted polytheist priests, declaring them social outcasts, imprisoning them, and killing many. Hatred of non-Christian books resulted in an overall impoverishment of civilization. The establishment of the Inquisition and, later, the sixteenth-century creation of the *Index of Forbidden Books* were the climax of this campaign to eradicate everything that deviated from the official policy of the Catholic, Apostolic, and Roman Church.

The desire to be done with non-Christian books and the mistrust of unfettered thinking beggared philosophy, forcing its practitioners to give up the struggle, to remain silent, or to express themselves with extreme prudence. (The entire roster of important philosophers from Montaigne to Sartre, in a line including Pascal, Descartes, Kant, Malebranche, Spinoza, Locke, Hume, Berkeley, Rousseau, Bergson, and so many others — not to mention materialists, socialists, and Freudians — enjoys pride of place in the *Index*.) The Bible, claiming to contain everything, banned everything it did not contain. Over the centuries, the results were devastating.

Countless fatwas were proclaimed against Muslim authors even when they did not defend atheist positions, did not discredit the Koran's teachings, and did not indulge either in blasphemy or invective. It was enough simply to think and write freely for the thunderbolts to come crashing down. The slightest deviation came at a heavy price. Exile, prosecution, persecution, libel, even assassination, all these horrors were perpetrated by the likes of Ali Abderraziq, Mohammed Khalafallah, Taha Hussein, Nasr Hamid Abu Zayd, Mohammed Iqbal, Fazlur Rahman, Mahmoud Mohammed Taha.

In their implacable opposition to free expression, the priests of the three religions preferred to authorize the conjurers whose deft manipulation of language, verbal contortions, and jigsaw-puzzle formulations blew smoke in their readers' eyes. What did these schoolmen achieve over the centuries beyond a verbal repackaging of ancient fables and ecclesiastical dogma?

Jews, Christians, and Muslims love memory exercises, particularly in regard to the chanting of the faithful. Muslims memorize the suras of the Koran at a very early age and learn to chant them with the correct elocution (*tajwid*) and the correct delivery (*tartil*). Proper articulation and intonation of the Koran (*tajwid*) requires a slow, melodious declamation with rich flourishes, such as singing several notes to one syllable of text. *Tartil* is a slow, rhythmic, measured, and meditative delivery. Traditionally, theological schools teach seven ways of reciting the Koran, the differences between them being a matter of linguistic and phonetic variables: consonants stressed, unstressed, without overtones; dropped vowels; change in inflection; very soft tone of voice; or verbal ornamentation, such as deliberate repetition of a phrase at the beginning of successive verses. All this contributes to subordination of the spirit and message of the text in favor of pure literary style. The words lose their meaning, and their repetition becomes an artistic performance.

The litanies we hear in Koranic schools — madrassas, often centers of hostility to *falsafa*, or philosophy — bear this out. Students learn by reciting aloud, as a group, in cadence, in a collective and communal rhythm. Their dirges help them memorize the teachings of Yahweh or Allah. Jewish mnemonic technique also offers a method of apprenticeship in reading and the alphabet by an association of letters and contents that rests on Talmudic doctrine.

Thus, books aim paradoxically (after they have been memorized wholesale) at what virtually amounts to their own elimination! Rationally enough, students learn the Torah or the Koran by heart. Thus, when the danger of persecution raises its head or when conditions such as exile make it impossible to have the volume at hand, the believer still enjoys mental possession of the book and its teachings.

3

Hatred of science. This law of the one book, total and all-inclusive, coupled with the unfortunate habit of believing that "everything" can be contained within a single text, means that there is no recourse to nonreligious (which is not to say atheistic) books, such as scientific works. Monotheism does not really like the rational work of scientists. Clearly Islam embraces astronomy, algebra, mathematics, geometry, optics, *but only* to calculate the direction of Mecca more accurately by means of the stars, to establish religious calendars, to decree prayer hours. Clearly Islam values geography, *but only* to facilitate the convergence on the Kaaba when pilgrims from all over the world flock to Mecca. Clearly it prizes medicine, *but only* to avoid the impurity that mars one's relation with Allah. Clearly it esteems grammar, philosophy, and law, *but only* to enrich commentary on the Koran and the Hadith. This religious instrumentalization of science subjects reason to domestic and theocratic uses. In Islamic lands, science is not pursued for its own sake today but for the improvement of religious practice. Centuries of Muslim culture produced inventions, research, and important discoveries in the area of secular science, such as algebra and astronomy, as well as being responsible for the preservation of classical texts. One hadith indeed celebrates the quest for scientific knowledge as far afield as China, but always in the logic of its instrumentalization via religion, never for the human and immanent ideal of social progress.

Christianity too considers that the Bible contains all knowledge necessary for the effective functioning of the church. For centuries the Bible inhibited all research that scrutinized and questioned its contents (without ever contradicting its claims). Faithful to the lessons of Genesis (knowledge is not desirable, science distances us from the essential — God), the Catholic religion impeded the forward march of Western civilization, inflicting on it incalculable damage.

From Christianity's earliest days, in the beginning of the second century of the common era, paganism in all its aspects was condemned. Everything it produced was rejected, tied to false gods, polytheism, magic, and error. Euclidean mathematics? Ptolemy's maps? Eratosthenes' geography? Aristotle's natural sciences? Aristarchus's astronomy? Hippocrates' medicine? Herophilus's anatomy? They were simply not Christian enough!

The discoveries made by Greek geniuses — Aristarchus's heliocentrism, to take just one example — were obviously applicable independently of the gods and the religious systems of the day. What did the existence of Zeus and his kin matter when one had to determine the laws of hydrostatics, calculate the length of a meridian, invent latitude and longitude, measure the distance between us and the sun, argue for the revolution of the earth around the sun, perfect the theory of epicycles, elaborate the map of the heavens, establish the length of a solar year, link tides and lunar attraction, discover the nervous system, offer theories on the circulation of the blood, all of them truths of no interests to the denizens of heaven?

Turning one's back on the results of such research, acting as though these discoveries had never taken place, starting every-thing again from scratch is at best stagnation, evidence of a dan-gerous hostility to change. But at worst it means speeding blindly backward — while others forge ahead — to the darkness from which every civilization, by its nature and by definition, strives to free itself in order to be. Refusal of the Enlightenment characterizes the monotheist religions: they prefer mental night for the nurturing of their fables.

4

Negation of matter. In science the church has always been wrong about everything: faced with an epistemological truth, it automatically persecutes the discoverer. The history of science's relationship with Christianity yields a prodigious abundance of blunders and stupidity. Between the church's rejection of the he-liocentric hypothesis of antiquity and its contemporary con-demnations of genetic laws, twenty-five centuries of wasted opportunities for humankind are heaped up. We scarcely dare imagine how swiftly the West would have advanced without such sustained brutalization of science!

One line of force in this crusade against science is the church's prolonged, unbridled condemnations of materialist the-ories. In the fifth century BCE the genius of Leucippus and Democritus led them to discover the atom without possessing the material means to confirm their intuition. It was a stroke that never ceases to amaze. Lacking a microscope, a lens, indeed any enlarging instrument at all, they extrapolated from the motes of dust in a ray of light the existence of particles invisible to the naked eye — but nonetheless there! And on this basis they con-cluded that the existence of these atoms explained the makeup of all matter, and consequently of the world itself.

From Leucippus to Diogenes of Oenanda, passing via Epicurus, Lucretius and Philodemus of Gadara, the atomist tradition remained alive, lasting through eight centuries of Greek and Roman antiquity. Lucretius's *De Rerum Natura* (*On the Nature of Things*) proposes the fullest account of Epicurean physics: form, nature, weight, atomic constitution, behavior in a vacuum, the theory of declivity, generation and decomposition — everything necessary for a complete decoding of the world. And of course, if everything is made up of matter, soul, spirit, and gods as well share that makeup. So do men. With the advent of pure immanence, fictions and fables cease along with religions, and with their disappearance the means of circumscribing the body and soul of the city's denizens also disappear.

Ancient physics proceeded from a poetic method. Yet despite everything, time confirmed it. The centuries rolled by, but in the age of electronic scanning, particle accelerators, positrons, nuclear fission, and technological pathways into the very heart of matter, that Democritean intuition has been validated. The "philosophical atom" has received the stamp of authenticity from the scientific — and in particular the nuclear — world. Nevertheless, the church to this day persists in its idealist, spiritualist, antimaterialist position — that a reality irreducible to matter somehow exists in the human soul. It is no surprise, then, that materialism has been the fly in Christianity's ointment from the beginning. The church stops at nothing to discredit this coherent philosophy and its complete account of all reality. And in order to block access to atomist physics, what better means than discrediting atomist morality? So the Epicurean ethos must be condemned. The Epicurean defines pleasure as ataraxia — the absence of care. So we must transform this negative definition into sheer aberration, and say it celebrates bestial, crude, and casual congress with animals! With this achieved, we no longer need concede importance to a physics dangerous in the eyes of the Christian caste, because it proceeds from an Epicurean swine.

The church thus strikes everywhere a hint of materialism appears. When Giordano Bruno died, burned by Christians at the stake on the Campo dei Fiori in 1660, he perished less for atheism — he had never denied God's existence — than for materialism: he asserted the coexistence of God and the material world. Nowhere did he blaspheme, in no part of his work did he offer insults to the God of the Catholics. He wrote, thought, and stated that this God, who is, could not fail to be of the wider world. It was the extended substance of the language to come later, with Descartes.

Bruno, who was also a Dominican (!), did not deny the existence of the spirit. Sadly for him, however, he situated it at the physical level of atoms. He understood particles to be so many centers of life, places where the spirit manifests itself as coeternal with God. Divinity then exists, of course, but it comes to terms with matter, representing its mystery resolved. The church believed in God's incarnation, but only as the Son who is the offshoot of a virgin and a carpenter. It most certainly did not believe in atoms.

The same can be said about Galileo, the emblematic representative of the church's hatred for science and of the conflict between faith and reason. The legend focuses on the issue of heliocentrism, with the pope and the Inquisition condemning the author of *A Dialogue Concerning the Two Chief World Systems* (1632) because Galileo argued that the earth was a satellite of a sun located at the center of the universe. Charges, trial, retraction: we all know the story, which ends, according to Brecht, with Galileo muttering as he left the seat of justice, *Eppur' si muove (And yet it moves)*.

In fact, things happened differently. What did the Vatican *really* hold against Galileo? Not so much his defense of Copernican astronomy—although this was a thesis that contradicted the church's Aristotelian position—as his adherence to the materialist camp . . . Before the courts of the day, heliocentrism was punishable by lifelong house arrest, a relatively mild sentence. Defense of atomism, on the other hand, led directly to the stake! That being so, why not confess to the less damaging charge? In other words, acknowledge the venial sin of heliocentrism rather than the fatal atomic error.

5

Bakeshop ontology. But why was the church so bent on persecuting the advocates of an atomist conception of the world? First of all because belief in the existence of matter, to the exclusion of every other reality, leads logically to assertion of the existence of a material God. And thus to denial of his spiritual, timeless, and immaterial qualities, along with other distinguishing features noted in his Christian passport. And thus to demolition of the intangible God manufactured by Judeo-Christianity.

But there is another reason, relating as it happens to the bakery business. For the church believes in transubstantiation. It affirms, according to the words of Jesus at the Last Supper— *This is my body, this is my blood* (Matthew 26:26–28) — that the true body and the true blood of Christ reside in the unleavened Host and the wine. Not symbolically, not allegorically, but really . . . At the moment of the Elevation, then, the priest hoists Christ's real body in his hands.

By what extraordinary machinations of the Holy Spirit does the baker's bread produce the mystery of an infinitely divisible body and a flow of blood that has flooded the planet? At the very moment when the priests officiate, all over the globe, every single Mass *really* produces the flesh of a resurrected corpse, reappearing in its eternal freshness, unchanged by eternity. Clearly a staunch believer in linguistics, Christ moves into the performative mode, creating reality through his words: he makes what *he* says become fact by the simple act of saying it.

In its very earliest days the church believed firmly in this miracle. It still does. The *Catechism of the Catholic Church* — in its twentieth-century incarnation — still insists on the *real* presence of Christ in the Eucharist (Article 1373). In validation of this fiction, there follow references to the Council of Trent, to the *Summa Theologica* of Thomas Aquinas, to the Mysteries of the Faith — labeled number 9 by the church — and to other texts by Saint John Chrysostom, who, in his *First Homily Against the Antinomians*, very rightly approves the call of Paul of Tarsus. Paul had told the Corinthians, as if this were an occasion for celebration, that *as for knowledge, it will pass away* (1 Corinthians 13:8). Such an initial postulate seems a very necessary prelude to all the nonsense that ensued!

Thus the church still believes in the real presence of Christ's body and blood in the baker's bread and the vintner's nectar. But to make the patient swallow such an ontological pill, many intellectual contortions (major contortions) are required. And it was the conceptual toolbox of Aristotle, the Vatican's cherished philosopher, that facilitated this magnificent feat of legerdemain. Hence a series of magicians' turns using the metaphysical categories of the Stagirite.

The explanation: Christ's body is *veritably, really, substantially* — the official terms — present in the Host. The same holds true for the hemoglobin in the wine. For the bread's *essence* disappears once the priest has spoken, whereas its *perceptible characteristics*, its *accidents* — color, taste, temperature — remain. Those characteristics are preserved in miraculous fashion by the divine will. He who can do the maximum — create a world — can also do the minimum — play tricks with a bakery product. Of course it tastes like bread, but it is not (or is no longer) bread! You could just as well maintain that the wine has become bread: it is white as Christ's red blood and does not intoxicate (or no longer does). Say what you will, it's still sweet red wine!

We need all this juggling with substance and perceptible characteristics in order to make the faithful believe that what is (bread and wine) does not exist, and what is not (Christ's body and blood) truly exists! An incomparable display of three-card monte! Once theology takes a hand, gastronomy and the vintner's arts, and even dietetics and hematology, throw up their hands. Thus the fate of Christianity plays out in the pathetic farce of an ontological shell game.

6

Epicurus: not an enthusiast for Hosts. What about Epicurus in all this? He liked bread, since his banquet of a crust and a modest crock of cheese has come down through the centuries and left indelible memories in the history of philosophy. But he would have laughed at the Eucharistic rabbit pulled out of the Christian hat! Laughed very long and loud . . . For, in virtue of the principles laid down in his *Letter to Herodotus*, a Host is reducible to atoms. Lucretius would explain how, with wheat flour and water, and without yeast, we manufacture this white, bland, tongue-coating, melting wafer out of a small pinch of atoms, each linked to its kin. He offers nothing useful in support of the fiction of transubstantiation. Nothing but matter.

Therein lay the danger of atomism and materialism. It made a metaphysical impossibility of the church's theoretical twaddle! By the standards of modern atomic calibration, there is nothing to be found in the bread and wine but what Epicurus predicted: matter. The hedging made possible by blathering on about essence versus perceptible characteristics became impossible when confronted with Epicurean theory. That is why the disciples of Democritus had to be destroyed by discrediting their lives and by the travesty of labeling their ascetic ethos as licentiousness and immorality.

In 1340, Nicolas d'Autrecourt was bold enough to propose an extremely modern (but atomist) theory of light. He believed in light's corpuscular nature (modern science validates him), which implies an identification of substance with its characteristics. This was bad news for believers in the Aristotelian metaphysical broth! The church at once forced him to recant, and burned his writings. It was the beginning of a persecution of all scientific research proceeding through atomism — which the Jesuits banned as early as 1632, maintaining the prohibition for centuries. Materialism (Articles 285 and 2124 of the *Catechism*) is still on the prohibited list of the contemporary church.

7

Forever missing the boat. Since the hodgepodge of biblical knowledge was entirely sufficient for science, the church missed all the major discoveries of ten centuries. Throughout that time, the urgings of the intelligence were contained, but not halted, by the Catholic, Apostolic, and Roman authorities. Progress continued thanks to rebellious individuals, determined research, scientists who prized the truths of reason over the fables of faith. But a scrutiny of the church's reactions to scientific discoveries over the last thousand years reveals an astounding accumulation of missed opportunities!

They include rejection of atomism in favor of Aristotelianism. To this must be added opposition to any proposition that excluded the intentionality of a creator God (since Genesis reports that God began from nothing and created the world in a week, anything that contradicted this unleashed the Vatican's fury). What of rational causalities? Of rational sequences? Of claims verifiable from observation? An experimental methodology? A dialectic of reasons? And what else? God decides, wills, creates—period! Could there be an alternative to creationism? Absolutely not!

Is there anything to be said for scientific belief in the eternity of the universe? In multiple universes? (Both Epicurean theses, incidentally . . .) Absolutely not! God created the universe from nothing. Before nothing, there was . . . nothing. Darkness and chaos, but also, in this welter of nothingness, there was God and his itch to innovate. Light, day, night, the firmament, heaven, earth, the deeps—we know the whole story, right down to the beasts of the field, reptiles, animals both wild and human. That is the official history, its genealogy minutely dated. Multiple worlds? Absolutely not!

After precise and meticulous calculations, scientists confirmed Aristarchus's idea that the sun indeed sat firmly at the center of our world. The church's response: absurd. Creation by a perfect God could take place only in the center, the zone of perfection. And then of course the notion of a centrally placed sun came dangerously close to reviving pagan solar cults . . . To exist on the outer rim would be a mark of inconceivable imperfection, *therefore* it could not be scientifically demonstrable! The factual was wrong, the fictitious was right. Heliocentrism? Absolutely not!

Lamarck, followed by Darwin, published their discoveries. The former proposed that species change, the latter that they evolve according to the so-called laws of natural selection. The readers of the only book shook their heads: God created the dog and the wolf from whole cloth, the city rat and the country rat, the cat, the weasel, and the bunny rabbit. No likelihood whatsoever that a comparison of their bones might prove evolution or transformation. And then there was that notion that men descend from monkeys! An unbearable narcissistic wound, Freud suggested. The pope cousin to a baboon? Horrors . . . Transformation of species? Evolution? Absolutely not!

In the industrious atmosphere of their laboratories, scientists advanced the idea of polygenesis — the original and simultaneous existence of groups of humans at different geographical locations. A contradiction, thundered the church: Adam and Eve were indeed, factually and really, the first man and the first woman. Before them no one existed. The existence of the primordial couple, the couple who brought us original sin, buttresses the biblical logic of error, guilt, and redemption. What can we do with men and women existing before sin, and thus spared by sin? Pre-Adamites? Absolutely not!

Brushing dirt from stones and poring over fossils, geologists proposed a scientific dating of the world. Seashells found on mountaintops, strata and layers all attest to an immanent chronology. But there is a problem: their dating does not correspond to the sacred numerology supplied by the Bible. Christians insist that the world is four thousand years old, no more, no less. Scientists prove the existence of a world before that Christian world. Science is wrong . . . Is geology a science to be relied on? Absolutely not!

Men of goodwill cannot tolerate death and disease, and to be able to fight off epidemics and pathologies they need to open bodies and learn from the dead lessons useful to the living — using death in order to save life. The church absolutely opposes research on human bodies. There can be no question of rational causalities, simply theological reasons: evil and death flow from peccant Eve. Pain, suffering, and disease proceed from divine will and a divine decision to put the faith of men and their loved ones to the test. The ways of the Lord are impenetrable, and he moves according to a plan known to him alone. From material causalities to pathologies? A rational etiology? Absolutely not!

Sitting at the foot of his couch at the turn of the nineteenth century, a Viennese doctor discovered the subconscious and the mechanisms of repression and sublimation, the existence of the death instinct, the role of dreams, and a thousand other factors that revolutionized a psychiatry then in its prehistoric phase. He perfected a method for treating, relieving, and curing neuroses, mental abnormalities, and psychoses. It is true that along the way, in *The Future of an Illusion*, Sigmund Freud also demonstrated that all religion proceeds from an "obsessional neurosis" closely related to "hallucinatory psychosis." The church condemned him, duly issued its fatwa, and consigned him to the *Index*. Man is animated by a dark force located in his subconscious? But that contradicted the dogma of free will so necessary to the Christian obsession with making everyone responsible, thus guilty, thus punishable ... And so useful in validating the logic of the Last Judgment! Freud and his discoveries? Come now ... Psychoanalysis? Absolutely not!

And finally: twentieth-century researchers discovered the genetic blueprint. They had gently pushed through a door to a universe that promised astounding possibilities in diagnostics and disease prevention, greater precision in treatments and in the avoidance of pathologies. They were working toward the advent of a predictive medicine that would revolutionize the discipline ... But the *Charter for Health Care Workers*, published by the Vatican, condemned them. Avoid pain and suffering? Believe ourselves exonerated from the price to be paid for original sin? Seek a human medicine? Absolutely not!

What an astonishing game of chess! On one side stood an unshakable determination to deceive (ourselves), to reject the truth, to maintain trust in the death instinct. On the other side stood the living impulse of research, the vitality of science, the dynamism of progress. The believers' condemnation of scientific truths — the atomist theory, the materialist option, heliocentric astronomy, geological dating, transformation of species, evolution, psychoanalytic therapy, genetic revolution — all loudly proclaimed the triumph of Paul of Tarsus, who had called for knowledge to pass away. It was a call successful beyond all expectations . . .

Clearly, the church deployed extraordinary determination to attain this phenomenal rate of success in failing! Persecution, consignment to the *Index*, burnings at the stake, the instruments of the Inquisition, imprisonments, and trials have never ceased . . . For centuries it was forbidden to read the Bible without priestly mediation. It was quite out of the question to approach the book with the weapons of reason, analysis, and criticism, as a historian, a geologist, a scientist. In the seventeenth century Richard Simon published the first Christian critical analysis of the Old and New Testaments. Naturally, Bossuet and the Catholic Church violently attacked him. The fruit of the Tree of Knowledge has left a lingering aftertaste of bitterness.

III

Seeking the Opposite of the Real

1

Inventing the afterlife. Monotheisms have no love for intelligence, books, knowledge, science. Preferring the ethereal over the material and the real, they have a strong aversion to man's instincts and basic drives. Thus not only do they celebrate ignorance, innocence, naïveté, obedience, and submission: the three religions of the book disdain the texture, forms, and forces of the world. The here and now is irrelevant, for the whole world, now and forever, bears the weight of original sin.

As a sign of their hatred of matter, the monotheisms cobbled together a world of antimatter. In antiquity the liegemen of the one God, embarrassed by these scientific questions, turned to Pythagoras (who was himself shaped by Eastern religious thought) and Plato to build their city of the spirit, where Ideas, surprisingly similar to clones of God, could flourish. Like God, these Ideas were eternal, immortal, without dimension, inaccessible to time, immune to growth and decomposition, resistant to all sensual, phenomenal, and corporeal conceptualization, requiring nothing but themselves to exist, endure, persevere in their being, and all the rest! Their identities were close kin to those of Yahweh, God, and Allah. On such stuff as this, the monotheisms built castles in the air intended to discredit all other habitation—real, concrete, or inherent.

Hence the schizophrenia of monotheisms. They judge the here and now by the standards of an elsewhere; they conceive of the earthly city only in terms of the heavenly city. They care about men, but only as a sideline to their preoccupation with angels; they give a thought to man's inherent nature if and only if it serves as a stepping-stone to transcendence; they are quite willing to turn their attention to the real world, but only to measure how well it corresponds to "intelligent design" theory; they are solicitous of earth only insofar as it offers an opportunity for heaven. Between these two contradictory concerns, a gap is created, an ontological wound impossible to close. Man can find no fulfillment there. An existential void gives rise to human malaise.

Here again, atomist monism (the atom is the universal substrate) and materialist unity (the only thing that can truly be said to exist is matter) permit us to circumvent metaphysical arguments that are full of holes. If a man considers the real to consist exclusively of matter, and if he concludes that reality has no manifestations other than earthly, sensual, worldly, phenomenal—such reasoning precludes mental wandering and keeps his feet on the ground, in contact with the one true world. Dualism, whether Pythagorean, Platonic, or Christian, does a disservice to those who subscribe to it. By aiming for paradise, we lose sight of earth. Hope of a beyond and aspiration to an afterlife engender a sense of futility in the present. If the prospect of getting taken up to paradise generates joy, it is the mindless joy of a baby picked up from his crib.

2

Birds of Paradise. This world outside the world produces two creations of fantasy: the angel and paradise. The angel functions as a prototype of anti-man. Paradise functions as antiworld, inciting humans to detest their condition and despise their reality in order to aspire to another essence and then to another existence. The angel's wing symbolizes the opposite of man's earthbound condition. In contrast to our own imperfect planet, paradise promises atopia, utopia, uchronia: that is, a land without territorial borders; an ideal society that lives in harmony, free of poverty, tyranny, and war; where time has no beginning and no end.

The Jews possess their own stables of winged creatures: the cherubim guarding the entrance to the Garden of Eden; the seraphim accompanying them (we recall the one who visited Abraham, or his colleague who wrestled with Jacob). Their job? To extol the Eternal One in a celestial Camelot. For although God disdains human trivialities, he does like his greatness to be celebrated. Both Talmud and Kabbala teem with angels. These are servants of God, but also protectors of the just and of the children of Israel. From time to time we see them leaving their heavenly abode to bear a message from God to men. (The pagan Hermes is never too far away; he too is feathered, but only on his hat and heels . . .)

Pure spirits of light — which in all logic does not exclude unarguably spiritual and luminous feathers and wings — the angels deserve our attention partly because they are without gender. Neither men nor women, androgynous, a little bit of each, even childlike, spared the throes of copulation. Happy creatures of the air, they are unaware of the sexual condition, for they are without desire, without libido. Seraphic poultry, they know neither hunger nor thirst, yet they feed on manna — the ambrosia of the pagan gods. But of course they do not defecate. Blissful avians, they know nothing of corruption, decrepitude, and death.

And then there are fallen, rebellious angels, untamed, undefeated. In the Garden of Eden the devil — "the slanderous one, the libeler" — teaches what he knows best: the option of disobedience, of refusal to submit, of saying no. Satan — "the adversary, the accuser" — breathes the wind of freedom across the dirty waters of the primal world where obedience reigns supreme—the reign of maximum servitude. Beyond good and evil, and not simply as an incarnation of the latter, the devil talks libertarian possibilities into being. He restores to men their power over themselves and the world, frees them from supervision and control. We may rightly conclude that these fallen angels attract the hatred of monotheisms. On the other hand, they attract the incandescent love of atheists.

3

Seeking the opposite of the real. As we might expect, these impossible bodies live in an equally impossible place—the walled-in Garden of Paradise. Pentateuch, Genesis, and Koran all affirm the existence of this hysterically conceived geography. But Muslims offer us its most perfect description. It is worth a visit! Streams, gardens, rivers, springs, budding meadows, magnificent fruit and drinks, great-eyed houris (always virginal), gracious young people, beds galore, superb garments, luxurious fabrics, extraordinary jewelry, gold, pearls, perfumes, priceless vessels . . . Nothing is missing in this glossy brochure, the work of an ontological chamber of commerce.

And the definition of paradise? The antiworld, the opposite of the real. In the real world Muslims scrupulously respect their rites. They observe the same rigorous logic of the licit and illicit, accept the same drastic division of things into the pure and the impure. In paradise all that comes to an end—no more obligations, no more rites, no more prayers. At the heavenly banquet they drink wine (83:25 and 47:15), they eat pork (52:22), they sing, they wear gold (18:31) — forbidden here below — they eat and drink from plates and goblets of precious metal — illicit on earth — they wear silk — repellent on earth, silk being excreted by a worm — they fondle houris (44:54), they enjoy eternally virginal women (55:70) or caress beautiful youths (56:17) on couches of precious stones — in the tents of the desert their couch is a mere rug and they are allowed a maximum of three legitimate wives. In short, everything hitherto forbidden is now there for the taking ... ad libitum ...

In the desert camp, eating vessels are of earthenware, in paradise, precious stones and metals. In the tent, squatting on rough skin rugs, families share a modest subsistence that cannot be counted on every day — camel's milk, mutton, mint tea. In heaven, prodigious quantities of food and drink are served up, set out upon green satin and brocade cloths. Beneath the tribal awning the smells are coarse, strong, overpowering — sweat, dirt, leather, animal hide, smoke, suet, soot. In Muhammad's company there are only magnificent scents: camphor, musk, ginger, incense, myrrh, cinnamon. Around the tribal hearth, if by chance alcohol is consumed, drunkenness threatens. In the Islamic version of the Celestial Kingdom, intoxication is unknown (37:47) and so (not unimportantly) are hangovers. Moreover, unrestrained consumption does not induce the temptation to sin!

Still in the logic of paradise as an antiworld, desirable in the interests of making the real and often undesirable world tolerable: Islam was originally a religion of deserts and their brutal, hot, and violent climate. In paradise, an eternal springtime prevails, without sun or moon, just an eternal light, never day, never night. Does the desert sirocco tan the skin or the harmattan scorch the flesh? In the Islamic heaven, the musk-laden wind breathes gently over rivers of milk, of honey, of wine and water, spreading its balm far and wide. Gathering food in the desert is often a dangerous and chancy undertaking: sometimes you find nourishment, sometimes you find nothing, or very little — single dates, rare figs. In Muhammad's domain grapes are so big that a crow wishing to fly around a bunch needs more than a month to complete his circuit! In the vast expanses of desert sand the coolness of shade is extremely rare and infinitely welcome. In the mansion of Muslim Ideas, a horse takes a hundred years to emerge from the shadow of a single banana tree. On earth, caravans crawl endlessly across the dunes, their progress slow, each mile over the sand taking what seems like an age. The Prophet's stables possess winged horses created from red rubies, free of material constraints, moving at galactic speeds.

And finally, the same differences apply to the body. A troublesome partner on earth, constantly needing his water ration, his food quota, his libidinal satisfaction, so many occasions for distancing himself from the Prophet and from prayer, so many occasions for slavery to natural needs. In paradise, the body's immateriality shines forth: no more eating, except for pure pleasure. If ingestion takes place, digestion is not a problem — even Jesus, who ate bread, wine, and fish, never excretes . . . nor are flatulence or gas emissions an embarrassment, for in heaven smells that are revolting on earth become the musk-scented exhalations of moist, languid bodies!

No more need for procreation to guarantee one's lineage; no need for sleep, since weariness is unknown; no need to wipe one's nose or spit. Illness is unknown to the very end of time; sorrow, fear, and humiliation, so often overriding all else on earth, are erased from our vocabulary; there is no more desire — desire is pain and privation, says the Platonic tradition — it is enough for desire to make itself felt to be instantly transformed into pleasure; looking hungrily at a fruit is enough to savor its taste, its texture, and its fragrance in our mouths.

Who could say no? How totally understandable that countless Muslims, lured by the promise of these celestial dream vacations, should have left happily for battle, from the Prophet's first raid at Nakhla to the Iran-Iraq war all the way to the present day! How natural that Palestinian suicide bombers should unleash death on Israeli café terraces; that aircraft hijackers should hurl passenger planes against New York's Twin Towers; that Islamic radicals should detonate a string of powerful bombs on packed commuter trains in Madrid! These events represent blood sacrifice. Human sacrifice made at the altar of falsehoods so improbable as to stagger even the meanest intelligence.

4

Solving the woman problem. Should we discern the logical consequence of hatred for intelligence in the hatred for women common to Judaism, Christianity, and Islam? According to the holy books, original sin, error, the desire for knowledge, all stem from the decision of one woman, Eve. Adam was an innocent fool, content to obey and submit. When the serpent speaks — nothing wrong with that . . . don't all snakes speak? — he addresses the woman and starts a dialogue with her. (In the Koran, the tempter is called Iblis or Shaitan. For centuries, millions of Muslims have performed a ritual "stoning of the devil" as part of the annual pilgrimage to Mecca.) Seducing serpent leads to seduced woman leads to woman the eternal temptress. It is an easy progression.

Hatred of women is like a variation on the theme of hatred of intelligence. To which might be added hatred of everything women represent for men: desire, pleasure, life. Curiosity as well — many dictionaries confirm that inquisitive women are widely dismissed as "daughters of Eve." They generate desire; they also generate life. Original sin is perpetuated through women — that sin which, as Saint Augustine assures us, is transmitted from the moment of conception, in the mother's womb, via the father's sperm. The sexualization of sin!

The monotheisms infinitely prefer the angel to the woman. Far better a world of seraphim, of cherubim, of thrones and of archangels than a feminine or mixed-gender universe! And above all, no sex. Flesh, blood, libido, naturally associated with women, give Judaism, Christianity, and Islam welcome excuses for stressing the theme of the illicit and the impure. Thus they wage war against the desirable body, against the menstrual blood that briefly liberates women from the burden of motherhood, and against hedonist energy. Bible and Koran overflow with rapturous anathema on these themes.

The religions of the book detest women. They admire only mothers and wives. To rescue women from their consubstantial negativity there are only two solutions—in fact a single two-step solution—marrying a man, and then bearing his children. Caring for their husbands, cooking for them, handling household problems, feeding, caring for, and educating his children, they have no more time for addressing the feminine within. The wife and mother kill the woman—which is exactly what the rabbis, priests, and imams count on to ensure the male's peace of mind.

Judeo-Christianity promotes the idea that Eve was created secondarily, as an afterthought, from Adam's rib (Genesis 2:22)! An inferior cut off the prime beef, a humble sparerib. (As Adam's wife, of course, she appears in the Koran [sura 2:35]. But the fact that she is never named is revealing . . . because the unnamed is unnamable!) The male came first, and only then, like a leftover fragment, a crumb—the female. Everything is against Eve, starting with her order of arrival. Her subordination to her husband set the pattern for womankind's existence. Above all, though, she was responsible for original sin. And she has paid heavily ever since.

Her body is cursed, and she is too, in her totality. The unfertilized egg emphasizes the feminine and negates the maternal; it is a sign of womanhood—but empty womanhood, divorced from motherhood. Therefore, a menstruating female is impure. The blood indicates periods when conception is not possible and is a reminder of the danger of infertility. For a monotheist there can be no more hideous oxymoron than a barren, sterile woman! And during menstruation she is at no risk of pregnancy, meaning that sexuality can be dissociated from fear and practiced for its own sake. The possibility of sex divorced from conception, and thus of sex alone, of pure sexuality—that is absolute evil.

In the name of this same principle, the three monotheisms condemn homosexuals to death (Leviticus 20:13). Why? Because their sexuality precludes (or precluded until very recently) the destinies of father, mother, husband, and wife, and clearly asserts the primacy and absolute worth of the free individual. The bachelor is only half of a person; he is incomplete without his female partner, says the Talmud. The Koran (sura 24:32) commands single men to marry. For his part, Paul of Tarsus saw in the solitary male the perils of lust, adultery, and free sexuality. Hence, given the impossibility of chastity, his endorsement of marriage—the least objectionable justification for the libido.

We find a similar horror of abortion in the three religions. The family functions as the fixed horizon, the basic cell of the community. It implies children, whom Jews consider to be the condition of their people's survival, whose number the Christian church wishes to see grow and multiply, whom Muslims see as a mark of the Prophet's blessing. Everything that disturbs this demographic metaphysics arouses monotheist anger. God does not approve of planned parenthood.

Yet immediately after childbirth the Jewish woman is considered unclean. Blood, always blood . . . If she gave birth to a boy, the ban on entering the temple lasts forty days; if she bore a girl ... sixty! Thus spake Leviticus ... To the present day, Orthodox Jewish men in their daily morning prayer recite, "Praised be God that he has not created me a gentile. Praised be God that he has not created me a slave ... Praised be God that he has not created me a woman" (Talmud, Menahot 43b). Not to be outdone, the Koran does not explicitly condemn the pre-Islamic tribal tradition that ascribed *shame* to a man who fathered a daughter and legitimized his deliberations on whether to *keep* the child or *bury it beneath the dust* (16:58).

As for our jovial Christian kin, delegates to the Council of Mâcon in 585 submitted for discussion a book by Alcidalus Valeus entitled *Paradoxical Dissertation in Which We Attempt to Prove that Women are not Human Creatures.* Paradoxical? In what way? We do not know if the attempt was successful; i.e., if Alcidalus won over his readers. But the Christian hierarchy was already sympathetic to his point of view: we need only recall Paul of Tarsus and his countless misogynistic pronouncements. In any case, the church's age-old prejudice against women remains to this day an undeniable fact.

5

Celebration of castration. We know of the travails of Origen, who took Matthew literally. The evangelist discusses eunuchs (19:12) and establishes a typology for them — born without testicles, castrated later by others, or self-mutilated in honor of the Kingdom of God — and concludes, "He who is able to receive this, let him receive it." Crafty. Origen cut to the heart of the matter, slicing off his genitals with a blade — probably before realizing that desire is less a question of one's sack than of one's brain. But too late ...

Monotheist literature abounds in references to the extinc-

tion of the libido and the destruction of desire: praise of continence, celebration of absolute or relative chastity. And since men
are neither gods nor angels but rather animals whose condition
we are forced to live with, monotheism encourages marriage
with fidelity to the spouse—or spouses in the case of Jews and
Muslims—and insists that all sexuality should be focused on
procreation. Family, marriage, monogamy, fidelity—all of them
variations on the theme of castration . . . Or how to become a
virtual Origen.

Leviticus and Numbers clearly state the rules on the question of Jewish sexual intersubjectivity: no sexual relations outside marriage; legitimization of polygamy; divorce at the
husband's discretion and without too many formalities (a letter,
a *guet*, to the repudiated spouse is sufficient); illegality of marriage to a non-Jew; transmission of Jewishness through the
mother (she has nine months to prove that she really is the
mother, the identity of the father being always uncertain); prohibition on women studying the Torah (mandatory for men); no
authorization for the daughters of Eve to recite payers, wear the
shawl, sport the phylactery, blow the shofar, build the ritual hut
(the *sukha*), or belong to groups of ten (the minimum necessary
for prayer); permission to own but not manage or administer her
own financial assets (the husband's role). Clear proof that God
made man in his own image, and not in the woman's.

A reading of the Koran shows the obvious kinship between
the two religions. Islam clearly proclaims the superiority of
males over females, for God prefers men to women (4:34).
Hence a series of diktats: prohibition on exposing the hair out of
doors—the veil (24:30) — or exposing bare arms and legs; no
sexuality outside legitimate relations with a member of the
community, who may himself possess several spouses (4:3); prohibition of polyandry for women, of course; praise for chastity,
of course (17:32 and 33:35); prohibition on marrying a non-

Muslim (3:28); prohibition on wearing men's clothing; no mingling of the sexes at the mosque; no question of shaking hands with a man unless wearing gloves; marriage mandatory, with no tolerance for celibacy (24:32) even in the name of religion; passion and love advised against in marriage, which is celebrated in the interests of family (4:25), tribe, and community; recommendation that the wife submit to all the sexual desires of the husband, who "*plows* his wife whenever he likes, for she is his tillage" — the metaphor is Koranic (2:223); permission to beat one's spouse on mere suspicion (4:34); the same ease of repudiation, the same existential minor status, the same legal inferiority (2:228), with a woman's courtroom testimony worth half that of a man, while a barren woman and a woman deflowered before marriage possess exactly the same value: none at all.

Hence praise of castration: women equal excess. Excessive desire, excessive pleasure, excessive wildness, excessive passion, excessive outbursts of ecstasy, excessive sexual delirium. They threaten the male's virility. The things women should strive for include God, meditation, prayer, performance of ritual, knowledge of the licit/illicit divide, awareness of the divine in the smallest details of everyday life. Heaven, not the earth. Still less the worst of what the earth has to offer — bodies . . . Woman, tempted long ago and long since transformed into eternal temptress, threatens the image man cherishes of himself, the triumphant phallus, borne like a talisman of his being. Terror of castration shapes every life led in the eyes of God.

6

Down with foreskins! Jews are not the only group to have a strong emotional attachment to circumcision. The Muslims followed their lead in this regard, as in so many others. It is no surprise that the issue enlivened the debates of the early Christians. On the question of whether to require Gentile converts to be circumcised, Paul of Tarsus (himself circumcised) declared that Gentiles could choose to spare the real flesh in favor of "circumcision of the heart" (Acts 15:1–9). Why not the lips, eyes, ears, and any other body part that might be useful? This "circumcision in spirit and not in the letter" (Romans 2:29) allows today's Christian (except for the Coptic Christians of Egypt) to sport a hood over his glans penis and shield it from the open air.

How strange that excision — female circumcision, with several languages using the same term for both kinds of mutilation — of little girls should revolt the westerner but excite no disapproval when it is performed on little boys. Consensus on the point seems absolute. But ask your interlocutor to think about the validity of this surgical procedure, which consists of removing a healthy part of a nonconsenting child's body on nonmedical grounds — the legal definition of . . . mutilation.

When Margaret Somerville, a Canadian philosopher, tackled the subject in a spirit free of polemical intent, with rational arguments, comparison, and analysis, when she provided genuine anatomical, scientific, neuropathological, and psychological information to support her charge of mutilation, she was subjected to a savage bombardment by her compatriots. Following this national cry of outrage, she stood by her conclusions, but withheld final judgment and later agreed to legitimize circumcision for . . . religious reasons. (For readers' information, 60 percent of Americans are circumcised, 20 percent of Canadians, and 15 percent of Australians on nonreligious, supposedly hygienic grounds.)

Chinese foot-binding, African stretching of the neck through the use of successive layers of rings, tooth-filing, piercing of nose, ears, or lips among Amazonian tribes, Polynesian scarification and tattoos, and Peruvian flattening of the skull

proceed from the same magical thinking as African clitoridectomy or Jewish and Muslim circumcision. Marking the body for
religious reasons, ritual suffering in order to earn integration
into the community, tribal practices designed to attract the
benevolence of the gods — there are a thousand reasons, even
without the help of psychiatry.

We shudder at other people's strange practices. In Russia,
the Skoptsi were a religious sect, active between the eighteenth
century and the 1920s, whose members advocated voluntary
castration. In some areas of Polynesia, young boys are not circumcised but superincised: a flat stick is pushed under the foreskin, then a single cut is made to split the foreskin on the top
side of the penis. In Australia, the rite of passage for young male
Aborigines is subincision, which entails cutting the underside of
the penis along its full length from meatus to scrotum. But we
have no right to shudder. Logic, assumptions about the nature of
being, and magical thinking are not that far apart. We tend to
judge as barbaric whatever is not our own custom. But how can
we accept and justify our own surgical mutilations while casti-
gating those of others?

For mutilation is a fact. First of all according to the law,
which forbids any surgical procedure unsupported by medical
evidence of a genuine pathology. And the foreskin is not of itself
a pathology. Then on physiological grounds: the area removed
corresponds to half or two-thirds of the skin covering the penis.
In an adult, this thirteen-square-inch zone — external and internal skin — concentrates more than a thousand nerve endings, or
two hundred and fifty feet of nerves. In other words, the
resection of one of the body's most innervated structures.

Moreover, the disappearance of the foreskin — which
primitive peoples bury, eat, dry, pulverize, preserve — produces a
circumferential scar that becomes keratinized over time: permanent exposure to the rubbing of fabric acts abrasively on the

skin, which hardens and loses its sensitivity. The drying of this surface and the disappearance of lubrication diminishes the sexual comfort of both partners.

7

God loves the maimed. The Koran does not require or encourage circumcision, but does not condemn it. However, tradition holds that Muhammad was born circumcised! The Koran does not recommend female circumcision or infibulation. On the other hand, such mutilations are practiced in the eastern Horn of Africa, involving the three types of female circumcision. (There is what is known as "gentle sunna" — *sunna* means "tradition" or "way of the Prophet" — which removes the head of the clitoris; moderate sunna, or clitoridectomy, which removes the clitoris and all or parts of the labia minora, infibulation, or total removal of the clitoris, labia minora, and labia majora, followed by sewing together of the remaining tissue, often with thorns, leaving a matchstick-caliber opening for urination and menstruation.)

The Jews too approve of this mutilation as a sign of full membership in their community. More or less the only such sign, so rigid on this point (so to speak) are the rules. God demanded it of Abraham, who submitted at the age of ninety-nine; he ordered it for all male members of his household, even slaves; he fixed it for the eighth day after birth; and he made of it the mark of God's specific Covenant with his chosen people. Circumcision is so important that if it falls on the Sabbath, all prohibitions on activity associated with that day are lifted. Even in the case of a child who dies before the foreskin's removal, the mohel performs his ritual task.

Montaigne describes a circumcision in his *Travel Journal*: the circumciser uses a knife placed beforehand on the mother's pillow in order to attract a maximum of propitiatory favor. He pulls the penis, grasps the foreskin, pushes back the glans, and cuts the flesh without anesthetic to remove the prepuce. After swallowing the wine he has been swilling in his mouth, he sucks the wound — this ritual aspiration is called the *meziza* — and then, says the Talmud, he draws the blood remaining in the wound into his mouth. He spits three times. And the child enters the community: he is given his name. The rite, *meziza* included, has remained unchanged since Montaigne.

Reams have been written and spoken about this primitive rite and its survival over the centuries. Followed by many other psychiatrists, Freud — whose biographers stress his bad memories of circumcision — has speculated about suppression of the feminine in the male (circumcision) as an echo of the suppression of the male in the female (excision). He proposed that the ritual could represent a paternal warning to male offspring against Oedipal urges via the threat of an even more drastic castration; or else the reenactment of the severing of the umbilical cord as the symbol of a new birth. Of course, such factors probably enter into play, in addition to the ritual's goal of establishing community membership and identity. But there is also — and significantly — the theory formulated by two Jewish philosophers, Philo of Alexandria in *Questions and Answers in Genesis* and Moses Maimonides in his *Guide for the Perplexed*. They hold that the procedure aims at weakening the sexual organ. It refocuses the individual on the essential — preventing his erotic inclinations from eroding an energy better employed in the celebration of God; it saps lust and facilitates mastery of desire. To which we may add that it adulterates sexual possibilities and precludes pure sexual fulfillment for its own sake; it carves into the flesh and with the flesh a hatred of desire, libido, and life. It implies the victory of the death-fixated passions at the very spot where the life force is located. It reveals one of the modalities of the death instinct turned against others — as always, for their own good.

With Christianity and the decisions arrived at by Paul, circumcision became a mental matter. No more need of a brand on the flesh; mutilation corresponded to nothing real. All that counted was "a circumcision of the heart." Achieving this meant stripping the body of all the sins resulting from carnal desire. Hence baptism, of course, but also and above all the daily asceticism of a life dedicated to the imitation of Christ, of his suffering and his Passion. With the man from Tarsus, then, the faithful kept his penis intact, but he lost the totality of his body. Henceforth the believer must separate himself entirely from his body, in the same way as the circumciser does away with the foreskin. With the advent of Christianity, the death fixation was ready to poison the whole planet.

PART THREE

CHRISTIANITY

I

The Construction of Jesus

1

Enter the forgers. Clearly, Christ existed—like Ulysses and Zarathustra, of whom it is hardly important to know whether they were flesh-and-blood people living at a precise time and in an identifiable place. Jesus's existence has not been historically established. No contemporary documentation of the event, no archaeological proof, nothing certain exists today to attest to the truth of a real presence at this meeting point between two worlds, abolishing one and naming its successor.

No tomb, no shroud, no archives, except for a sepulcher invented in 325 by Saint Helena, mother of Constantine. She must have been a woman of supreme gifts, since we are also indebted to her for the discovery of Golgotha and of the *titulus*, the wooden fragment bearing the charges brought against Jesus. Then there is that piece of cloth from Turin, which carbon-14 dating has situated in the thirteenth century CE, and which only a miracle could have wrapped around Christ's corpse more than a thousand years earlier! Finally, there are of course two or three vague references in ancient texts—Flavius Josephus, Suetonius, and Tacitus—but in copies made several centuries after the alleged crucifixion of Jesus and—significantly—after the success of his supporters was assured.

On the other hand, how can we deny Jesus's conceptual

existence? For the same reason as Heraclitus's Fire, Empedocles's Friendship, Plato's Ideas, or Epicurus's Pleasure, Jesus functions wonderfully as an Idea on which a vision of the world is articulated, a conception of the real, a theory of a sinful past and of future salvation. We must leave it to lovers of impossible debates to decide on the question of Jesus's existence and address ourselves to the questions that matter. What exactly is this construction named Jesus? What was its purpose? Its aims? To serve whose interests? Who created this fiction? How did the myth take shape? How did this fable evolve in the centuries that followed?

The answers to these questions require a detour via a hysterical thirteenth apostle, Paul of Tarsus (a "bishop of foreign affairs," as he called himself), the author of a successful coup d'état (the emperor Constantine), and his successors (Justinian, Theodosius, Valentinian) who incited Christians to despoil, torture, and slaughter pagans and burn pagan libraries. From Jesus the invisible ectoplasm to Jesus the absolute master of an empire and then of the world, history evolves alongside the family tree of our civilization. It begins in a historical fog in Palestine, continues in Rome, and then settles into the gold, pomp, and purple of Christian power in Byzantium. It thrives even today in millions of minds formatted by the unbelievable story — built on the wind, on the improbable, on contradictions that the church has invariably dispelled through bouts of political violence.

So we know that most existing documents are skillfully executed forgeries. Burned libraries, repeated orgies of vandalism, accidental fires, Christian persecutions and autos-da-fé, earthquakes, the media revolution that replaced papyrus with parchment and presented the copyists, sectarian zealots of Christ, with a choice between the documents to be saved and those to be cast into outer darkness . . . Then there were the liberties taken by monks who established editions by ancient authors to which they added what they considered (with the hindsight of the conquerors) to be missing. It all added up to a philosophical nightmare.

Nothing of what remains can be trusted. The Christian archives are the result of ideological fabrication. Even the writings of Flavius Josephus, Suetonius, or Tacitus, who mention in a few hundred words the existence of Christ and his faithful in the first century of our era, obey the rules of intellectual forgery. When an anonymous monk recopied the *Antiquities* of the Jewish historian Josephus (arrested and turned into a double agent, a collaborator with Roman power), when that monk had before him the *Annals* of Tacitus or Suetonius's *Lives of Twelve Caesars* (and was astonished to find no mention of the story he believed in), he added a passage in his own hand and in all good faith, without shame and without a second thought, without wondering whether he was doing wrong or committing a forgery. He could do it the more easily because in those days one did not approach a book with the eye of a modern reader, concerned with the truth and respectful of the authenticity of the text and the author's rights . . . Even today we read these writers of antiquity in manuscripts copied several centuries after they were written, and contemporaneous with Christian copyists who redeemed their contents by arranging them to swim with the flow of history.

2

Hysteria crystallized. The ultra-rationalists — from Prosper Alfaric to Raoul Vaneigem — were probably right to deny the historical existence of Jesus. The closed corpus of texts, documents, and information we possess has been pored over for decades without ever producing a definitive conclusion or winning general approval. From Jesus the fiction to Jesus the Son of God the spectrum is broad, and the number of theories advanced offers equal justification to the aggressive atheism of the Rationalist Union and to the beliefs of Opus Dei.

What can be said is that the period in which Jesus supposedly appeared teemed with individuals of his kind, fire-breathing prophets, exalted madmen, hysterics convinced of the rightness of their grotesque truths, heralds of apocalypse. A history of that incandescent century would include countless such examples. The Gnostic philosophers themselves proceeded from the millenarian effervescence and fiery lunacy which marked that period of anguish, fear, and change in a world nobody understood. The old was crumbling, splintering, threatening to collapse. And that threatened collapse generated fears to which certain individuals responded with frankly irrational proposals.

On the banks of the Jordan, a region familiar to Jesus and his apostles, a man named Theudas claimed to be Joshua, the prophet of promised salvation (and also an etymon, or earlier form, of the name Jesus) . . . Arriving from his native Egypt with four hundred followers, all spoiling for a fight, he sought an end to Roman power and claimed the ability to divide a river with his words alone, thus allowing his men to advance and put an end to the colonial power. Roman soldiers beheaded this poor man's Moses before he could display his hydraulic talents.

On another occasion, in 45, Jacob and Simon, sons of Judas the Galilean — yet another place-name familiar to Jesus — began an uprising that ended as badly as that led by their father in the year 6. The Romans crucified the rebels. Menahem, grandson of a family prolific in freedom fighters, followed in his ancestors' footsteps and rebelled in 66, triggering the Jewish War that ended in 70 with the destruction of Jerusalem.

In this first half of the first century, prophets, messiahs, and bearers of good tidings abounded. Some invited their supporters to follow them into the desert, there to witness prodigies and manifestations of divinity. A visionary from Egypt with forty thousand followers occupied the Garden of Olives, another area associated with Jesus. He claimed that his voice alone could shatter the walls of Jerusalem and lay the city open to his men. Once again, the Roman soldiery dispersed them. Multitudes of stories describe this Jewish determination to unseat Roman power with the sole help of religious, mystical, millenarian, and prophetic discourse announcing the good tidings predicted in the Old Testament.

Their resistance was legitimate: the wish to eject occupying armies seeking to force their language, laws, and customs on the conquered always justifies resistance, rebellion, refusal, and struggle, even armed struggle. But to believe — spurred only by their belief in the impossible — that they could oppose the world's most battle-tested troops, hardened in all the major conflicts of the day, trained and professional, possessing impressive equipment and full powers, merely transformed their magnificent struggle into battles lost in advance. Brandished like a battle flag before the Roman legions, God was outmatched.

Jesus thus embodied the period's hysteria, its belief that with goodwill alone and with action undertaken in the name of God, one could conquer and triumph. Breaking down walls with one's voice instead of with battering rams and siege artillery, crossing rivers with a word and not in military craft worthy of the name, opposing battle-hardened troops with hymns, prayers, and amulets and not with spears, swords, or cavalry: there was nothing there to trouble the Roman army of occupation. Mere scratches on the Roman hide.

The name of Jesus crystallized the diffuse and disparate energies wasted against the imperial machinery of the day. It furnished the emblematic patronymic of all Jews who (armed only with their will and the belief that their God could miraculously free them from the colonial yoke) refused to accept Roman occupation. But if God's power and his love of his people were so great, surely he could have spared them from having to endure, even briefly, the occupiers' unjust laws. Why would he tolerate such injustice before encompassing its abolition?

Thus, whether Jesus really lived or not must be reduced to the status of a mere hypothesis. This Jesus may well have been the son of a carpenter and a virgin. He may well have been born in Nazareth, he may well have given lessons as a child to the doctors of the law and spoken as a grown-up to fishermen, craftsmen, and other humble folk working on the shores of the Sea of Galilee. He may well have had more trouble with Jewish communities than with the Roman authorities, accustomed as they were to these sporadic and unimportant rebellions. But he synthesized, focused, sublimated, and crystallized what roiled the period and the history of the first century of his era. Jesus gave a name to Jewish rejection of Roman domination.

Etymology supports this claim. "Jesus" means "God saves, has saved, will save." There could be no clearer expression of the name's symbolic freight: his very name pointed to his destiny. The patronymic heralded a future that was already known, and implied that the adventure ahead was written somewhere in a corner of heaven. Thenceforth, history was content to allow its revelation to unfold day by day. How could one imagine that such a given name did not mandate the fulfillment of these earlier prophecies and potentialities? Or what better way of saying that the construction of Jesus implies a forgery reaching down to the smallest details, itself serving as a pretext and an occasion for this ontological catalyst?

3

Catalysis of the miraculous. Jesus thus concentrated in his name the messianic aspirations of the period. In the same way, he epitomized the ancient term *topoi*, used to describe one who was miraculous. For to be born of a virgin mother told of her good fortune by a heavenly or angelic figure, to perform miracles, to possess a charisma that attracted passionate followers — all these were commonplaces scattered throughout the literature of antiquity. Obviously, if we consider the Gospels as sacred texts we have no need to undertake the comparative study that would set them in context — that would set what is miraculous in the New Testament squarely within the logic of what was miraculous in antiquity. Jesus, as characterized by Paul of Tarsus, shares some similarities with Homer's Ulysses and with Encolpius, one of the protagonists in Petronius's *Satyricon*. The writer Philostratus wrote a biography of Apollonius of Tyana, which some have seen as an attempt to construct a rival to Jesus Christ. In other words, Jesus is an epic hero among other epic heroes.

Who was the author of Jesus? Mark. The evangelist Mark, first author of the wonderful adventures of the said Jesus. Probably the companion of Paul of Tarsus on his missionary wanderings, Mark wrote his text around the year 70. Nothing indicates that he knew Jesus in person, and small wonder! An open and obvious acquaintance would have been legible and discernible in Mark's writings. But we cannot frequent a fiction . . . All we can do is credit it with an existence, just like the beholder of a desert mirage who honestly believes in the truth and reality of the palm tree and oasis he sees in the burning heat. The evangelist therefore relates, in the hysterically incandescent tones of the period, this fiction whose authenticity he attests to in all good faith.

Mark wrote his Gospel with conversion in mind. His audience? People who needed convincing, people essentially indifferent to the Christ message who had to be attracted, captivated, and seduced. His text is in the unmistakable register of propaganda — which routinely resorts to artifice in order to please, persuade, and convince. Hence Mark's recourse to the miraculous. How else could he interest his readers in the commonplace story of a simple man, a man just like the general run of mortals? The Gospels recycle the literary fashions of pagan antiquity, which took it for granted that one embellished, decorated, and dressed up a man one wished to transform into a crowd-inspiring herald.

To convince ourselves of this, let us read the best-known pages of the New Testament, as well as Diogenes Laërtius's work *Lives, Teachings, and Sayings of Eminent Philosophers*. And let us give both texts equal literary status, that of historical writings composed by men not inspired by the Holy Spirit but eager to reach their readers and persuade them that they speak of exceptional individuals, of great men, of remarkable people. Pythagoras, Plato, Socrates, and Jesus seen by the same eye, the eye of a reader of ancient texts. What do we find?

A homogeneous world, identical authorial literary devices, the same compulsion to give their subject the relief and brilliance necessary for their readers' edification. Mark wants Jesus to be loved, Diogenes Laërtius wants the same for his great philosophers of the ancient tradition. Does the evangelist recount a life full of supernatural events? So does the biographer, stuffing his text with astonishing, extraordinary adventures. For both paint portraits of exceptional men. How could they be born, live, speak, think, and die like ordinary mortals?

To be specific: Mary, the mother of Jesus, conceives in virginity through the working of the Holy Spirit. Nothing extraordinary there: Plato too was born of a mother in the prime of life but endowed with an intact hymen. The archangel Gabriel told the carpenter's wife that she would give birth without the help of her husband, a good-natured fellow who agreed without making a fuss? What of it? The same Plato was gratified when Apollo himself called in person! Joseph's son is essentially the

Son of God? No problem: so is Pythagoras, whose disciples take him for Apollo in person, coming in directly from among the Hyperboreans. Jesus performs miracles, restores sight to the blind, life to the dead? Just like Empedocles, who also brings a corpse to life. Jesus excels in prophecies? So does Anaxagoras, who accurately predicts meteor showers.

Nor is this all. Does Jesus speak with inspired fervor, lending his voice to those greater, stronger, and more powerful than he? What about Socrates, inhabited and haunted by his daimon? Does the man destined to die on the cross teach his disciples, converting them with his oratorical talent and rhetoric? All the philosophers of antiquity, from Cynics to Epicureans, deploy a similar talent. Jesus's relations with John, his favorite disciple? The same bond links Epicurus and Metrodorus. The man from Nazareth speaks metaphorically, devours symbols, conducts himself as an enigma? Pythagoras too . . . Jesus never wrote, except for one occasion, with a stick that immediately erases the characters traced on the sand? It was the same for Buddha and Socrates, philosophers of the spoken word and of healing speech. Jesus died for his ideas? So did Socrates. Did the Messiah suffer through a night of decision at Gethsemane? Socrates, while serving in the Athenian army, had raptures or out-of-body experiences on the battlefield of Potidea in Thrace. Did Mary learn of her destiny as a virgin mother through a dream? Socrates dreamed of a swan and met Plato the next day.

Anything more? Yes, there is more . . . Clearly Jesus's body ingests symbols, but it does not digest them: quite impossible to excrete a concept . . . What extraordinary flesh, impervious to every caprice: the Messiah neither hungers nor thirsts, he never sleeps, does not defecate or copulate or laugh. Neither does Socrates. Remember the *Apology*, in which Plato plays the part of a character ignorant of the effects of alcohol, of fatigue, of sleeplessness. Pythagoras too appears clad in an anti-body, in spiritual flesh, in ethereal, incorruptible matter, untouched by the agonies of time, reality, and entropy.

Plato and Jesus both believe in a life after death, in the existence of an immaterial, immortal soul. After the Crucifixion, the wise man of Galilee returns among men. Well before him, Pythagoras used the same tactic. But more gradually, for Jesus let only three days go past, whereas the linen-shrouded philosopher waited two hundred and seven years before returning to Greater Greece. And there are so many other fables at work, whether about Greek philosophers or the Jewish seer, when the author of the myth wishes to convince his reader of the exceptional nature of his subject and of the character he is describing.

4

Construction outside history. The miraculous turns its back on history. One cannot rationally do battle with downpours of frogs or anvils, any more than with dead men emerging from their tombs to dine with their families. As for the paralyzed or sufferers from dropsy or hemorrhoids, suddenly restored to health by the stroke of a magic wand, we should steer clear of such topics. A word that heals, speech that cures, a gesture that leads to physiological miracles, is beyond us if we stick to the terrain of pure reason. To understand them we must think in terms of symbols, allegories, stylistic effects. Reading the Gospels requires the same approach as the classical prose of antiquity or Homeric poems: surrender to literary effect and renunciation of the critical spirit. The labors of Hercules signify extraordinary strength, the pitfalls of Ulysses illustrate his cunning and intelligence. The same goes for Jesus, whose reality and truth do not reside in their connection with established facts but in what they signify: the extraordinary power, the enormous strength of a man participating in a world bigger than he is.

The Englishman John Langshaw Austin coined the term *performative utterances* for a class of statements that *perform* an action as opposed to merely reporting or describing it. The Gospel genre is performative (to borrow Austin's term): simply declaring something is true creates its truth. The testamental stories are indifferent to the real, the probable, or the true. On the other hand, they deploy a power of language that by dint of affirmation creates what it declares. The prototype of the performative is the priest who proclaims a couple married. By the very act of articulating a formula he makes the event correspond with the words that signify it. Jesus did not obey history but the performativity of the testaments.

The evangelists despise history. Their apologetic choice permits it. There was no need for their stories to have actually happened, no point in having the real coincide with the formulation of the narrative given to it. It is enough for the words to produce their effect — to convert the reader and elicit from him agreement on the character and his teaching. Were the authors of the New Testament conscious of this myth? I do not think so. It was neither conscious, nor deliberate, nor systematically thought out. Mark, Matthew, Luke, and John did not knowingly deceive. Neither did Paul. *They* were deceived, for they said that what they believed was true and believed that what they said was true. None of them had encountered Jesus physically, but all credited this fiction with a real existence, in no way symbolic or metaphorical. Clearly they believed what they wrote. Intellectual self-intoxication, ontological blindness.

All of them credited a fiction with reality. By believing in the fable they told, they infused it with more and more substance. Proof of the existence of a truth is often reducible to the sum of errors repeated until they become received truth. Thus the probable nonexistence of an individual, about whom one spins details over several centuries, finally evolves into a mythology to which assemblies, cities, nations, empires, and a whole planet subscribe. The evangelists created a truth by harping on fictions. Paul's militant ardor, Constantine's coup d'état, and the repressions of the Valentinian and Theodosian dynasties did the rest.

5

Tissue of contradictions. Construction of the myth took place over several centuries, with the connivance of diverse and multiple writers. They recopied one another, added, subtracted, omitted, and travestied, wittingly or not. It finally added up to a considerable corpus of contradictory texts. This leaves us with the ideological challenge of distilling the material for an unambiguous story from this mass. The result: we retain some evangelists as reliable and we set aside those who obtrude upon the hagiography or the credibility of the project. Hence the synoptic Gospels and the Apocrypha, and even the intertestamental writings, on which researchers have conferred the curious status of metaphysical extraterritoriality!

Was Jesus a vegetarian, or did he resuscitate a cooked rooster at a banquet? Did the infant Jesus strangle little birds in order to take upon himself the noble role of reviving them? Did he redirect the course of streams with his voice, make birds out of clay and then transform then into real flying creatures, or perform other, similar miracles before the age of ten? What of Jesus curing snakebites by blowing on the spot where the fangs had buried themselves? What of the death of his father Joseph at the age of one hundred and eleven? And the death of his mother Mary? And Jesus roaring with laughter—and so many other stories set down on several thousand pages of apocryphal Christian writings? Why were they left out? Because they compromised the goal of an unequivocal narrative . . . Who put together this corpus and decided on the canon? The church, its councils, and its synods toward the end of the fourth century of our era.

Yet this culling has failed to remove an incalculable number of *contradictions* and *improbabilities* in the body of the text of the synoptic Gospels. One example: according to John, the wooden tablet on which the judges set down the reasons for Jesus's sentence—the *titulus*—is nailed to the wood of the cross, above Christ's head. According to Luke, it hung around the neck of the condemned man. Mark remains vague, offering no deciding opinion . . . And if we compare Matthew, Mark, Luke, and John on this *titulus*, the writing on it says four different things . . . On the road to Golgotha, says John, Jesus bore his cross alone. Why then do the others add that Simon of Cyrene helped him? Depending on which Gospel we consult, Jesus appeared after his death to a single person, to a handful, or to a group . . . And those appearances occur at different locations . . . There is no end to this kind of contradiction in the body of the Gospels themselves, even though those writings were retained by the official church in order to manufacture a single unequivocal myth.

Beyond these contradictions, there are also *improbabilities*. For example the verbal exchange between the condemned man and Pontius Pilate, an important Roman governor. Apart from the fact that in such cases the interrogation is never undertaken by the great man but by his underlings, it is hard to envisage Pontius Pilate conversing with a Jesus who was not yet the Christ nor what history would make of him—a planetary star. At the time, Jesus would have been merely a common-law defendant, like so many others in the occupying power's jails. It is thus hardly probable that an exalted official would deign to talk with a petty local jailbird. Moreover, Pontius Pilate spoke Latin and Jesus Aramaic. How could they have conversed as John's

Gospel says they did, back and forth, without an interpreter, translator, or intermediary? Sheer myth.

That same Pilate could not have been a procurator as the Gospels call him, for the title of procurator was first used around the year 50 of our era. Pilate's title was prefect of Judaea. And this Roman official could not have been the mild, affable man, benevolently inclined toward Jesus, that the evangelists describe, unless the authors of these texts were intent on blaming the Jews for their hero's death and (in a mild case of collaboration) flattering the Roman occupiers ... For what history relates of this prefect of Judaea is rather his cruelty, his cynicism, his ferocity, and his taste for repression. Tinkering with the facts.

Another improbability: the Crucifixion. History again bears witness: at that time Jews were not crucified but stoned to death. What was Jesus accused of? Calling himself King of the Jews. The fact is that Rome could have cared less about this business of messiahs and prophecy. Crucifixion implied a challenge to the imperial power, which the crucified man never explicitly posed. But let us concede that he was put on the cross. In that case, like all other such victims, he would have been left hanging there, at the mercy of wild beasts and dogs that had no trouble tearing the body to pieces since the crosses were barely over six feet tall. Then the remains were thrown into a common grave. In any case, there was no question of bodies being laid to rest in tombs. Fabrications.

The tomb then. Another improbability. A secret disciple of Jesus, Joseph of Arimathea, obtained his master's body from Pilate for entombment. Without the ritual mortuary cleansing? Unthinkable for a Jew ... One of the evangelists mentions aromatic herbs, myrrh, aloe—some seventy pounds of it—and swaddling bands, common in Egyptian-style embalmment. The three others omit these details ... But the solution to the contradictions appears to lie in the meaning of the name of Joseph's birthplace: Arimathea, which means "after death." On the performative principle, then, Joseph of Arimathea names the man who appears after Christ's death and cares for his body, a kind of first among the faithful. Sheer invention.

A comparative reading of the texts leads to a host of other questions. Why were the disciples absent on the day of the Crucifixion? How can we believe that after such a thunderbolt — the death of their master — they returned to their homes without reacting, meeting, or continuing the mission begun by Jesus? For each of them resumed his old trade in his village. Why did none of the twelve carry on the work which Paul — who had never known Jesus — took upon himself: spreading the gospel, bearing the good tidings as far afield as possible?

What can be said about all this? What can be done about these contradictions, these improbabilities — some texts rejected, others preserved but full of inventions, myths, approximations, all signs of a later, lyrical and militant construction of Jesus's story? We readily understand why, for centuries, the church categorically forbade any historical reading of the so-called sacred texts. It was simply too dangerous to read them in the way contemporaries read of Plato or Thucydides!

Jesus was thus a concept. His whole reality resides in that definition. Certainly he existed, but not as a historical figure — unless it was in such an improbable manner that whether he existed or not is of little importance. He existed as a crystallization of the aspirations of his era and of the reverence for the miraculous common to the authors of antiquity, articulated in the performative register that creates by naming. The evangelists wrote a story. In it they narrated less the past of one man than the future of a religion. A trick born of the rational mind: they created the myth and were created by it. The believers invented their creation, then made it the object of a cult: the very essence of willing self-deception.

II

The Pauline Contamination

1

Ravings of a hysteric. Paul took hold of this concept, clothed him, and supplied him with ideas. The early Jesus hardly ever spoke out against the customs of everyday life. Two sentences (Mark 7:15 and 10:7) show him unopposed to marriage and indifferent to the appeal of the ascetic ideal. We seek in vain for rigid prescriptions concerning the body, sexuality, sensuality. This relative benevolence toward the things of everyday life went hand in hand with praise for and the practice of gentleness. Paul of Tarsus transforms Jesus's silence on these questions into a deafening hubbub thundering out hatred of the body, of women, and of life. Christianity's radical antihedonism proceeds from Paul — not from Jesus.

Initially Paul, a hysterical, fundamentalist Jew, had taken pleasure in the persecution and brutal treatment of Christians. When fanatics stoned Stephen to death Paul was one of their number. And on other such occasions, it seems. His conversion on the road to Damascus in 34 arose from pure hysterical pathology: he fell to the ground (not from a horse, as Caravaggio and the painterly tradition have it), was blinded by an intense light, heard the voice of Jesus, and remained sightless for three days, neither eating nor drinking throughout that time. He recovered his sight after the laying on of hands by Ananias—a Christian sent by God *in missi dominici* . . . Paul at once sat down to table, ate, and then set out on long years of fevered proselytizing all over the Mediterranean basin.

The medical diagnosis seems clear. Such crises are invariably witnessed and attested to by other people—and this was the case with Paul. His fall, the blindness which modern experts have diagnosed as hysterical (unless it was just a passing loss of vision), his deafness, his three-day loss of the sense of smell and of appetite, his tendency to mythomania (he claimed that Jesus spoke to him in person), and after all that his thirty-year mission to dramatize an imaginary character, the elect of God, chosen by him to transform the world . . . it all adds up to histrionics, to moral exhibitionism. Indeed his crisis reads unmistakably like a passage from a manual of psychiatry, chapter heading Neuroses, subsection Hysteria . . . This was true hysteria . . . a hysterical conversion!

2

Infecting the world with neuroses. How are we to live with our neuroses? By making them the model for the world to follow, by inflicting our neuroses on the world . . . Paul created the world in his own image. A deplorable image, fanatical, moving with a hysteric's irresolution from enemy to enemy—first Christians, then Gentiles—sick, misogynistic, masochistic . . . How could we fail to see in our own world a reflection of this portrait of a man so clearly controlled by the death instinct? For the Christian world eagerly experiments with such ways of being and doing—ideological brutality, intellectual intolerance, the cult of poor health, hatred of the vital body, contempt for women, pleasure in inflicting pain, disdain for the here and now in the name of a gimcrack beyond.

Small, thin, bald, and bearded, Paul of Tarsus provides no details on the illness he metaphorically describes. In 2 Corinthians 12:7, he confides that Satan gave him *a thorn in the flesh*—an expression later adopted by Kierkegaard. No details, except for one occasion when he draws attention to his haggard appearance while addressing the Galatians—after he had suffered a beating that left visible marks . . . So that for centuries critics have piled up theories on the nature of that thorn. It is hard to resist offering a solemn inventory of their diagnoses: arthritis, renal colic, tendonitis, sciatica, gout, tachycardia, angina pectoris, itchy rash, skin sores, boils, eczema, leprosy, shingles, plague, rabies, erysipelas, gastritis, intestinal cramps, kidney stones, chronic ear infection, sinusitis, bronchitis, bladder infection, urinary retention, Maltese fever, filariosis, malaria, pilariosis, ringworm, pilonidal cyst, headache, gangrene, suppuration, abscesses, chronic hiccups (!), convulsions, epilepsy . . . His joints, tendons, nerves, heart, stomach, bowels, anus, ears, sinus, bladder, head, all were involved.

All except the sexual register . . . The etiology of hysteria includes a weakened—if it exists at all—libidinal potential. Disturbances arising from sexuality, a tendency for example to see it everywhere, to indulge in extremes of eroticism . . . How can we not recall all this when Paul's pen drips ad nauseam a hatred, a contempt, a permanent mistrust for the things of the body? His loathing of sexuality, his praise of chastity, his worship of abstinence, his approval of the widowed condition, his passion for celibacy, his appeal to his listeners to conduct themselves as he did (clearly expressed in the First Epistle to the Corinthians 7:8), his reluctant consent to marriage, but only as the best of bad choices (he would have preferred renunciation of all things corporeal). These are all obvious symptoms of hysteria.

The above conclusions are borne out by a number of undeniable facts, foremost among them Paul's failure to acknowledge any kind of deep-seated pathology whatsoever. We can frankly admit to abdominal pain or arthritic joints. Rampant skin disorders are noticeable, as are repeated hiccups. It is less easy to admit to *sexual impotence*, which can however be very obliquely hinted at under the cover of metaphor (the "thorn" accomplished this). Sexual impotence or any fixation of the libido on a socially indefensible object — a mother, a human being of the same sex, or any other perversion in the Freudian sense of the term. Freud locates the roots of hysteria in the struggle against repressed terrors of sexual origin, and their partial realization in the form of a conversion — in the psychoanalytical sense, but the other meaning also fits.

There is a kind of law that appears to have held sway over the planet since the beginning of time. In homage to La Fontaine, let us call it the "fox and grapes complex": it consists in making a virtue of necessity in order to avoid losing face. Life inflicts sexual impotence or a problematic libido on Paul of Tarsus. His response? He gave himself the illusion of freedom, of autonomy and independence, by believing that he had freed himself from what defined him. Celibacy was not imposed upon him; it was a choice, a decision he had made. Unable to lead a sex life worthy of the name, Paul declares null and void all forms of sexuality for himself (of course) but also for the rest of the world. A desire to be like everyone else by demanding that everyone else emulate him, whence his determination to make all humankind bow to the rule of his own limiting circumstances.

3

A weakling's revenge. This logic is clearly apparent in a proclamation of the Second Epistle to the Corinthians (12:210), in which he affirms, "For the sake of Christ, then, I am content with weaknesses, hardships, insults, persecutions and calamities, for when I am weak, then I am strong." This comes close to a straightforward acknowledgment of the logic of compensation that held captive the hysteric who collapsed on the road to Damascus. From the starting point of his own dilapidated physique, Paul militated for a world that resembled him.

His hatred of self turned into a vigorous hatred of the world and all its concerns: life, love, desire, pleasure, sensations, body, flesh, joy, freedom, independence, autonomy. There is no mystery about Paul's masochism. He saw his whole life through the prism of difficulties: he loved problems, he rejoiced in them, craved them, longed for them, manufactured them. In the epistle in which he confirms his taste for humiliation, he makes a list of what he suffered in order to preach to the crowds: five flog-gings — thirty-nine strokes each time — three scourgings with rods, one stoning at Lystria in Anatolia — where he actually came close to dying, his body being left for dead on the ground — three drownings, one of them involving a day and a night im-mersed in icy water — without mentioning the dangers en-demic to travel over roads infested with brigands, dangerous river crossings, the fatigue of marches beneath a leaden sun, countless nights without sleep, forced fasting, thirst, the cold of Anatolian nights. Add to those his prison terms, two years in a dungeon, exile . . . A masochist's dream!

Sometimes he found himself in humiliating situations. On the Agora in Athens, for example, where he tried to convert Stoic and Epicurean philosophers to Christianity by speaking of the resurrection of the body, sheer nonsense for Hellenes. The disciples of Zeno and Epicurus laughed in his face, but he took their insults without flinching . . . On another occasion, to flee popular rage and the anger of the ethnarch of Damascus, he escaped in a basket lowered from a window down the city ramparts. Since ridicule never kills, Paul survived.

This hatred of self Paul transformed into hatred of the world—and of the need to be able to live with it, partly to dispel it, keep it at a distance. The opposite of what tormented him would henceforth haunt his reality. The contempt of the individual Paul for his body, so incapable of scaling the heights that it might have aspired to, became a discrediting of all flesh in general, of all bodies and of all people. In 1 Corinthians 9:27 he confesses, "I pummel my body and I subdue it," and he asks of men, "Pummel your body and subdue it. Do as I do . . ."

Whence, as we know, praise of celibacy, chastity, and abstinence. No Jesus in all this; just the revenge of the weak. In 1 Corinthians 15:8–9, Paul says, "Last of all, as to one untimely born, he appeared also to me," and he feels unworthy to be numbered among the apostles: "I am the least of the apostles . . . I am not meet to be called an apostle."

Unable to have women? He loathes them . . . Impotent? He despises them. An excellent occasion for recycling the misogyny of Jewish monotheism, later bequeathed to Christianity and Islam. The first verses of the first book of the Bible set the tone: Genesis radically and irrevocably condemns woman, the first sinner, the source of all the world's evil. And Paul embraced this disastrous, this infinitely disastrous idea as his own.

Hence the prohibitions rained upon them throughout the Pauline writings, epistles, and acts: fragile beyond repair, women's destiny is to obey men in silence and submission. Eve's descendants must hold their husbands in awe and refrain from teaching or from trying to control the supposedly stronger sex. Temptresses, seductresses, they may of course hope for salvation, but only in, through, and for motherhood. Two thousand years of punishments visited on women simply to exorcise the neuroses of a weakling!

4

In praise of slavery. Paul the masochist articulates the ideas with which Christianity will one day triumph. These include delight in the joys of submission, obedience, passivity, total subservience to the powerful on the false grounds that all power comes from God and that the social position of the poor, the modest, and the humble emanates from a heavenly will and a divine decision.

God, good, compassionate, etc., approves the diseases of the diseased, the poverty of the poor, the tortures of the tortured, the servility of servants. Addressing the Romans in the heart of their empire, Paul spoke with most timely enthusiasm of the need to obey magistrates, officials, the emperor. He called on everyone to pay his due: taxes to the tax inspectors, fear to the army, the police, and dignitaries, honor to senators, ministers, monarchs.

For all power came from God and proceeded from him. Disobeying the powerful was rebelling against God. Hence his extolling of submission to order and authority. Hence his injunction to flatter the powerful, legitimize and justify the destitution of the poor, respect those wielding the sword. The church now entered a partnership with the state, which from the start set it squarely on the side of tyrants, dictators, and autocrats.

Sexual impotence transfigured into power over the world, the inability to enjoy women turned into an engine of hatred for women, contempt for self transformed into love of one's tormentors, hysteria sublimated into the construction of a social neurosis — what wonderful material for a psychiatric portrait! Jesus took on substance by becoming Paul's hostage. Bland and without substance on questions of society, sexuality (and with good reason, for ectoplasm does not become flesh overnight), and politics, the man of Nazareth assumed ever clearer features. Construction of the myth went on apace, gaining ever greater precision.

Paul read no Gospel during its author's lifetime. He himself never knew Jesus. Mark wrote the first Gospel, either in the very last years of Paul's life or after his death. Beginning with the second half of the first century of our era, the teacher from Tarsus propagated the myth, visited multitudes of men, told his fables to thousands of individuals in dozens of countries: the Asia Minor of pre-Socratic philosophers, the Athens of Plato and Epicurus, the Italy of the Epicureans of the Campagna or the Stoics of Rome, the Sicily of Empedocles . . . He visited Cyrene, the city where hedonism was born with Aristippus. He also made a detour via Alexandria, Philo's city. Everywhere, he contaminated. Soon Paul's disease infected the whole body of the empire.

5

At war with intelligence. Hatred of self, of the world, of women, of freedom: Paul of Tarsus added to this deplorable roster hatred of intelligence. Genesis had already preached loathing of knowledge, for we must never forget that tasting the fruit of the Tree of Knowledge was the original sin, the unforgivable fault transmitted from generation to generation. Wishing to know, and not remaining content with the obedience and faith demanded by God — that was what was unforgivable. To rival God in knowledge, to prefer education and intelligence to the imbecility of the obedient, these were so many mortal sins.

And Paul's education? Nonexistent, or almost: the Old Testament and the certainty that God spoke through it . . . His intellectual training? We have no idea whether he was a bright student or undertook prolonged studies . . . Rabbinical training, in all likelihood . . . His profession? Maker and seller of tents for nomads . . . His verbal style? Heavy, derivative, complex, oral in fact. His Greek? Clumsy, graceless, possibly dictated to him as he went about his manual trade. Some have even concluded that he could not write . . . The opposite of a Philo of Alexandria, the philosopher and Paul's contemporary.

This uneducated man, openly scoffed at by the Stoics and Epicureans in the public square of Athens, faithful to his technique of making a virtue of necessity, transformed his lack of culture into a hatred of culture. He called on the Corinthians and Timothy to turn their backs on "the addled and foolish questionings" and "hollow frauds" of philosophy. The alleged correspondence between Paul and Seneca is clearly a forgery of the first order. Paul was not a learned man and he addressed not philosophers but his peers. His audience, throughout his wanderings around the Mediterranean, was composed of humble folk and never included intellectuals, philosophers, men of letters. In the second century, Celsus wrote *Alethes logos* ("True Discourse" or "The True Word"), a polemic against Christianity, in which he characterized Christians as tanners, cleaners, craftsmen, carpenters, and the like. So Paul did not need culture. Demagoguery was enough, and with it its perpetual ally: hatred of intelligence.

III

The Totalitarian Christian State

1

Hysteria (continued). Just as French rationalism was shaped on the basis of three dreams recalled by Descartes (!), so Christianity strode on to the historical stage with an event recalling the purest pagan traditions: astrological signs . . . The year is 312. Constantine is advancing on Rome. He is fighting his rival Maxentius, from whom he hopes to wrest Italy. His conquest of the north of the peninsula was lightning-fast: Turin, Milan, and Verona fell easily into his hands. The emperor was an old hand at direct contacts with the absolute: in the temple of Grand in the Vosges mountains of Gaul, Apollo appeared in person to promise him a reign of thirty years. At the time, paganism did not trouble him. Indeed he was a devotee of *Sol Invictus*, the Unconquered Sun.

But this time the message was transformed. Like Paul struck down on the road to Damascus, Constantine saw in the heavens a sign announcing that he would conquer in its name. And — a detail of some importance — his troops also witnessed the event: all of them saw the same holy talisman! Eusebius of Caesarea, the prince's house-trained intellectual, and furthermore a bishop, a peerless forger, an outstanding specialist in Christian apologia, gives us a detailed interpretation of this sign, which was in the form of a luminous cross above the sun. Moreover —

here Eusebius warms to his task—a celestial text promised that the emperor would win his war against Maxentius by invoking the sign. Two precautions are better than one: the next night Jesus appeared in a dream, teaching his protégé the sign of the cross that would prove useful in winning every one of his battles, provided he armed himself beforehand with the sign. We readily understand that once he became the most Christian emperor, Constantine, imbued as he now was with philosophical rationality, turned savagely on astrology, magic, and paganism. All that philosophical rationality made him unreasonable.

A few days later, he won. Naturally . . . Maxentius was drowned beneath the Milvius bridge on October 28, 312. Helped by the ghost of the Nazarene, Constantine became master of Italy. He marched into Rome, disbanded the Praetorian Guard, and gave Pope Miltiades the Lateran Palace. Admittedly, the Christian kingdom was not of this world, but why should it be neglected, especially when it offered the occasion for pomp, gold, purple, money, power, dominance, all of them virtues naturally deduced from the messages of the carpenter's son?

And that sign? Was it a text message from Christ or a collective hallucination? A message from Jesus, riveted in celestial eternity but with a keen eye for the most trivial goings-on in the here and now, or further proof that in this age of anguish a fissured world was susceptible to communal neuroses and divinely mandated hysteria? A proof of regeneration or a mark of decadence? Christianity's first step or one of paganism's last? The misery of men without God—and more miserable still with him.

Today this sign is interpreted in rational and even ultra-rationalist manner: not as astrology but astronomy. Contemporary scientists propose a hysterical (and thus religious) reading of an event reducible to the simplest of causalities. On October 10, 312, eighteen days before the glorious victory over Maxentius, Mars, Jupiter, and Venus stood in the Roman sky in a configuration that encouraged interpretation of the sign as a fabulous presage. Delirium completed the job.

While Constantine was not a monument of bookish culture, he is acknowledged to have been a cunning strategist, an astute politician. Did he really believe in the power of the sign from Christ? Or did he exploit it skillfully and stage-manage it for opportunistic ends? A pagan familiar with the workings of magic, a believer, like everyone else in this period of antiquity, in the claims of astrology, the emperor may also have counted on obtaining the maximum possible support from his troops, who included a large and loyal Christian contingent respectful of power and never questioning orders.

His father, Constantius Chlorus, had pursued a fruitful policy of tolerance toward Christ's faithful. Was Constantine (counseled by active Christian intriguers) emulating that politically astute policy? Did he have a visionary's glimpse of the possibilities inherent in exploiting this interesting force, annexing it to his cause through the award of timely and generous gifts that tied them to his project—let us call it Gramscian—of unifying the empire? In any event, in these early years of the fourth century, that unlikely candidate Jesus (his praises shouted from the rooftops by Paul) became the emblematic instrument in the fanfare of a new empire.

2

Constantine's coup d'état. Constantine's coup was masterly. We still live today with its fatal heritage. Naturally he understood what he could obtain from a people obedient to Paul's call for submission to the temporal authorities, for uncomplaining acceptance of dire poverty, for obedience to the magistrates and officials of the empire, for disapproval of temporal disobedience as an insult flung in God's face, for accepting slavery, deceit, and the existence of social disparities. Examples of Christian martyrdom and Christian behavior in the relatively rare persecutions they endured were clear indications to the powerful of how useful this rabble could be to the legally untouchable figures at the summit of the state.

Constantine accordingly heaped them with assurances. To put it another way, he bought them. And the policy worked . . . He wrote into Roman law new articles that satisfied the Christians and made official the ascetic ideal. He enacted harsh laws against the degradation of social mores that marked the late empire, against unfettered sexuality, the triumph of the circus games, and the orgiastic practices of certain pagan cults. He made divorce procedures more difficult, forbade possession of concubines, made prostitution a crime, and condemned sexual dissipation. At the same time he abrogated the law forbidding the celibate to inherit. So, after a few timely demises, people of the church could now legally fill their pockets. He did not outlaw slavery, despite the wishes of Christ's sectarians, but mitigated some of its harshness . . . Magic, on the other hand, was banned, and so were gladiatorial combats. At the same time, Constantine ordered the building of Saint Peter's and of other, secondary basilicas. The Christians rejoiced: their kingdom was henceforth of this world.

At about this time Fausta, the new Christian's second wife, persuaded him that her stepson had tried to seduce her. Without waiting for proof, he sent his cutthroats to torture and then behead his own son, as well as a nephew also implicated in the "plot." When he realized the empress had deceived him, he sent the same gang in. They took advantage of Fausta's visit to her bath to release a flow of boiling water . . . Infanticide, uxoricide, homicide: the most Christian emperor bought his salvation and the church's silence with a host of gifts: tax exemptions for church landholdings, generous subsidies, and the creation of new churches — Saint Paul and Saint Lawrence. All variations on the theme of love for one's neighbor.

Thus benevolently disposed, afloat in gifts, fattened and enriched by gratuities from the prince, the clergy conferred full powers upon him at the Council of Nicaea in 325. The pope was absent, for reasons of what we would today call health. There, Constantine proclaimed himself the "thirteenth apostle," thus endowing Paul of Tarsus with a strong right sword arm. And what an arm! Church and state formed what Henri-Irénée Marrou, a historian scarcely to be suspected (being a Christian) of anticlericalism, atheism, or left-wing leanings, has called a "totalitarian state." The first Christian state.

While this was going on, Constantine's mother Helena, concerned for the salvation of the son who had authorized the axe and the boiling water, undertook a journey to Palestine. A devout Christian, and magically inspired, she discovered there three wooden crosses with one of the famous *tituli*, clearly Christ's. The site of Calvary was most opportunely buried under the temple of Aphrodite, which of course had to be destroyed .. . The eighty-year-old Helena spent the considerable sums given her by Constantine on the building of three churches: the Holy Sepulchre, the Garden of Olives, and the Nativity, where she put her relics on display. Even if those sites were "discovered" for that specific purpose, without a shred of historical justification or topographical evidence, their cult has endured . . . To repay the emperor for this major asset, and deciding that God had pardoned his crimes, the church made his mother a heroine of its mythology. As a result, Helena was canonized, becoming the first Roman empress to enter the thanatophilic Christian pantheon.

Constantine died on the day of Pentecost, May 22, 337. A few weeks before his death, he was baptized by the bishop of

Nicomedia, an ally of Arius. The Council of Nicaea had condemned Arianism as a heresy, yet the matter was not closed, and the disputes continued. Constantine's choice of an Arian bishop to perform the ceremony was a mark of the emperor's political genius. By this gesture, he reconciled Orthodox and Arian Christians, thus restoring the unity of the church. Even on his deathbed, he had an eye to the future, especially his post regnum. Even after death, he strove to preserve the unity of the empire.

Like many tyrants, Constantine was unable to settle the question of a successor. He left behind a power vacuum and a disorganized group of high officials of church and state. For more than three months at the height of summer, May 22 to September 9, the various ministers (civil, military, and ecclesiastical) reported daily to the imperial corpse as it lay in state. This neurotic behavior was a preview of the later cult of the dead, evidenced by Christian fascination with corpses and relics.

3

From victims to victimizers. Christians had admittedly suffered persecution, but it was not always as severe as the Vulgate claims. The figures for those devoured by lions in the arena have been substantially lowered by historians eager to leave the field of Christian apologetics and do their work conscientiously. Tens of thousands of dead, wrote Eusebius of Caesarea, Constantine's domestic intellectual. Modern estimates come closer to three thousand — by way of comparison, ten thousand gladiators fought to the death simply to celebrate the end of the war against the Dacians in 107.

What defines totalitarian regimes today corresponds point by point with the Christian state as it was constructed by Constantine's successors: use of constraint, torture, acts of vandalism, destruction of libraries and symbolic sites, unpunished murders, ubiquitous propaganda, the leader's absolute power, the remolding of the whole of society along the government's ideological lines, extermination of opponents, monopoly of legal violence and means of communication, abolition of the frontier between private life and the public sphere, overall politicization of society, destruction of pluralism, bureaucratic organization, expansionism — all signs of totalitarianism from its origins, as well as the totalitarianism of the Christian Empire.

The emperor Theodosius I proclaimed Catholicism the state religion in 380. Twelve years later he categorically banned pagan worship. Nicaea had already set the tone. In 449 Theodosius II and Valentinian III ordered the destruction of everything that might excite God's wrath or wound Christian hearts. That definition was apparently broad enough to include multiple exactions in every field. Tolerance, love of one's neighbor, and forgiveness of sins had their limits.

Constantine had previously been in contact with pagan intellectuals such as Nicagoras of Athens, Hermogenes, and Sopatros, but as of the year 330, he severed his relationship with them. That got the ball rolling. In 335, Sopatros was executed for witchcraft, and writings by the Neoplatonist philosopher Porphyry (who had died in 305) were burned. Such autos-da-fé came thick and fast, one much like the other. The emperor Theodosius I took severe measures against all heretics, including Montanists, Eumonians, and, above all, Arians. In 435, during the reign of Theodosius II, Nestorius the patriarch of Constantinople was exiled to Egypt and all of his writings were consigned to the flames, wherever they could be found in both the Eastern and Western Empire. Another symbol of the repression of rational thought by irrational religion was the murder of Hypatia of Alexandria, the first female mathematician known to history. A Hellenized Egyptian, she was a Neoplatonist, mathematician, astronomer, and teacher, one of the foremost intellects of her time. During an antipagan riot in 415, a Christian mob pulled Hypatia from her carriage and dragged her through the streets to a church. She was stripped naked, and the flesh was scraped from her bones with sharp oyster shells and broken tiles. After tearing her body to pieces, the mob burned her mutilated remains. A sterling example of the Christian belief in love of one's neighbor!

4

The name of the law. Lawmakers are quick to legitimize oppression and confer on it the force of law under the label of justice. Thus, legal formulas are devised to cover all manner of crimes and misdeeds, persecutions and assassinations. The reader should consult the Theodosian Code if he needs proof that the law *always* supports the ruling caste's domination over the masses. In United States history, the black codes (referring to laws enacted in the former Confederate states after the Civil War) were intended to assure the continuance of white supremacy. A review of the anti-Semitic laws passed by the Vichy government during the Second World War would dispel any remaining doubts.

To be specific: in 380 the law condemned non-Christians to "infamy," in other words rescinded their civic rights and therefore their chances of participating in the life of the city, for example in teaching or the law. It decreed the death sentence for all who threatened the persons or the goods of Catholic ministers and their places of worship. Meanwhile, Christians destroyed pagan shrines and confiscated, looted, and ravaged temples and their furnishings with the blessings of authorities backed by the legal texts.

The ban on pagan practices proceeded alongside a merciless battle against heresies, defined as what did not conform to imperial decrees. Meetings were forbidden, so of course was Manichaeism, and Jews were persecuted under the same heading as magic or dissolute morals. The law encouraged informers. It forbade marriage between Jews and Christians . . . It authorized the confiscation of non-Christian goods. Paul of Tarsus very early pointed down this path, for in the Acts of the Apostles (19:19) he admits his presence at a burning of supposedly magical books.

In keeping with the tactics of Constantine's mother, Catholic churches replaced the razed temples. Here and there, synagogues and Gnostic shrines went up in flames. Often-priceless statues were destroyed and broken up and their fragments recycled into Christian buildings. Places of worship were so utterly ravaged that their debris served for a time to repave roads and build highways and bridges. An index of how widespread the damage was: in Constantinople, the temple of Aphrodite served as a parking space for horse-drawn vehicles. Sacred trees were uprooted.

From the end of the eighth century BCE and for the next thousand years, the oracle of Apollo at Didyma near Miletus (on the west coast of Turkey) was second in importance only to Delphi. In 303 AD, the emperor Diocletian consulted an oracle to ask why his soothsayers' methods were not working. When he sought advice, the gods did not answer. The oracle said that the Christian God was too powerful and was preventing the Roman gods from communicating. Whereupon Diocletian initiated what was to be the last and greatest persecution of Christians by the Roman Empire. Ultimately, that sealed Didyma's fate. Its long history ended abruptly when Constantine the Great converted to Christianity and, blaming the oracle for the persecutions, retaliated by closing the temple of Apollo at Didyma and executing all the priests.

Subsequent emperors followed suit. A text dated February 19 of the year 356 decreed the death sentence for persons convicted of worshipping idols or participating in sacrifices. In consequence, Christians in Antioch seized a prophet of Apollo and tortured him. At Scythopolis in Palestine, Domitius Modestus conducted "interrogations" of the top officials and intellectual leaders of Antioch and Alexandria. His aim was to leave no educated man alive. Many Neoplatonist philosophers perished in this ferocious repression. In his *Homily on Statues*, Saint John Chrysostom condoned physical violence in certain circumstances and explicitly wrote that "Christians are the repositories of public order."

At Alexandria in 389, Christians attacked the Serapeum (temple of Serapis) and the Mithraeum (temple of Mithras). The idols inside were removed, publicly displayed, and mocked. The pagan faithful protested ("particularly the philosophers," according to contemporary sources), and riots ensued with many deaths on both sides. At Suffectum (Sufes in modern-day Sbiba, Tunisia) around 401, Christian monks destroyed a statue of Hercules, the patron god of the city, and sixty people died in the resulting riots. Encouraged by the aforementioned John Chrysostom, bands of monks ransacked the shrines on the Phoenician mountains. All this was the consequence of Paul's call to despise culture, knowledge, books, and intelligence.

5

Vandalism, autos-da-fé, and the culture of death. Like Paul of Tarsus, Christians were convinced that academic learning hindered access to God. All books (not just books by authors accused of heresy, such as Arius, Mani, and Nestorius) were at risk of being burned. Neoplatonist works were condemned as books of magic and divination. People who possessed libraries feared for their safety. In 370 the citizens of Antioch, terrified of persecution, preempted the Christian commissars and burned their own books in the public square. As for the Great Library of Alexandria, its daughter library was housed in the Serapeum, a temple dedicated to the god Serapis. In 391, by order of the bishop of Alexandria, the temple was leveled and the library went up in smoke.

In 591, the Neoplatonic school in Athens was closed, and the Christian Empire confiscated its holdings. Paganism had survived in the Greek capital for centuries. Plato's teachings could point to a thousand years of uninterrupted transmission. The philosophers set out on the road to Persian exile. What a triumph for Paul of Tarsus, once mocked by Stoics and Epicureans in the home of philosophy during his attempt at proselytization. The posthumous victory of God's weakling and his disastrous neuroses! A culture of death, of hatred, of contempt and intolerance . . . At Constantinople in 562, Christians arrested "Hellenes" — an insulting name — parading them through the city to the accompaniment of hoots and jeers. On Kenogion Square, Christians lit a huge bonfire and tossed the philosophers' books and the images of their gods into the flames.

Justinian hammered in the final nail, stiffening Christian legislation against the unorthodox. Non-Christians were forbidden to bequeath their wealth to pagans; it was forbidden to testify in court against the church's followers; forbidden to own Christian slaves; forbidden to draw up a legal deed; forbidden to profess freedom of conscience (!). And in 529 Justinian made it mandatory for pagans to take instruction in the Christian religion and then undergo baptism, on pain of exile and confiscation of their goods; he forbade those converted to the religion of

PART FOUR

THEOCRACY

I

Selective Exploitation of the Texts

1

Historical extraterritoriality. Everyone knows of the existence of monotheism's three books, but very few know their dates of origin, their authors, or the ups and downs attendant on establishing the three texts — the absolutely final, immutable texts. For the Torah, Old Testament, New Testament, and Koran took an unthinkably long time to emerge from history and claim that their texts issued from God alone, that they had no need to explain themselves to those who entered their paper temples armed only with faith, unburdened of reason and intelligence.

One instance: in a library specializing in the history of religions, scholars face great problems hunting down dates of composition and origin for the body of texts that make up the holy books. As if even historians, men of reason, were indifferent to the conditions in which these texts were composed. Yet knowledge of those conditions is essential to our understanding of the texts. Take Genesis for example. It was contemporaneous with which book, which author? The *Epic of Gilgamesh* or the *Iliad*? Hesiod's *Theogony* (*Origin of the Gods*), the *Upanishads* or Confucius's *Analects*?

We address the opening texts of the Torah, the Old Testament, and the Bible knowing nothing more about them than their existence. We are not even aware of our lack of knowledge of the subject. For these pages, like all that follow, enjoy extraterritorial historical status. This methodological quirk confirms the pious in their belief that these books have no human author, no established birth date, that they fell from heaven one day in miraculous fashion or were dictated to an inspired man in a divine voice impervious to time and entropy, immune to growth and corruption. A mystery!

For centuries, the clerics banned direct reading of the texts. Questioning their historical veracity was all too human, they felt—and we still live more or less under the shadow of that veto. Those who serve religions know intuitively that direct contact and a reading that is both intelligent and imbued with common sense will expose the incoherence of these pages. They were written by a considerable number of people after centuries of oral transmission, extending over an extremely long historical span, the whole having been copied a thousand times. The scribes who copied them were often unscrupulous or foolish; they could even be genuine and outright forgers. When we cease to approach their work as sanctified objects we swiftly drop the illusion that they are holy. Hence the need to read them properly, pen in hand.

2

Twenty-seven centuries in the making. When we finally become aware of these facts, our surprise persists. For example, the French edition of the Bible produced by Emile Osty and Joseph Trinquet proposes a ten-century time frame for its composition—between the twelfth and second centuries before Jesus Christ. In other words, between the last Egyptian books of wisdom—the royal scribe Ani of Thebes, for example—and the

New Academy of the Skeptic philosopher Carneades. Jean Soler
—an excellent demolisher of myths—gives us his own esti-
mate: between the fifth and the first centuries before the common era, in other words between Socrates and Lucretius. And
some historians shrink the time frame still further, proposing just
the third and second centuries BCE . . .

This means that the estimated birth dates for the first book
of the Bible are almost ten centuries apart! Which makes it difficult to think as a historian and perform a task of sociological,
political, and philosophical contextualization. The labor of era-
sure (deliberate or not), traces or proofs of historicity, and the
stripping away of the scaffolding mean that we no longer know
which men made these books nor what immanent conditions
made them possible. This being so, the road is wide open for the
mythical fabrications of those who believe in a divine source!

The same vagueness clouds the origins of the New Testament texts. The oldest estimates date from a half century after Jesus's supposed existence. In any case, none of the four evangelists
ever knew Christ in the flesh. At best, their knowledge of him
stems from the mythological and fabulous account transmitted
orally and then one day written down, some time between the
fifties of the common era—Paul's epistles—and the end of the
first century—the Apocalypse. Yet no copy of the Gospels exists
before the end of the second or the beginning of the third. We
date them with an eye to the supposed facts and with a prior belief in what those texts tell us.

Since they are by Mark, Luke, Matthew & Co., and since
we are in those murky waters, the texts must naturally date from
given periods—even if the oldest document we possess is a late
arrival, contemporary with what some historians call the "forg-
ing" of Christianity, the notorious decades of the second century
of our era. In 1546, the Council of Trent cut to the heart of the
matter, deciding on the definitive corpus on the basis of the

Vulgate, itself manufactured from the Hebrew text and translated in the fourth and fifth centuries by a Saint Jerome not overburdened with intellectual honesty.

The Jews built their corpus equally slowly and over as long a span. While certain texts of the Torah are supposed to date from the twelfth century before Jesus Christ, we would have to wait until after the destruction of the Temple in Jerusalem (in around 70 CE) before the rabbis settled the details of the Hebrew Bible. In the same period, Epictetus lived the life of an emblematic Stoic in imperial Rome.

Early in the third century, they compiled and codified the Jewish oral laws (the Mishna) that supplement the laws in the Torah. At about the same time, Diogenes Laërtius collated his documents and began to write his *Lives, Teachings, and Sayings of Famous Philosophers*. Around 500, rabbis from Palestine completed the Babylonian Talmud, a commentary on the Mishna. By then, Boetius was writing his *Consolation of Philosophy* in prison. We would have to wait until about the year 1000 to see the definitive text of the Hebrew Bible established. At about this time, in his own corner of the old empire, Avicenna was trying to reconcile philosophy and Islam.

This was also the time when, from a handful of Korans — the "s" is mandatory — Muslims established their definitive version. In order to do this, they had to choose from among several texts, compare one dialect with another, standardize the spelling, separate abrogating and abrogated verses in order to avoid a too glaring incoherence. A genuine operation of textual but also ideological calibration. Time does its work on documents, and the meticulous history of this forgery has still to be written.

Conclusion: if we go upstream and take the most ancient Old Testament dating (twelfth century BCE) and then voyage downstream to the final establishment of the New Testament corpus at the Council of Trent (sixteenth century), the construction sites of the monotheisms were constantly at work for twenty centuries of action-filled history. For books directly dictated by God to his people, the opportunities for human intervention are numberless. At the very least, they call for and deserve serious archaeological spadework.

3

Monotheistic grab bag. What is certain is the staggering historical sweep we confront. We do not even possess an official date of birth for worship of a one God . . . Some locate it around the thirteenth century BCE, but Jean Soler insists on the neighborhood of the fourth and third — in other words very late, and even here, fuzziness persists. But the family line is clear: the Jews invented it — even drawing inspiration from the Egyptian solar cult — to ensure the coherence, cohesion, and existence of their small, threatened people. The mythology they fashioned engendered belief in a warrior God, a fighter, bloodthirsty, aggressive, a war leader highly effective at mobilizing a people without a land. The myth of a chosen people founded the essence and existence of a nation thereafter blessed with a destiny.

Of that labor of invention, several thousand pages of canonical text survive — very few, considering their worldwide influence over the course of more than twenty centuries. The Old Testament boasts a total of three thousand five hundred pages, the New nine hundred, the Koran seven hundred and fifty, that is, a little more than five thousand pages in which everything and its opposite is said once and for all.

In each of these three founding texts contradictions abound. Every fact articulated is almost immediately confronted with its opposite. A given opinion appears to triumph — but so, immediately afterward, does its exact opposite. One value is given pride of place, only to be followed a little later by its antithesis. The labor of definitive dating and the construction of a definitive corpus make no difference, not even the decision to decree three synoptic Gospels in order that they may be read side by side. Jew, Christian, and Muslim may draw on the Torah, the Gospels, and the Koran as they wish: all three find material permitting them to justify black and white, day and night, vice and virtue.

Should a war leader need a verse to justify his action, he will find an unbelievable number to choose from. But a peacemaker, a hater of war, can just as easily brandish a sentence, a quotation, a word to justify the opposite! Does the former lift a few words from the texts to justify a war of total extermination? The books are there, and so are the texts. Does the latter call for universal peace? He too lifts the maxims he needs. Does an anti-Semite need justification for his hysterical loathing? Does a believer seek to establish his contempt for the Palestinians, Bible in hand? Or a misogynist need to prove the inferiority of women? An abundance of texts permits it . . . But another word lifted from this clutter authorizes the reader to arrive at the opposite conclusion. And the same applies if we seek a clear conscience on issues of hatred, murder, and contempt: there is just as much material to support vilifying one's neighbor as there is to extol undying love for him. Too many pages written over too many years by too many anonymous people, too much consolidation and too many second thoughts, too many sources, too much material: in the absence of a single source of inspiration (God) . . . The three so-called holy books offer us too many scribes, middlemen, and copyists. None of the books is cohesive, uniform, unequivocal. We are therefore forced to acknowledge the incoherence, lack of uniformity, and ambiguous nature of the books' teachings. A close reading, beginning with the beginning and aiming for the end by following a signposted path, is a simple but little-practiced method.

Who has really read the book of his religion from beginning to end? And who, having once read it, has directed his reason, his memory, his intelligence, and his critical faculties to the parts and the whole of what he has read? Reading does not imply thumbing through page after page, chanting their contents like an ecstatic dervish, consulting them like a catalog, selecting this or that story, here and there and from time to time, but taking the time to *meditate on the whole.* If we do that, we lay bare the incredible improbability, the tissue of incoherences that constitute these three books, which for more than two millennia have built empires, states, nations, and history.

4

Cherry-picking the scriptures. In this open-air archaeological dig, selective extraction is the order of the day. Since each of these books is held to have been inspired from or dictated by God, it cannot be anything other than perfect, absolute, definitive. God has mastered the use of reason, the principle of non-contradiction, the dialectic of consequences, and logical causality — or else he is no longer God. Since the whole is perfect, its constituent parts are equally perfect. Thus the book in its entirety reflects the perfection of every moment that goes into its construction: the Bible is true and thus each of its fragments is also true — and so is a word lifted out of context.

Starting from this principle, we meditate on the spirit according to the letter — and vice versa. Does one selected quotation say the opposite from its predecessor? Yes, but a third expresses the opposite of that opposite. And then we extract yet another phrase, which — offering us another contradiction — restores the first proposition. This game of justifying our thesis by use of a quotation taken out of context allows everyone to use the so-called sacred texts for his own purposes. Hitler defended some of his measures by invoking Jesus driving the moneylenders from the Temple. Martin Luther King validated his campaign of nonviolence by quoting from the Gospels . . . The state of Israel invokes the Torah to legitimize its colonization of Palestine. The Palestinians quote the Koran to provide justification for the murder of innocents with the ultimate goal of eliminating Israel. Sophistry, convoluted dialectical skills, and relish for argument are enough to bestow blessings on vice and consign virtue to the pillory.

A Jewish example. We all know the story. Haloed in mist, surrounded by flames, and speaking with a mighty voice — hard to imagine him falsetto and unsure of himself — Yahweh intervenes in person on the mountain to deliver his Ten Commandments to Moses. The fifth on the list is the best-known: "Thou shalt not kill" (Deuteronomy 5:17). No sentence could be plainer: its subject, a personal pronoun; verb cast in the future tense; imperative mood; active voice; negative. God expresses himself in terms immediately accessible to the meanest intelligence: a ban on committing murder, on taking someone's life — an absolute, untouchable principle, requiring no adjustment, suffering no exceptions, no restrictions. The thing is said and understood.

Lifting these few words from the Ten Commandments is enough to define an ethic. Nonviolence, peace, love, forgiveness, mildness, an entire program rejecting war, violence, armies, capital punishment, battles, the Crusades, the Inquisition, colonialism, the atom bomb, assassination — all things that believers in the Bible have been practicing shamelessly for centuries in the very name of their holy book. Why then this blatant logical contradiction?

Blatant because only a few verses later in Deuteronomy 7:1, the same Yahweh steps in to justify the Jews in their extermination of certain peoples explicitly named in the Torah: the Hittites (settlers who came originally from Asia Minor), Amorites, Perizzites, Canaanites, Girgashites, Hivites, and Jebusites, no fewer than seven peoples, constituting most of the population of Palestine. Against these tribes, Yahweh authorizes anathema, racism — mixed marriage is forbidden — and a ban on contracts. Spurning compassion, he demands the demolition of their altars and monuments and legitimizes book burnings. His reasons: the Jews are the chosen people (Deuteronomy 7:6) singled out by God and exalted above all others and despite all others.

The injunction not to kill is very clear. But the vocabulary of the rest of Deuteronomy includes: smite, perish, destroy, burn, dispossess, and other terms straight out of the repertory of total war. Yahweh justifies the slaughter of every living thing. Men and beasts, women and children, the old, donkeys, bulls, the ox, the ass, and the sheep — the text recording them all faithfully — must perish by the sword (Joshua 6:21). The conquest of the land of Canaan and the taking of Jericho come at the price of all life there. The city of Jericho is burned. The gold and silver are spared the general destruction and dedicated to Yahweh in return for his greatness, his acts of generosity, and his complicity in what we may rightly call *the first genocide*: the extermination of a people.

What are we to conclude from this? Should we see an undeniable contradiction? Or should we read more closely, more subtly, leaving the beaten paths habitually taken in approaching this subject? For the imperative of not killing can seem to be made compatible with justifying the extermination of a people. In his own day, Leon Trotsky gave voice to the solution in his book *Their Morality and Ours*: a morality of combat, one ethic for one side, a different code for the other.

A hypothesis: the Ten Commandments are valid as a local,

sectarian, and communal recommendation. Understood is "thou, a Jew, shalt not kill Jews." The commandment plays an architectonic role in ensuring the life and survival of the community. On the other hand, when killing others, non-Jews, the goyim — the word itself connotes two irreconcilable worlds — killing is not really the crime, or at least it is no longer tied to the Commandments. The imperative of not taking life ceases to be categorical and becomes hypothetical. It does not found the universal but upholds the particular. Yahweh speaks to his chosen people and has no concern at all for the others. The Torah invented the ethical, ontological, and metaphysical inequality of races.

5

The whip and the other cheek. Another example, Christian this time, of possible contradictions or logical contradictions. The four Gospels apparently celebrate only gentleness, peace, and love. Jesus shines forth as a symbol of forgiveness of sinners, a figure gifted with words of consolation for the indigent and afflicted, for the poor in spirit, and other variations on the theme of charitable thinking. That is the usual panoply of the Messiah, as served up to small children and stage-managed every Sunday in sermons addressed to families.

A selected morsel to illustrate this aspect of the character: the parable of the other cheek. It is well-known. Matthew (5:39) reports it and Luke borrows it from him (6:29). Jesus taught that he was not supplanting the Old Testament but fulfilling it. On the question of the Jewish law of retribution, the *lex talionis*, he suggests that what he meant by "fulfilling" was overtaking. To those who practiced the principle of an eye for an eye and a tooth for a tooth, he proposed a new tactic: the man smitten on the right cheek must turn the other cheek (which will probably be smitten in its turn . . .).

Here again, as with the sixth commandment, the recommendation allows of no ambiguity. No prevarication, no close scrutiny of the parable that might justify returning the blow. One slap, and the Christian responds with an act of abstention that defuses the situation. No wonder the Roman Empire encountered no problems dispatching Christian martyrs to the lions! Turning the other cheek leads inevitably — and without striking a blow — to our own destruction as long as our adversary is a ruthless brute. Lying defiantly across strategically vital railroad tracks in one of their many acts of civil disobedience, Mahatma Gandhi and his followers could take heart from the example of the evangelists — in the knowledge that their adversary was not a Nazi battalion commander who would quickly have denied them the use of either cheek.

But the Gospels contain another story also validated by the church authorities, since it figures in the canon — the story of Jesus and the Temple moneylenders. According to John 2:15, he drove them all out with a scourge (or whip). It is useless to argue (as some are tempted to do) that turning the other cheek is an authentic reflection of the Messiah's teachings — whereas Christ's fury and violence in the Temple is inconsistent with his character, and therefore must surely be attributable to someone else, an apostle perhaps. The same Jesus who refused to return blow for blow violently ejected the vendors and moneylenders for selling oxen, sheep, and doves and changing money in the Temple! Gentle, peaceful, tolerant Jesus?

For believers who might find this episode too trivial to invalidate the image of a peaceable Christ, let us recall a few more passages from the New Testament in which their hero's conduct is not always genteel . . . For example, when he utters seven *curses* against hypocritical Pharisees and scribes (Luke 11:42–52); when he consigns to hellfire those who do not believe in him (Luke 10:15 and 12:10); when he *heaps abuse* on the cities north of Lake Genesareth for their failure to repent; when he predicts the *ruin* of Jerusalem and the *destruction* of the Temple (Mark 13); when he declares that whoever is not for him is *against* him (Luke 11:23); when he teaches that he has come not in peace but bearing the *sword* (Matthew 10:34); and many other instances.

6

Hitler, Saint John's disciple. Adolf Hitler thought highly of the story of the Temple moneylenders, taken from the Gospel according to John. A Christian who never renounced his faith, Hitler praised the Catholic, Apostolic, and Roman Church, marveled at its creation of an unrivaled civilization, and prophesied its continued vigor in the centuries to come.

For the moment, I shall merely note that in *Mein Kampf* (volume 1, chapter 11, page 307),[*] he mentions Jesus's actions in the Temple and refers explicitly to the *whip* (*scourge*) — Saint John was the only evangelist to provide this detail. This was the kind of Christianity Hitler admired: *true Christianity* (*loc. cit.*) and *apodictic faith* (volume 2, chapter 5, page 454). Apodictic, the exact word Hitler used, meaning "expressing essential truth or absolute certainty."

A Christian who does not deny the dual message of his Bible can also draw on Exodus (21:23–25) to evoke the *lex talio-*

---

[*]The page numbers cited correspond to the paperback edition of *Mein Kampf*, American translation by Ralph Manheim, published by Mariner Books, a division of Houghton Mifflin.

nis. As we know, it calls on us to exchange an eye for an eye, a tooth for a tooth, but also hand for hand, foot for foot, burn for burn, wound for wound, bruise for bruise. And as we have seen, Jesus proposed turning the other cheek as an alternative to this ancient tribal formulation. But if we abrogate this Gospel parable and replace it with the vengeful Old Testament prescription, and couple this with the New Testament episode of the Temple moneylenders, the worst of excesses can easily be justified. With such a cargo of sophistries, we could justify Kristallnacht as a modern-day eviction of the moneylenders — let us remember that Jesus reproached them with transacting business and money-changing . . . Then, pursuing the same hysterical line of argument and invoking the *lex talionis*, the Final Solution becomes the logical response to the National Socialists' nightmare of the racial and Bolshevik Judaization of Europe . . . Unfortunately, the metaphoric scourge permits the dialectician and the determined theoretician to legitimize the gas chambers. Moreover, Pius XII and the Catholic Church succumbed to the charms of these Hitlerian contradictions from the very beginning. Indeed the church continues to do so, if we accept as an admission of collusion its enduring unwillingness to acknowledge the error implicit in the Vatican's support for Nazism. I shall return to this later.

7

Allah's problems with logic. Hitler — Abu Ali in Arabic — admired the Muslim religion in its very essence, virile, warlike, conquering, and militant. And many of the Muslim faithful subsequently repaid that kindness: there was the pro-Nazi grand mufti of Jerusalem during the Second World War, of course, but there were also the eternally anti-Semitic and anti-Zionist militants who recycled former Nazis into the highest ranks of Middle Eastern military staffs and secret services after the Second World War, who protected, concealed, and cared for many of the Third Reich's war criminals in their territories — Syria, Egypt, Saudi Arabia, Palestine. Not to mention an unbelievable number of conversions of former Reich dignitaries to the religion of the Koran.

Pursuant to our examination of the Torah, New Testament, and Koran, let us consider additional contradictions and examples of selective borrowing from the sacred texts as a pretext for evil deeds. The Old Testament prohibits killing but simultaneously condones the annihilation of certain enemies of the Jews. Christian brotherly love is juxtaposed with sanction of violence, when dictated by God's anger. The Koran, too, is full of inconsistencies. The mixed messages in all three monotheistic books have the potential of leading to monstrous consequences.

A Muslim example, then: an extremely imprudent sura (4:82) states that the Koran issued directly from Allah. The proof? The absence of *contradictions* in the divine book . . . Alas! It takes no time at all to conclude that every page teems with contradictions! At several points, the Koran refers to itself with evident self-satisfaction: "intelligently exposed" (6:114) — just like Spinoza! — "coherently narrated" (22:16) — like a proposition by Descartes! — and with "no hint of tortuousness" — like a page out of Bergson! Except that the book abounds in contradictory statements. Figuratively speaking, you have only to bend down and gather them up.

The Koran consists of one hundred fourteen suras or chapters. Except for sura 9, each chapter begins by repeating the first line of the first sura: In the name of Allah, the Beneficent, the Merciful. Duly noted. According to Islamic tradition, God has ninety-nine names; the hundredth will be revealed only in a future life. Many of these names are variations on the theme of mercy and compassion. Al-Rahîm: the Most Merciful, the Most Compassionate. Al-Ghaffâr: the All-Forgiving, the Absolver. Al-Ghafûr: the Pardoner. Al'-Adl: the Just, Equitable, Impartial. Al-Latîf: the Subtle, Gracious, Refined. Al-Halîm: the Lenient, Clement, Most Serene, Most Kind and Gentle. Al-Karîm: the Generous, the Bountiful. Al-Barr: the Gracious Benefactor, the Source of Goodness. Al'-Afûw: the Eraser of Sins, the Remover of Error, Fault, and Wrong Action. Dhû'l-Jalâli wal-Ikrâm: the Lord of Majesty and Generosity.

"Mercy" may be defined as "forgiveness extended to those one might punish." The specifically religious definition is "the goodness through which God extends his grace to men and to sinners." In that case, how is it that, among the ninety-nine Beautiful Names of Allah, there is also Al-Mudhill: the Humiliator, the Degrader, Bringer of Dishonor and Disgrace. Al-Mumît: the Taker of Life, the Creator of Death. Al-Muntaqim: the Avenger, the Inflictor of Retribution. Al-Dârr: the Punisher, Bringer of Harm to Those Who Offend Him. Debasing, killing, avenging, harming—strange ways of showing mercy! But justified on page after page of the Koran.

8

Roster of contradictions. Allah is constantly presented in the Koran as a warrior immune to pity. Of course he can exercise his magnanimity: it is after all one of his attributes. But when? Where? With whom? There is much more putting to the sword, subjecting to the yoke, torturing, burning, pillage, and slaughter than love of one's neighbor. And all this as much in the deeds and gestures of the Prophet as in the text of the holy book. Muslim theory and Islamic practice are not shining examples of compassion.

For Muhammad himself did not excel in chivalrous virtues, as his story attests: the Muhammad of Medina was a great raider during tribal wars, rounding up captives, sharing out booty, sending his friends into the thick of the fighting to commit deeds of extraordinary violence. And again, slightly injured by a flying stone, he watches his demoralized troops seek refuge in a trench, entrusting close friends with the liquidation of this or that dangerous rival, happily slaughtering Jews, and so forth. Allah was great, no doubt about it, and so therefore was his Prophet. But it would not be wise to scrutinize the qualities of the emissary too closely, for God might suffer by comparison.

Magnanimous, then? Here is a listing of contrary qualities: Allah excelled in strategy, battle tactics, and *punishment* — including killing (8:30) — he deployed his *cunning*, that virtue born of cynicism, more closely resembling a vice than anything else, with flair. He resorted willingly to violence and decided on questions of life and *death* (3:156); he devised *ignominious punishments* for doubters (4:102); he was the *Master of vengeance* (5:95 and 3:4); he *annihilated* evildoers (3:141); indeed he practiced that sublime virtue so assiduously that he did not even tolerate a belief that diverged from his wishes; thus he punished those who conceived a *false idea* about him (48). Magnanimity — nothing like it!

9

Everything and its opposite. On one occasion the Prophet teaches that the reward for good is paradise (3:136), *but* on another he asks (55:60), "Is the reward of goodness aught but goodness?" He affirms that everything proceeds from the will of God, who knowingly leads men astray (45:23), *but* in a later chapter, he says the opposite: that every man is responsible for his own acts and deeds (52:21). Not for nothing is the Prophet the heir of Moses and Jesus.

Multiple verses in the Koran conflict with the notion that Allah is beneficent and merciful, as he is characterized in the invocation that opens each sura. However, the contrary is also true. There is the Koran's injunction to kill unbelievers (8:39) and polytheists (9:5), *but* praise in the very next verse for those who offer them asylum (9:6). We see (in 8:39) an order to battle violently against unbelievers, *whereas* Allah's advice to "pardon them and turn away" (5:13) could possibly be construed as an appeal for toleration and living in peace. Sura 7:199 reiterates the same idea, expressed as "forgiveness and turning aside." Many verses authorize mass slaughter (4:56, 4:91 and 2:191–94). But sura 5:32 (often quoted to refute charges that Islam has a zest for butchery) states that: killing a man who has committed no violence on earth is the same as killing all men, in the same way as saving one man means saving them all. The Koran endorses *lex talionis* (2:178); one example: cutting off the hands of thieves (5:38), *but* elsewhere (5:45) it tells us that renouncing that harsh law "shall be an expiation for him who forgoes it." In 5:51, the Koran says, "Do not take the Jews and the Christians for friends," *but* earlier in the same chapter (5:5) it permits a man to marry a chaste woman who follows one of the other two books! Two more suras that contradict the prohibition against friendship with those of other faiths: 49:10 proclaims the brotherhood of all believers, and 29:46 suggests that one should debate courteously with them. The Koran gives its stamp of approval to hunting down the impious (4:91), *but* another verse concerning those who have strayed from God recommends leaving them alone: "We have not sent you as a keeper over them" (4:80). Verse 13:5 refers to infidels with chains on their necks, *but* verse 2:256 (often cited as proof of Islam's tolerance) states, "There is no compulsion in religion . . ." Here of course we are dreaming . . .

One sura contains prayers to God for the extermination of Jews and Christians (9:30), *but* a later verse in the same chapter (9:71) says that the peoples of the book are guardians of each other. The Koran affirms the equality of all in the face of life and death (45:21), *but* describes a father on being told of the birth of a daughter: "his face becomes black and he is full of rage" (43:17). To say nothing of the inequality in store after death: inmates of fire versus dwellers in the garden (59:20). So in countless places the Koran contradicts the invocation of a Magnanimous One with which each sura begins.

The sura entitled "Women" teaches that the absence of contradictions in the Koran proves the book's divine origin (it was dictated over a period of twenty years, at Mecca and Medina, to a man who, as a sweeper-up of camel dung, could neither read nor write). If that is true, the number of contradictions accumulated and cursorily indicated above authorizes us to insist yet again on the human, all too human, origins of the book. Paradoxically, the Koranic thesis of an absence of contradictions in the text (itself contradicted by a scrutiny of the text, which teems with contradictions) means that the text is correct, validating the conclusion that its origins are human and not divine.

10

Contextualization and sophistry. Scholars are thus faced with an onslaught of truths, refuted by as many countertruths, in a disordered metaphysical laboratory where every assertion is promptly contradicted. Some pick and choose from the Koran, ignoring other passages, in an attempt to reduce the totality of Islam to the small portion of texts that they wish to put into evidence. Some try to justify the logic of their own selection from the texts to show that the totality of Islam is reducible to the small proportion of texts they choose. One approach results in a moderate Islam, another in a fundamentalist Islam, a third in a secular (!), open, democratic Islam.

Attempts have even been made to paint Islam as feminist— based largely on the biography of the Prophet who, blessings be upon his name, helped his wife Aïsha with her household chores. Supporters of this view, no slouches in the intelligence department, then superimpose their ideas onto an alien context. From the camel races that Muhammad and his wife participated in, they extrapolate the possibility, today, of coed soccer tournaments! Another has gone so far as to assert that the Koran predicted the conquest of space (15:33) and the invention of cybernetics! But perhaps this is the right place to stop.

Some endeavor to select material from the book in order to depict Islam as peaceable and tolerant. All they need do is isolate the verses in which the Prophet recommends giving sanctuary to unbelievers; practicing forgiveness, forgetfulness, and peace; rejecting violence and crime; renouncing the *lex talionis*; loving one's neighbor (whether Jew, Christian, nonbeliever, atheist, or polytheist); and tolerating different points of view. Unhappily, another will claim exactly the opposite with the same appearance of legitimacy, affirming the rightness and justice of crime, murder, violence, hatred, contempt . . . For there is no Koranic truth, no right reading—merely fragmentary interpretations, ideologically slanted to derive personal benefit from the authority of the book and the religion.

For example, what does it mean to contextualize a verse that calls for a massacre of the Jews? Does it mean explaining the call as a function of the period, of the historical context, of the reasons for writing and thinking such things in the tribal moment? And afterward? Does anti-Semitism disappear when we show that its roots reach down into a loam fertilized by its history and geography? Does the call to crime suddenly and magically cease to be a call to crime? Whatever we think of the context, we cannot alter the fact that the words were written down black on white. Even if a contrary injunction is to be found elsewhere in the text, anti-Semitism is also there, and is expressed with an equal sense of legitimacy.

Yet somewhat paradoxically, Muslim enthusiasts for contextualization consider their book sacred, divine, inspired, revealed, dictated by God. As a result, the Koran becomes rationally untouchable. But to serve their own interests, these enthusiasts shift registers and abruptly lean toward a historical reading. Depending on their dialectical needs, they seek both faith and reason, belief and documentation, fable and truth. At one moment navigating on mystical terrain, at another on the philosophical level, they are impossible to pin down, never on the same wavelength as a reader free of prejudices or convictions and determined on a real reading of the text.

I favor a pitiless historical reading of the three so-called holy books. I also argue for the need to consider their effective repercussions in the history of the West and the world. The Jewish fables about Canaan, the genocidal Mosaic utterances, the prospect of a communitary set of Commandments, the rule of *lex talionis,* the scourge wielded to expel the moneylenders, the parables of the blade and the sword, the "mercy" of a murderous, anti-Semitic, intolerant God, all help forge the monotheistic epistemology, despite the Torah's prohibition on killing, the Gospels' brotherly love, and the mixed messages sporadically delivered by the Koran. These three books all too often serve a death instinct consubstantial with the neurosis of the religion of a one God—now transformed into the religion of the only God.

II

In the Service of the Death Fixation

1

Selective bones of contention. The ability to select at will from all three monotheist books could have yielded the best of results. It would have sufficed to choose Deuteronomy's injunction against killing, transforming it into a universal absolute allowing not a single exception; to stress the evangelists' theme of brotherly love (excluding everything that contradicted that categorical imperative); to give unequivocal support to the Koranic sura which holds that killing one man means killing all of humankind . . . Then the three religions of the book might have appeared to us as respectable, pleasurable, desirable.

If rabbis insisted that one could not be Jewish and at the same time slaughter, colonize, and deport whole populations in the name of their religion . . . if priests condemned everyone who did away with his neighbor . . . if the pope, first among Christians, always took the side of the victims, the weak, the poor, the lowly, the descendants of the humble folk who were Christ's first followers . . . if caliphs, imams, ayatollahs, mullahs, and other Muslim dignitaries pilloried the wielders of swords, the Jew-killers, the murderers of Christians, the impalers of the unfaithful . . . If all these representatives of their one God on earth chose peace, love, and tolerance, we would first and foremost have known of it and witnessed it, and next we would have been able to support the three religions on the basis of their principles. And finally we could have condemned the exploitation of those principles by the bad, the wicked. Instead of all this, these representatives of their one God do the opposite. They select the worst options, and, save for extremely rare, intermittent, particular, and personal exceptions, they have historically supported war leaders, saber-rattlers, soldiers, warriors, rapists, pillagers, war criminals, torturers, promoters of genocide, dictators (except for Communist ones) — the very dregs of the earth.

For monotheism is fatally fixated on death. It loves death, cherishes death; it exults in death, is fascinated by death. It gives death, doles it out in massive doses; it threatens death and moves from threat to action: from the bloody sword of the Israelites killing off the Canaanites to the use of airliners as flying bombs in New York, stopping off on the way to release an atomic cargo over Hiroshima and Nagasaki. Everything is done in the name of God, blessed by him, but blessed most of all by those claiming to act in his name.

Today, the Grand Rabbinate of Jerusalem castigates the bomb-clad Palestinian terrorist in the streets of Jaffa but remains silent when Tsahal missiles kill the inhabitants of a West Bank neighborhood. The pope thunders out against the pill, responsible for "the greatest genocide of all time," but actively defends the massacre of hundreds of thousands of Tutsi by the Catholic Hutu of Rwanda. The most exalted spheres of world Islam denounce the crimes of colonialism, the humiliation and exploitation visited on Muslims by the Western world, but rejoice in a worldwide jihad carried out under the auspices of Al-Qaeda. Fascination with the deaths of people, miscreants, and infidels — all three of them additionally convinced that atheism is their single common enemy!

Monotheist indignation is selective, with esprit de corps

working full blast. The Jews have their Covenant, the Christians their church, the Muslims their ummah. Three brotherhoods operating outside the law and enjoying an ontological and metaphysical extraterritoriality. Among members of the same community everything is permissible and justifiable. A Jew — Ariel Sharon — may order the killing of a Palestinian — the hard-to-defend Sheikh Ahmad Yassin — without offending Yahweh, for the murder is committed in his name. A Christian — Pius XII — has the right to justify an exterminator of Jews — Eichmann, exfiltrated from postwar Europe with the Vatican's help — without offending his Lord, for the Nazi genocide avenges the deicide attributed to the Jewish people. A Muslim — the Mullah Omar — may order the hanging of women accused of adultery, thus gratifying Allah in whose name the gallows are erected . . . Behind all these abominations stand verses from the Torah, passages from the Gospels, and suras from the Koran, legitimizing, justifying, blessing.

As soon as religion triggers public and political results, it substantially increases its power to harm. When we point to a phrase culled from one or another of the three books in order to explain the rightness and legitimacy of a crime, we automatically render the crime immune to attack, for how can we attack the revealed word, the utterance of God, the divine urging? God does not speak — except to the Jewish people and the handful of visionaries, virgins for example, to whom he occasionally sends messages — but the clergy has him talk his head off. When a man of the church gives his opinion, quoting pieces from his book, opposing him becomes the equivalent of telling God no in person. Who possesses the moral strength and conviction to refuse the word of (a man of) God? Every theocracy is a denial of democracy. Even better: the smallest hint of theocracy neutralizes the very essence of democracy.

2

The Jewish invention of holy war. Let us give credit where it is due. The Jews invented monotheism and everything that went with it. First divine right and its mandatory correlative: the chosen people exalted, other peoples discounted; a logical enough sequence. Then, more importantly, came the divine strength needed to buttress this heaven-sent right, because the sword arm is what guarantees its realization here below. God utters, speaks, and his prophets, messiahs, and other emissaries translate his otherwise not very intelligible speech. The clergy transforms that speech into orders upheld by iron-plated, caparisoned, determined troops, armed to the teeth. Hence the three founding pillars of all civilizations: the prince representing God on earth, the priest providing the prince with ideas, and the soldier guaranteeing the priest's brute strength. And the people, of course, *always* pay the costs of theocratic perfidy.

The Jews invented the temporal dimension of monotheist spirituality. Well before them, the priest acted in concert with the king: the association was primitive, prehistoric, antediluvian. But the chosen people adapted this skillful and very practical logic for their own purposes: the earth had to be organized in the same way as heaven. Theological schemas had to be reproduced on the terrain of history. Immanence had to demarcate the rules of transcendence. The Torah tells the story without beating about the bush.

On Mount Sinai, God spoke to Moses. At the time the Jewish people were weak, threatened with annihilation in wars with surrounding peoples. It badly needed God's backing to envisage the future with confidence. An only God, bellicose, mail-clad, merciless, fighting and giving no quarter, capable of exterminating the enemy without a twinge of conscience, galvanizing his troops: such was Yahweh, whose type—like Muhammad's—suggested a tribal war leader promoted to cosmic rank.

God promised a land that would be theirs "for an everlasting possession" (Genesis 17:8) to his people. They were the elect, the chosen, singled out from among all others, raised above the common herd, a "peculiar treasure unto me" (Exodus 19:5). Did some unassuming race already inhabit that land? Did people cultivate its fields? Did its soil nourish children and the aged? Did men of mature age tend herds of livestock there? Did women give birth? Did their young receive schooling? Did the people worship gods? But these Canaanites were of little importance, and God had decided on their extermination: "and I will cut them off," he declared (Exodus 23:23).

God deployed his heavy artillery to conquer Palestine. Let us say (to borrow modern strategic terminology) that he invented total war. He split the sea in two (why not, after all?), drowned a whole army in it (no half-measures!), stopped the sun in its tracks to give the Hebrews time to annihilate their Amorite enemies (Joshua 10:12–14) ("love of one's neighbor" in action, with God's help). Earlier, God had released a deluge of hailstones and frogs (a touch of whimsy), called up swarms of mosquitoes and horseflies (no point in skimping), turned water into blood (an injection of poetry and color), unleashed plagues, ulcers, and pustules (bacteriological warfare so soon!), to which he added what soldiers have always done best: killing everything that moved, women, the aged, children, livestock (Exodus 12:12). Clearly, scorched earth, fire, and wholesale slaughter of populations are not a recent invention.

Yahweh blessed war and those who waged it. He sanctified combat, led it, supervised it, although admittedly not in person —ectoplasm has trouble wielding a sword—but by inspiring his people. He sanctioned crimes, murders, assassination, gave his blessing to the liquidation of innocents, killed animals like men and men like animals. He could be humane (unless he was dealing with Canaanites). He proposed an alternative to battle, offering slavery — a token of goodness and love — in its place. To the indigenous population of Palestine, already living there when the Hebrews arrived, he promised total destruction — *holy war*, to use the terrifying and ultramodern expression of Joshua (6:21).

For two thousand five hundred years, no leading figure descended from the chosen people has declared that these pages are rooted in fable, in prehistoric and highly dangerous — because criminal — fictions and nonsense. Quite the contrary. There exist on this planet a considerable number of people who live, think, act, and conceive of the world on the basis of these texts that call for generalized butchery. And there isn't the slightest danger that they will be denied the right to publish on the grounds that they encourage murder, racism, and other incitements to breaches of the peace. Yeshiva students memorize these passages, no more inclined to change a single comma than to touch a single one of Yahweh's hairs. The Torah offers the first Western version of the many arts of war published in the course of the centuries.

3

God, Caesar & Co. The Christians themselves were not slow to enroll God in their misdeeds. There was no question for them of being a chosen people, nor any divine justification for the annihilation of a people who threatened to frustrate their destiny as history's favorites. But they firmly believed that God's word condoned the distinctly temporal actions of their religion (at first sight so distinctly spiritual). From the humiliation of Jesus to the humiliations carried out in his name, the process of Christian evolution was swift and easy, and the resultant mania enduring.

Here again, selective borrowing from the texts proved its usefulness. The Christians drew on John, for example, for the following: "My kingdom is not of this world" (18:36). But they reverted to Matthew for the opposite, as follows: "Render therefore unto Caesar the things which are Caesar's, and unto God the things which are God's" (22:21). One asserts the primacy of the spiritual and a professed indifference to earthly matters. The other, while admittedly asserting the separation of powers, also promulgates a de facto legalism — for rendering unto Caesar justifies payment of taxes to support the army of occupation, accepting the burden of financing the imperial forces, and submitting to the laws of the empire.

The apparent contradiction is resolved when we seek clarification from Paul of Tarsus. For as it evolved into Paulinism, Christianity distanced itself from Judaism. And the epistles to the different peoples visited by the Tarsiot furnish us with church doctrine on the question of relations between the spiritual and the temporal. Paul believed that Jesus's kingdom would be of this world: he wanted to achieve this and worked for its accomplishment in the here and now, hence his travels from Jerusalem to Antioch, from Thessalonica to Athens, from Corinth to Ephesus. The convert from Judaism, not content with a promised land stolen from the Canaanites, wanted the whole planet to march under the banner of a sword-wielding Christ.

The Epistle to the Romans states it clearly: "There is no power but of God" (13:1). So much for theory. What follows in practice is approval of submission to Roman authority. On the principle that those who wield power are first and foremost God's ministers, Paul efficiently wraps up his case. Disobeying a soldier, challenging a magistrate, resisting a prefect of police, standing up to a procurator—Pontius Pilate for example—constitute so many affronts to God. So let us rewrite Christ's words in the Pauline manner: render therefore unto Caesar the things that are Caesar's and to Caesar the things that are God's—in full settlement.

Armed with this ontological asset, the Christians very early began to sell their souls—no longer useful for practice of the gospel message—to the temporal power. They settled into the gilt and purple of palaces; they clad their churches in marble and gold; they blessed armies; they sanctioned expansionist wars, military conquests, police operations. They raised taxes; they unleashed the soldiery against the discontented poor; they lit bonfires—as early as Constantine's reign, in the fourth century of their era.

History bears witness: millions of dead in the name of God, millions on every continent and in every century. Bible in one hand, sword in the other: the Inquisition, torture, the rack; the Crusades, massacres, pillage, rape, hangings, exterminations; the African slave trade, humiliation, exploitation, serfdom, the trade in men, women, and children; genocides, the ethnocides of the most Christian conquistadors, of course. But also, and more recently, we see Rwanda's Catholic clergy hand in glove with Hutu exterminators; the Vatican a fellow traveler with *every* brand of twentieth-century fascism—Mussolini, Pétain, Franco, Hitler, Pinochet, the Greek colonels, South American dictators, etc. Millions of dead in the name of brotherly love.

4

Christian anti–Semitism. It is hard for a Christian to love his neighbor, particularly if the neighbor is a Jew . . . Saul-become-Paul channeled all his passion into dismantling Judaism—the same passion that (before the road to Damascus) he brought to persecuting Christians, helping mistreat them, and even hastening their encounter with the beyond. To sell the sect he had newly embraced, he had to persuade his listeners that Jesus was the Messiah foretold in the Old Testament, and that Christ had abolished Judaism by fulfilling the prophecy. Since Yahweh's faithful did not buy the nonsense about a Son of God who died on the cross to save humankind, Jews emerged as fundamental adversaries. Then, very quickly, they became the enemy.

It is said that the Wandering Jew was afflicted with his curse because the first of them refused to slake Christ's thirst on the path to Golgotha. For this failure to help the Crucified One, the curse fell upon him—not very charitable of Jesus—but also and above all on his kind, his descendants, his people. This was all the more portentous because the Christian version of Jesus's death assumes that the Jews were responsible—not the Romans . . . And Pontius Pilate? Neither responsible nor guilty. Paul affirmed it when speaking of the Jews who "killed the Lord Jesus" (1 Thessalonians 2:15). The Gospels abound in openly anti-Semitic passages. Daniel Goldhagen lists forty or so in Mark, eighty in Matthew, one hundred and thirty in John, one hundred and forty in the Acts of the Apostles . . . Jesus himself, gentle Jesus, described the Jews as being "of your father, the devil" (John 8:44). In such circumstances, loving one's neighbor was difficult.

From the first Christian transformation of the Jews into a people of God-killers to the long-delayed recognition of the state of Israel by John Paul II at the end of 1993 (and taking into account the church's long love affair with every manifestation of anti-Semitism in history, including most significantly the twelve years of German National Socialism), the picture is clear. The extreme expression of this hatred was the active collaboration between the Vatican and Nazism. And then—which is less widely known—that of Nazism with the Vatican. For Pius XII and Adolf Hitler shared a certain number of points of view, in particular the loathing of Jews in all their guises.

5

The Vatican admired Adolf Hitler. The love-marriage between the Catholic Church and Nazism cannot be denied. Instances — and they are not minor ones — abound. Their complicity did not reside in unspoken approval, explicit omissions, or calculations made on the basis of partisan positions. The facts are clear to anyone who approaches the issue by interrogating history: it was not a marriage of reason, determined by concern for the survival of the church, but a shared loathing of the same implacable enemies: Jews and Communists — most often packaged together in the same grab bag labeled Judeo-Bolshevism.

From the birth of National Socialism to the extrusion of the Third Reich's war criminals after the regime's collapse to the church's silence on these questions ever since, the domain of Christ's heir Saint Peter was also that of Adolf Hitler and his henchmen, German Nazis and French fascists, collaborators of the Nazis, Vichyites, fascist militias, and other war criminals. Even today, it is still impossible to consult the Vatican's archives on the subject.

The facts, then. The Catholic Church approved the rearmament of Germany in the 1930s, which was of course contrary to the spirit of the Versailles Treaty but also to a part of Jesus's teachings, particularly those celebrating peace, mildness, love of one's neighbor. The Catholic Church signed a concordat with Adolf Hitler as soon as the chancellor took office in 1933. The Catholic Church held its tongue over the boycott of Jewish businesses, remained silent over the proclamation of the Nuremberg racial laws in 1935, and was equally silent over Kristallnacht in 1938. The Catholic Church provided the Nazis with its genealogical records, which told them who in Germany was Christian, and therefore non-Jewish. (On the other hand, the Catholic Church did invoke the principle of "pastoral secrecy" in order not to communicate the names of Jews converted to Christ's religion or married to Christians.) The Catholic Church supported, defended, and aided the pro-Nazi Ustachi regime of Ante Pavelic in Croatia. The Catholic Church gave its absolution to France's collaborationist Vichy regime in 1940. The Catholic Church, although fully aware of the policy of extermination set in motion in 1942, did not condemn it in private or in public, and never ordered any priest or bishop to condemn the criminal regime in the hearing of his flock.

The Allied armies liberated Europe, reached Berchtesgaden, discovered Auschwitz. What did the Vatican do? It continued to support the defeated regime. The Catholic Church, in the person of Cardinal Bertram, ordered a requiem Mass in memory of Adolf Hitler. The Catholic Church was mute and showed no disapproval at the discovery of the mass graves, the gas chambers, and the death camps. Even better, the Catholic Church did for the Nazis (shorn of their Führer) what it had never done for a single Jew or victim of National Socialism: it set up a network designed to smuggle war criminals out of Europe. The Catholic Church used the Vatican, delivered papers stamped with its visas to fugitive Nazis, established a chain of European monasteries that served as hiding places for dignitaries of the ruined Reich. The Catholic Church promoted into its hierarchy people who had performed important tasks for the Hitler regime. And the Catholic Church will never apologize for any of these things, particularly since it has acknowledged none of them.

If there is ever to be repentance, we shall probably have to wait four centuries for it, the time it took for a pope to acknowledge the church's error in the Galileo affair. Chiefly because the doctrine of papal infallibility proclaimed at the first Vatican Council in 1869–70 (*Pastor Aeternas*) forbids challenging the church — for when the supreme pontiff speaks or makes a decision he does so not as a man capable of being wrong but as the representative of God on earth, constantly inspired by the Holy Spirit — the famous doctrine of "saving grace." Are we to conclude from all this that the Holy Spirit is fundamentally Nazi?

While the church remained silent on the Nazi question during and after the war, it missed no chance to act against Communists. Where Marxism is concerned, the Vatican has given proof of a commitment, a militancy, and a vigor better expended in fighting and discrediting the Nazi Reich. Faithful to church tradition (which, through the grace of Pius IX and Pius X, condemned human rights as contrary to the teachings of the church), Pius XII, the pope so famously well-disposed toward National Socialism, excommunicated the Communists of the whole world en masse in 1949. He asserted collusion between the Jews and Bolshevism as one of the reasons for his decision.

To recapitulate: no run-of-the-mill National Socialist, no Nazi of elevated rank or member of the Reich's staff was ever excommunicated. No group was ever excluded from the church for preaching and practicing racism or anti-Semitism or operating gas chambers. Adolf Hitler was not excommunicated, and *Mein Kampf* was never put on the *Index*. We should not forget that after 1924, the date Hitler's book appeared, the famous *Index Librorum Prohibitorium* added to its list — alongside Pierre Larousse, guilty of the *Grand Dictionnaire Universel* (!) — Henri Bergson, André Gide, Simone de Beauvoir, and Jean-Paul Sartre. Adolf Hitler never appeared on it.

6

Hitler admired the Vatican. A widely held notion that fails to stand up to the most rudimentary analysis, still less to a reading of the texts, represents Hitler as a pagan fascinated by Nordic cults, a lover of Wagnerian horned helmets, of Valhalla and of generous-breasted Valkyrie, an antichrist, the very antithesis of Christian. Apart from evoking the difficulty of being at once atheist and pagan — denying the existence of God or gods while at the same time believing in them — to believe this means that we must ignore Hitler's writings (*Mein Kampf*), his political action (the Reich's failure to persecute the Catholic, Apostolic, and Roman Church, as opposed, for example, to its treatment of Jehovah's Witnesses), and the Führer's private confidences (his published conversations with Albert Speer), in which he consistently and unambiguously expressed his admiration for Christianity.

Was it an atheist Führer who decided to stamp the words *Gott mit uns* on the belt buckles of the Reich's soldiers? Do people know that the slogan comes from the scriptures? Notably from Deuteronomy, one of the books of the Torah, which says, "For the Lord thy God is he that goeth with you" (Deuteronomy 20:4). These words were lifted from the speech Yahweh addressed to the Jews leaving to fight their enemies, the Egyptians, to whom God held out the promise of unspecified extermination (Deuteronomy 20:13).

Was it an atheist Führer who ordered all schoolchildren in the National Socialist Reich to begin their day with a prayer to Jesus? Not to God, which might have made a deist of Hitler, but to Jesus, which explicitly labels him a Christian. The same supposedly atheist Führer asked Goering and Goebbels, in the presence of Albert Speer who recorded the conversation, to remain within the bosom of the Catholic Church, as he himself would until his dying day.

7

Christianity and National Socialism: points in common.
The understanding between Hitler and Pius XII went far beyond personal compatibility. The two doctrines shared more than one point of convergence. The infallibility of the pope, who we should remember was also a head of state, could not have been displeasing to a Führer also convinced of his infallibility. The possibility of building an empire, a civilization, a culture with a supreme guide invested with full powers — like Constantine and several Christian emperors who succeeded him — was something that fascinated Hitler during the writing of his book. The Christian eradication of everything redolent of paganism? The destruction of altars and temples? The book burnings (remember that Paul recommended them)? The persecution of all who opposed the new faith? All excellent things, Hitler concluded.

The Führer admired the theocratic evolution of Christianity. He wrote (*Mein Kampf*, volume 2, chapter 5, page 454) that it was only by virtue of "passionate intolerance" for pagan altars that an "apodictic faith" could grow up — Hitler's term for "unshakable faith." He marveled at the church's determination to give up nothing, even and especially in the face of science when it contradicted certain of its positions or took its dogma to task (page 459); the flexibility of the church, for which Hitler predicted a future well beyond what people might imagine (page 459); the permanence of the venerable institution (volume 1, chapter 3, page 115) despite the occasionally deplorable behavior of clergy (which did nothing to affect overall church policy). In all this, Hitler asked his readers to "take lessons from the Catholic Church" (page 459, but also pages 114–20).

What is the "true Christianity" Hitler mentions in *Mein Kampf* (volume 1, chapter 11, page 307)? That of the "great founder of the new doctrine": Jesus, the same Jesus to whom children in the schools of the Third Reich prayed. But which Jesus? Not the one who turned the other cheek, no, but the angry Jesus who ejected the moneylenders from the Temple with a whip. Hitler specifically mentioned this passage from John in his argument. Also, let us not forget what sort of people this most Christian whip served to drive out: unbelievers, non-Christians, vendors, merchants, money-changers — in short, Jews, the unspoken key word in this complicity between Reich and Vatican. John's Gospel (2:14) does not invalidate Hitler's philo-Christian and anti-Semitic reading; indeed, it makes it possible. Particularly if we take note of the many passages in the New Testament consigning the Jews to hellfire. The Jews were a race of deicides. Here lies the key to this fatal partnership: they use religion, said Hitler, in order to do business; they are, he adds, the enemies of any kind of humanity; he goes on to specify that it was the Jews who created Bolshevism. Let everyone make up his own mind. But to Hitler himself things were clear: "to the political leader, the religious ideas and institutions of his people must remain inviolable" (page 116). So the gas chambers could be operated in the name of Saint John.

8

Wars, fascisms, and other pursuits. The partnership of Christianity and Nazism is not an accident of history, a regrettable and isolated mistake along the wayside, but the fulfillment of a two-thousand-year-old logic. From Paul of Tarsus, who justified fire and the sword in turning a private sect into a religion contaminating the empire and the world, to the Vatican's twentieth-century justification of the nuclear deterrent, the line has endured. Thou shalt not kill . . . except from time to time . . . and when the church tells you to.

Augustine, a saint by trade, dedicated all his talent to justifying the worst in the church: slavery, war, capital punishment, etc. Blessed are the meek? The peacemakers? Augustine is no more enthusiastic than Hitler about this side of Christianity, too soft, not virile or warlike enough, squeamish about bloodshed — the feminine face of religion. He offered the church the concepts it lacked to justify punitive expeditions and massacres. These things the Jews had practiced to acquire their land, on a limited geographical scale, but the Christians drew from that local action inspiration for action across the face of the globe, for their goal was converting the world itself. The chosen people generated catastrophes that were *first of all* local. Universal Christianity created *universal* upheavals. Once it triumphed, every continent became a battlefield.

With the church's blessing, Augustine, bishop of Hippo, sanctioned *just persecution* in a letter (185). A choice formulation, which he presents in contrast to *unjust persecution!* What differentiates the good corpse from the bad? Flaying of victims — when is it defensible and when is it indefensible? All persecution by the church was good, because motivated by love; while persecution directed against the church was indefensible, because inspired by cruelty. We should relish the rhetoric and talent for sophistry of Saint Augustine, who preferred his Jesus to brandish the whip and not to suffer it at the hands of the Roman soldiery.

Which brings us to the concept of *just war,* itself formulated by the same church father, a man who decidedly never shrank from brutality, vice, or perversion. As the heir of the ancient pagan fable — Greek as it happened — Christianity recycled trial by ordeal. In a war, the victor was designated by God; so too, therefore, was the vanquished. By deciding in the conflict between winners and losers, God designates the true and the false, good and bad, legitimate and illegitimate. Magical thinking, to say the least.

Jesus at Hiroshima. Jesus and his scourge, Paul and his belief in power emanating from God, and Augustine with his just war together constitute a Trinitarian assault group capable of justifying every operation committed in the name of God over the last two millennia. They gave us the Crusades against the Saracens, the Inquisition against supposed heretics, the so-called holy wars against unbelievers — what glory! Saint Bernard of Clairvaux confiding in a letter (363): "the best solution is to kill them," or again, "a pagan's death is a Christian's glory" — the most Christian campaigns of extermination against peoples called primitive, colonial wars to evangelize every continent, the fascisms of the twentieth century, including of course Nazism, all of them furiously unleashed against the Jews.

Little wonder, then, that official Christianity in the era of postmodern war opted for the nuclear deterrent, defended it, and excused it. John Paul II accepted its principle on June 11, 1982, via a truly extraordinary logical fallacy: the atom bomb, he said, opened the road to peace! France's bishops followed close behind, armed with their own reasons, which included the need to struggle against "the domineering and aggressive nature of Marxist-Leninist ideology." Sweet Jesus! What power of decision, what lucidly stated positions! How we would have welcomed an equally clear and straightforward condemnation of Nazism during its twelve-year reign. We would even have been grateful for a similar moral assertion *after* the death camps were liberated.

When the Berlin Wall fell and the Bolshevik threat could at least be said to have diminished, the church upheld its position. In part III, section II, chapter 2, article 5, item 2315 of its latest *Catechism*, the Vatican expresses "strong moral reservations" about the arms race. Note the understatement! The accumulation of nuclear weapons is not an effective deterrent to war, but the Vatican condemns it not at all. In the same document, under the article heading "You shall not kill" — long live logic and coherence! — item 2267 states, "The traditional teaching of the Church does not exclude recourse to the death penalty." It is scarcely surprising that the index has no listing for "capital punishment," "death sentence," or "punishment." On the other hand, euthanasia, abortion, suicide, issues addressed in the same chapter, are fully referenced.

As we know, the crew of the *Enola Gay* dropped an atomic bomb on Hiroshima on August 6, 1945. In a few seconds the nuclear explosion caused the death of more than a hundred thousand people, women, the old, children, the sick, innocents whose only crime was being Japanese. The crew returned safely to base: the Christian God had protected these new Crusaders. We should add that Father George Zabelka had solemnly blessed the crew before its deadly mission! Three days later, a second atomic bomb struck Nagasaki and killed eighty thousand people.

10

Love of one's neighbor (continued). The Pauline texts, so useful in justifying submission to de facto authority, triggered results that went far beyond the legitimization of wars and persecution. In the field of slavery, for example, which Christianity did no more than the other two monotheisms to deter. Indeed, in later centuries the small-scale slavery resulting from tribal raids evolved into the slave trade pure and simple, the sale and deportation of whole populations for use as chattels and beasts of burden.

But give antiquity its due. Since the ancients preceded us, they must be accorded the honor of inventing — if not confirming and legitimizing—a host of evils, including slavery. The Commandments do not advocate any particular respect for one's neighbor if he looks different, if he is not branded in the flesh by the rabbi's knife. The non-Jew did not enjoy the same rights as members of the Covenant. So that, outside the confines of the book, the Other may be called on to account for himself, to be treated like an object, a thing: the goy by the Jew, the polytheist or animist by the Christian, the Christian by the Muslim, and the atheist, needless to say, by everyone.

The subject is introduced into the Torah from the outset, for Genesis (9:25–27) defends slavery. It would have been difficult to get off the mark much faster . . . You bought people, they became part of the household, sleeping under the same roof as Jews, you circumcised them, yet they remained slaves. The curse that fell on Noah when he sobered up and realized that a son had caught him naked in his drunken slumber was extended to a whole people—Canaanites yet again—doomed to servitude. Elsewhere, many other passages codify the implications of the curse.

Leviticus, for example, carefully specifies that a Jew must avoid using one of his own kind as a slave (25:39–55). A Jew might work as an indentured servant, yes, but this was more or less a rental agreement that ended after six years, whereupon his freedom would be restored. A non-Jew, on the other hand, could remain in a state of serfdom until his death. The children of the Covenant had been slaves of the Egyptians before Yahweh extracted them from that condition and made of the Jews a free people, capable of submission but obliged to submit to no other power than God's. The rights of the chosen people . . .

Christianity, which also condoned slavery, brought no change. As we may recall, all power came from God, everything proceeded from his will. Someone finds himself a slave? The ways of the Lord are mysterious, but there is always a reason to fall back on: original sin, an abstract concept, but each individual has a personal responsibility to atone for it. Augustine (back so soon?) encouraged the slave to toil with a zeal pleasing to God! Every slave was a slave for his own good (whether he realized it or not). God created the slave; a state of servitude is what suited the slave's inherent nature; God's plan would have it no other way.

Then came the ultimate sophistry. Since men were equal in the eyes of God, what matter that there existed on earth differences that were in the final analysis incidental? Man or woman? Slave or owner? Rich or poor? Of little importance, said the church — at the same time aligning itself throughout history with men, the rich, the propertied . . . Every man was as God willed. To rebel against this was to resist the divine plan, to insult God. The good slave who honestly played his part as a slave — like Sartre's café waiter — entered his (fictional) paradise thanks to his (real) submission . . . Saint Augustine's *City of God* (19, 21) — what a truly edifying work!

In harsh reality, Christianity showed a harder side. As early as the sixth century, Pope Gregory I banned slaves from the priesthood! Before him, Constantine forbade Jews to keep slaves in their households. In the Middle Ages, thousands of them labored in the agricultural domains of the supreme pontiff. Great monasteries exploited them unblushingly. In the eighth century, for example, the monastery of Saint-Germain des Prés employed no fewer than eight thousand.

Inheriting this, as they inherited all the rest, the Muslims practiced slavery and the Koran did nothing to suppress it. On the contrary: it legitimized slave- and booty-hunting raids, loot in gold, silver, women, animals, men. Indeed, we owe the invention of the slave trade to Islam. In the year 1000 there was a regular traffic between Kenya and China. Muslim law banned the sale of Muslims, but not that of other believers. Nine centuries before the transatlantic trade, trans-Saharan traffic began its dismal career. It is estimated that ten million men were deported over a period of twelve hundred years by the faithful of Allah, the Compassionate, the Most Great, the All-Wise.

One comment: at heart, the three monotheisms disapproved of slavery, since Jews and Muslims forbade it for members of their own community, while the Christians, who detested Jews, prohibited them from owning domestic slaves. Then they made it illegal for a slave to enter holy orders in order to serve the word of God. Torah, New Testament, and Koran justified enslaving their enemies as a mark of infamy, and therefore of humiliation, a destiny befitting the subhuman nature of anyone worshipping any other god than their own.

11

Colonialism, genocide, ethnocide. The logical sequence to justification of slavery was colonialism, which entailed exporting one's religion to the four corners of the world and the use of force, of physical, mental, spiritual, psychic, and of course armed constraint to achieve those ends. Exporting slavery and extending it to every continent was the work first of Christianity and then of Islam. As for the Jewish people, they have sought to establish their dominion over *only one* territory, their territory, without ever seeking further. Zionism is neither expansionist nor internationalist. On the contrary, the dream brought to fruition by Theodor Herzl implies nationalism, a centrifugal movement, the desire of a closed society existing for oneself alone — and not a desire for mastery of the whole planet, a desire shared by Christianity and Islam.

The Catholic, Apostolic, and Roman Church excels in the destruction of civilizations. It invented ethnocide, the spiritual rather than the physical extinction of cultures. The year 1492 does not merely spell the discovery of the New World but the destruction of other worlds. Christian Europe laid waste a considerable number of Amerindian civilizations. Soldiers, accompanied by the scum of society—jailbirds, petty criminals, strong-arm men, mercenaries—disembarked from the caravels. Once the ensuing ethnic cleansing was over, the priests followed at a safe distance in solemn procession, with crucifixes, ciboria, Hosts, and portable altars, all most useful in preaching brotherly love, forgiveness of sins, the sweetness of the angelic virtues, and other tokens of biblical joy—original sin, hatred of women, of the body and of sexuality, guilt. Meanwhile, Christendom gave the peoples it called savages its housewarming gifts of syphilis and other transmissible diseases.

The partnership of the church and Nazism likewise aimed at extermination of a race reconfigured for the purposes of the cause into a people of God-killers. Six million dead. To which we must add complicity in the deportation and murder of gypsies, homosexuals, Communists, Freemasons, left-wingers, laymen, Jehovah's Witnesses, antifascists, and other people guilty of not being very Christian.

The Christian passion for mass extermination is old and enduring. A recent example was the genocide of Tutsis by the Hutu of Rwanda, supported, defended, and covered up by the Catholic establishment on the spot and by the supreme pontiff himself. The pope was much quicker to ensure that priestly genocide-bent war criminals, monks, nuns, and other members of the Catholic community might escape the firing squads than to offer one word of compassion to the Tutsi community.

For in Rwanda, a country with an overwhelmingly Christian population, the church even *before* the genocide had practiced racial discrimination in accepting candidates for seminaries, in training, in the administration of Catholic schools, in ordination or promotion in the ecclesiastical hierarchy. *During* the genocide some members of the clergy played an active part:

purchase and delivery of machetes by members of the Catholic establishment, sniffing out the victims' hiding places, actively participating in orgies of brutality — people locked into churches, the churches burned down, their remains obliterated by bulldozers — denunciations, sermons to fire up the masses, exploitation of racial language.

After the massacres, the Catholic Church stayed on course. Convents were taken over to hide guilty Christians from justice, networks galvanized to help smuggle this or that criminal out to European countries, air tickets provided by Christian humanitarian organizations. Guilty priests were farmed out to provincial Belgian and French parishes, bishops implicated in the genocide were whisked from view. And the church resorted to public attitudes of denial — insisting, for example, on referring to "fratricidal war" in preference to "genocide."

Silent on the preparations, silent during the massacres — nearly one million dead in three months (between April and June 1994) — silent after the scope of the disaster (carried out with the blessings of French president François Mitterrand) was revealed, John Paul II emerged from his silence to write a letter to the president of Rwanda on April 23, 1998. Its contents? Did he deplore? Did he express compassion? Did he repent? Regret? Blame his clergy? Wash his hands of their actions? No, not at all: he requested a stay of execution for Hutus found guilty of genocide. Not a single word for the victims.

12

Repressions and the death fixation. The fixation of the three monotheisms on the death instinct can be explained. How can we escape the domination of that instinct after so effectively killing off the life urge both within and outside ourselves? Fear of death, of the void, horror at the idea of the emptiness that follows death, all help generate consoling fables, fictions that incite us to deny use of our full powers. The real is not. Fiction, on the other hand, is. This false world, which forces us to live in the here and now buttressed by hopes of a tinsel afterlife, leads to denial, contempt, or hatred of the here and now.

Hence countless opportunities for seeing this hatred at work: on the body, desires, passions, drives, on the flesh, women, love, sex, on life in all its forms, on matter, on the things that enhance our existence in this world, in other words, on reason, intelligence, books, science, culture. This suppression of everything living forces on us the celebration of everything that dies — bloodshed and war — of whatever kills, of those who kill. Whereas intelligent reading from the three books would let us select whatever confers maximum power on the life force, religion seeks out the death force in all its forms. Suppression of the living engenders love of death. And generally speaking, all contempt for women — we prefer virgins, mothers, and wives — goes hand in hand with a cult of death.

Civilizations are not founded on the death drive. Sacrificial blood, the scapegoat, laying the foundations of a society through an act of ritual murder — these are sinister social constants. The Jewish extermination of the Canaanites, the Christian crucifixion of the Messiah, the Muslim jihad of the Prophet all shed the blood that blesses and sanctifies the monotheist cause. Primitive, magical aspersion, disemboweling of the propitiatory victims — who happen to be men, women, and children. The primitive survives in the postmodern, the animal survives in man, the beast still dwells in *Homo sapiens*.

III

Toward a Post-Christian Secular Order

1

Muslim thirst for blood. A worthy synthesis of the two monotheisms that preceded it, Islam acclimatized them to an Arabian desert conditioned by the tribal and the feudal. It also adopted as its own the worst legacies of the above-mentioned Jews and Christians: a community of the elect, a sense of superiority, the local transformed into the global, the private expanded to the universal, submission of body and soul to the ascetic ideal, the cult of the death instinct, theocracy indexed to the extermination of everything different, slavery, raiding, total war, punitive expeditions, murders, etc.

Let us remember that Moses slew an Egyptian foreman with his own hands. And that Muhammad and his followers regularly slaughtered people, beginning with the killing of an unarmed merchant at Nakhla (Saudi Arabia) in 623. He continued to kill until the day he died on June 8, 632. It is not possible to list all of the wars, battles, raids, surprise attacks, sieges, and other feats of arms by Muslim warriors. Battle of Badr (March 624): three hundred and fifty Muslims from Medina defeated an army of nine hundred commanded by Amr ibn Hisham, one of the polytheist leaders in Mecca. Also known as Abu Jahl, meaning "father of folly and ignorance," he was the one who had killed the first Muslim martyr (an old woman named Sumayyah), and he was himself killed at the battle of Badr. Uhud (March 625): Muhammad wounded; a few dozen martyrs. East Medina (late 626–early 627): Jews slain. The battle of the Trench (627): a "Jewish plot." The conquest of the Khaybar oasis (May–June 628). The raid on Mu'ta (September 629). Readers of the Koran do not seem to be overly concerned with verse 32 of sura 5: "Whoever slays one soul, it is as though he slew all men." (Paraphrase: To kill one man is to kill all men.)

Nearly two hundred and fifty verses — of the six thousand two hundred and thirty-four of the book — justify and legitimize holy war, jihad. Enough to drown the handful of very inoffensive phrases recommending tolerance, respect for one's neighbor, magnanimity or nonrecourse to violence in questions of religion (!). In such an ocean of blood, who can still take the trouble to linger over two or three sentences that recommend tolerance over barbarity? Particularly since the Prophet's biography bears eloquent witness: murder, crime, the sword, and the punitive expedition constantly recur. Too many pages encourage anti-Semitism, hatred of Jews, despoiling and exterminating them, for a Muslim fighter not to feel justified in putting them to the sword.

The Muslim community thought like the children of the Covenant. They too proclaimed themselves the chosen people, singled out by Allah, preferred by him (9:19 but also 3:110). But two claimants to elite status are one too many! Believing that others are of inferior race, that subhumans exist, that God establishes a hierarchy among humans by distinguishing the small designated community from the rest of humanity, means that the Other may not claim the same status as ourselves. Yesterday's hatred of the Hebrews for the Canaanites generates today's hatred of the Palestinians for the Jews, each side believing itself summoned by God to dominate the other — the others — and thus seeing itself as empowered to exterminate them.

For Islam *in its essence* rejects metaphysical, ontological, religious, and therefore political equality. The Koran teaches it: at the top, Muslims, below them Christians, because they too are people of the book, and then Jews, who as monotheists are also members of the group. Finally, after the Muslim, the Christian, and the Jew, comes the fourth group, all lumped together in general disapproval, unbelievers, the infidel, miscreants, polytheists, and of course atheists . . . The Koranic law, which forbids killing, committing crimes against, or massacring one's neighbor, is strictly confined to members of the community of the book: the *ummah*. As with the Jews.

But at the very heart of the Muslim community of supposed equals, hierarchy still prevails: men dominate women, the clergy dominate the faithful, pious believers dominate the lukewarm, the old dominate the young. Male supremacy, theocracy, gerontocracy, the original tribal and primitive models have remained unchanged over thirteen centuries. Islam is *fundamentally* incompatible with the societies that arose from the Enlightenment. The Muslim is not brotherly: he is the brother of his coreligionist, granted, but not of the others, negligible or hateful quantities, counting for nothing.

2

The local as universal. Muslims divide the world in two: friends and enemies. On one side, brothers in Islam, on the other the rest, all the rest. *Dar al-islam* against *dar al-harb*: two separate and incompatible worlds, governed by savage and brutal relations — a predator and a prey, an eater and an eaten, a dominator and a dominated. As in the most elemental of jungles, the big cats keep to themselves while the rest wait to be conquered, enslaved, and possessed. The law that governs relations among animals.

It is a world vision not too distant from Hitler's, justifying the logics of branding, possession, administration, and extension of territory. The fox and the chickens, the falcon and its prey, lion and gazelle, weak and strong, Islam and the others. No law, no justice, no communication, no exchange of information—just muscles, instinct, strength, battle, war, and blood.

The universal? To paraphrase Miguel Torga, the local minus walls. Seventh-century tribalism, the feudalism of the Arabian desert, the primitive view of the clan, invariably transplanted unchanged into the civilization of the hour, including our own postmodern, hyperindustrial, and digital model. The desert village become world blueprint. The oasis, where nothing has penetrated for centuries (apart from nomad caravans laden with subsistence-level goods), functioning as social, human, metaphysical, and political archetype.

A book dating from the beginning of the 630s, theoretically dictated to an illiterate camel herdsman, regulates down to the smallest detail the daily lives of billions of people in the era of supersonic travel, space conquest, worldwide information networks, the real and universal time of generalized communications, the sequencing of the human genome, nuclear energy, the first glimpses of the post-human . . . The remark applies equally for the Torah- and Talmud-obsessed Lubavitchers, who share a similar ignorance of the passage of time.

As in the nomad tent of fifteen hundred years ago, the family constitutes the core. Not the national or patriotic community, and still less the universal or cosmopolitan entity, but that of the paterfamilias, owner of his two, three, or four obedient wives—for primitive polygamy survives in the Talmud as in the Koran (4:3) — surrounded by numerous children. The latter are a blessing from God, authority of course proceeding from Allah, but through the voice of father, husband, and spouse, figurations of God under the goatskin tent.

Every action occurs in the gaze of the tribe, which judges it by its degree of conformity to Koranic or Muslim rules. The father, but also — following pure male chauvinist logic, the senior brother, the brother, and other variations on the theme of the male — is the incarnate locus of religion and therefore of politics and theocracy. He is the basic cell of society. Neither Plato — in *The Republic* — nor Hegel — in *Elements of the Philosophy of Right* — nor Mussolini, nor Hitler, nor Pétain, nor any other kind of fascist had doubts on that score. They all knew that the beginnings of the community, the genealogy of the community, were rooted in the intimate space of the family — the primitive tribe. Read or reread Engels and *Origins of the Family, of Private Property and the State* if you need convincing.

3

Yellow stars and Muslim tattoos. Of equal importance to the communal logic of inclusion and exclusion was the distinguishing mark or sign. Wearing the distinctive color yellow — sometimes as a turban — on one's person initially resulted from a decree by an eleventh-century caliph in Baghdad (the usual way of characterizing that period is to speak of the golden age of Islam), who sought to distinguish Jews and Christians by an outward sign that swiftly became one of opprobrium.

Muslims have a concept known as *dhimma*, which originally referred to the pact of surrender between non-Muslims and their Muslim conquerors. Today, a *dhimmi* is a non-Muslim citizen of a country governed in accordance with sharia, Islamic law. At one time, the status of *dhimmi* was available only to people of the book (Jews and Christians), but later it was extended to include Zoroastrians and certain others. Muslims characterize *dhimma* as a contract that protects *dhimmis*, allowing them to retain their religion and guaranteeing their personal safety and the security of their property. In theory, Islam is a religion of peace and tolerance. In practice, *dhimma* imposes an extra tax on the Jew, Christian, or Zoroastrian for the privilege of living in Islamic territory. Forcing non-Muslims to pay for protection is financial extortion.

Armed with this protection (!), the dhimmi enjoys civic rights that are almost nonexistent. In a tribal society, where ownership of a horse makes it possible to exist, to travel, to fight, to display one's social rank, the non-Muslim owns no such thing. He is permitted to ride an ass or mule (degrading mounts), but he has to ride sidesaddle, woman-style. He may walk in the street, but is not allowed to overtake a Muslim. Bearing arms is of course categorically forbidden—more or less implying that, being disarmed, the *dhimmi* is at the mercy of the first bandit to cross his path. Sometimes, beyond wearing the yellow fabric of sinister memory, he has a lion tattooed on his forearm, just as a later generation of Jews sported a tattooed number there.

In theory, the abolition of dhimmitude dates from 1839. In fact it was not until the end of the First World War that the Ottoman Empire finally abandoned a practice whose observance it was no longer able to impose . . . Obviously, the famous protection guaranteed on paper was not invariably granted—not by a long shot—to non-Muslim believers, who nevertheless conscientiously paid the tax and consented to live as subhumans.

4

Against the closed society. Islam has evolved within its own hermetic set of assumptions—within a history of its own that in effect ignores and denies the overall sweep of history. This has generated a closed, static society, shut in upon itself, fixated on the immobility of death. Marxism once claimed to be fulfilling history by abolishing it: its adepts professed a quasi-religious cult of history the better to achieve that goal. In the same way, the Muslim ambition to rule the planet aims ultimately for a frozen system, a system running counter to the flow of history, abandoning the dynamic of the real and of the world in favor of a universe conceived in the manner of an afterlife. A society applying the principles of the Koran would give us a universal nomad encampment, astir with the distant echo of subterranean spasms and the song of the spheres, dead husks orbiting themselves in celebration of nothingness, emptiness, the meaninglessness of a long-defunct history.

Every theocracy that refers back to the model of a timeless, dimensionless fictional universe seeks to impose on an immanent world a carbon-copy reproduction of that conceptual archetype. For the blueprints of the city of men are stored in the city of God. The Platonic Idea, such close kin to the idea of God (with no date of birth, no expected time of death, without answerability of any kind whatsoever, impervious to time or entropy, flawless, perfect), engenders the mirage of a closed society, it too endowed with the attributes of the Concept.

Democracy lives on movement, change, on contractual agreements, flexible time frames, enduring dynamics, dialectical interplay. It creates itself and thrives at the behest of a will that stems from living forces. It relies on the use of reason, on dialogue among the parties concerned, on active use of communication, on diplomacy and negotiation. Theocracy lives by the opposite principle: it is born, lives, and thrives on immobility, death, and the irrational. Theocracy is democracy's most dangerous enemy — the day before yesterday in prerevolutionary Paris, yesterday in Tehran in 1978, and today every time Al-Qaeda gives violence a voice.

5

Muslim fascism. The question of fascism still exercises a handful of contemporary historians, unable to agree on a firm and final definition. Was French marshal Philippe Pétain fascist? He was certainly a nationalist, and according to some a patriot, but although his Vichy regime pursued extreme right-wing policies, they were not necessarily fascist . . . These are byzantine debates, for there were many brands of fascism in the twentieth century, each with its own specific attributes. Indeed, we could call the last hundred years the *fascist century*. Brown and red in Europe and Asia, military khaki in South America. But green as well, which we too often overlook.

For the overthrow of the shah of Iran in 1978 and the seizure shortly thereafter of all powers by the Ayatollah Khomeini (and by one hundred and eighty thousand mullahs) gave birth to an authentic Muslim fascism. A quarter century later, with the blessings of a silent and forgetful West, it is still in the saddle. Because far from heralding the emergence of the *political spirituality* so lacking in the West (as Michel Foucault wrongly believed in 1978), the Iranian revolution gave birth to an Islamic fascism never before associated with that religion.

We know that Foucault seriously misread the event. Not only because of an article he wrote in *Corriere della Sera*, on November 26, 1978, stating that "there will be no Khomeini party, there will be no Khomeini government." (He was cruelly contradicted by events four months later.) But because he identified the new Islamic government as "the first great insurrection against planetary systems, the most modern form of revolt" — without considering for a second the possibility of a government inspired by Islamic law, the sharia . . . What did Foucault really know about the Koran and Islam?

By the time he wrote those words for the Italian daily, Foucault had already meditated fruitfully on the issues of incarceration, madness, prison, homosexuality, and folly. He should have known better than anyone else that by its very nature an Islamic government would enlist the services of everything he had fought against: sexual discrimination, imprisonment of outsiders, leveling of differences, the logic of confessions, the prison system, disciplining the body, unchallenged biopower, the panoptical principle, the punitive society, and so forth. Knowledge of the Koran and the Hadith (the two sources of sharia) should have made it clear that, far from signifying a return to the spiritual in politics, an Islamic government marked Islam's entry into the field of postmodern politics. And this, in perfect accord with the theocratic principle, ushered in the Islamic fascism whose implications at first eluded this very skilled student of the microphysics of power.

6

An ayatollah speaks. Politicians theorizing about power usually bequeath to us dry, straightforward books that go right to the heart of the matter, summarizing either their authors' intentions or else their achievements. In Cardinal Richelieu's *Political Testament*, Lenin's *The State and Revolution*, General de Gaulle's *The Edge of the Sword*, Mussolini's *The Doctrine of Fascism*, and Hitler's egregious *Mein Kampf*, we encounter respectively a theory of monarchic legitimacy, a Marxist-Leninist manual for Bolshevists, a treatise on the theory of modern war, a fascist manual, and a National Socialist racial doctrine.

After his death the Ayatollah Khomeini left a *Politico-Spiritual Testament* that outlines the theory of Islamic government that so excited Michel Foucault in the first days of the Iranian revolution. The Shiite dignitary put into words, simply, even concisely, the political program of an Islamic republic. His book explained how to govern minds, bodies, and souls according to Muslim principles and with the help of the Koran and the Hadith (in other words on the basis of sharia). It is a breviary of Islamic theocracy — an undeniably fascist breviary.

Muslim theocracy — like any other — presupposes an end to the separation between private belief and public practice. The believer emerges from the private center of his being to take over every single area of the community's life. We no longer enjoy a direct relationship with God, based on a mystical intimacy touching us alone, but an indirect relationship mediated by the political community and regulated by somebody else. The end of religion for one's own sake; the beginning of religion for others.

At which point religion becomes the business of the state. Not of a restricted community, a limited group, but the whole of society. This extension of politics to the totality of the human sphere is the very definition of totalitarianism. The state serves an idea — racial, fascist, Islamic, Christian, etc. — and family, work, privacy, school, barracks, hospital, newspaper or publishing office, friendship, leisure, reading, sexuality, courts, sports are all controlled by the dominant ideology. And thus Islamic family, Islamic work, Islamic privacy, Islamic school, and so on.

7

Islam: structurally archaic. How can we legitimize the totalitarian and immanent use of the Koran? By claiming to possess the only legitimate reading of the holy book. Selective excerpting makes possible an Islam à la carte, with a broad range of offerings. Today we can profess allegiance to the Prophet yet drink alcohol, eat pork, refuse the veil, reject sharia, bet at the racetrack, root for our soccer team, espouse human rights, praise the

European Enlightenment. Or so it is claimed by those who aspire to modernize the Muslim religion and live a secular, modern, republican Islam, and similar untenable twaddle.

Following this same incoherent logic, one can be a Christian yet not really believe in God, scoff at papal bulls, mock the sacraments, refuse to subscribe to the mysteries of the Eucharist, spurn dogma, brush aside all church teachings! The practice of selective borrowing from the texts today allows us to worship a mere signifier, emptying it utterly of what it once signified. At which point we are worshipping an empty shell, prostrating ourselves before nothing — one of the many signs of the nihilism of our era.

At the other end of the spectrum we find the reverse: scrupulous respect for Koranic teachings. Hence the practice of polygamy, routine sexist and male chauvinist behavior, the denial of existential reality to all non-Muslims, justification for the killing of infidels — from monotheists to atheists — zealous observance of the rituals and obligations of churchgoers, condemnation of all use of reason, etc.

The Koran does not countenance à la carte religion. Nothing in the book permits us to dismiss every sura hostile to comfortable living, to middle-class integration into postmodernity. On the other hand, nothing forbids (in fact, everything authorizes) a scrupulous reading on whose basis all the duties specified in the holy book are justified. No one is obliged to be a Muslim, but when he professes to be one, he must adhere to the theory and teachings and practice his beliefs accordingly. It is a question of the pure and simple principle of coherence. Islamic theocracy illustrates the maximum coherence possible on this subject.

For Islam is structurally archaic, contradicting point by point everything the philosophy of the Enlightenment has achieved in Europe since the eighteenth century. In other words, condemnation of superstition, rejection of intolerance, abolition

of censorship, resistance to tyranny, opposition to political abso-
lutism, an end to state religion, proscription of magical thinking,
extension of freedom of thought and expression, promulgation
of equal rights, the notion that all law arises from contractual
immanence, the wish for social happiness here and now, the aspiration toward the universal reign of reason. Sura by sura, the
Koran clearly states its opposition to them all.

8

Fascist thematics. In Iran, the Ayatollah Khomeini was officially addressed as "Imam" rather than Grand Ayatollah. In Sunni
Islam, an imam is the leader of worship in a mosque. But in Shiite Islam, an imam is a spiritual and political leader whose authority comes from Muhammad through his son-in-law Ali.
Being divinely inspired, the imam has the same attributes as the
pope — in other words, infallibility. Like the Führer, Il Duce, the
Caudillo, the Conducator (Romania's Ceausescu), and the Great
Helmsman (Mao), the imam's word is law: *performative logic*. He
has a monopoly on correct interpretation of the Koran. He
alone is qualified to select from the Koran whatever passages appear to support the creation of a total theocracy.

For everything is in the Koran. Reading it gives us every
possible reply to every possible and imaginable question.
Money? Trade? The law? Justice? Education? Sovereignty?
Women? Divorce? Family? Diet? Ecology? Culture? Nothing is
missing, everything is there. Western governments would find
priceless policy guidelines in the Koran. The supreme leader thus
possesses the supreme source, the holy text, and his utterances
are therefore to be identified with justice and law. He embodies
the theory of the man of destiny.

To which must be added a *binary logic* pitting friends against enemies. No quarter, no details, no subtlety. No need for hair-splitting to decide for whom and against whom to fight. In the logic of the Iranian revolution, the enemies are America, Israel, the West, modernity, the superpowers. Multiple names, all reducible to the same entity: Satan. The devil, the demon, the Prince of Darkness. Every brand of fascism proceeds in this manner, designating the enemy and demonizing him to the maximum in order to galvanize troops for battle. Embodiment of the scapegoat theory.

Then (a theme common to fascism and Islamism) we have the claim of a *postpolitical logic*. Meaning? Neither right nor left but elsewhere, beyond, or — in Iran's case — above. On God's side. So Iran will have no truck with the Marxist, Bolshevik, Soviet (in its day), atheist, materialist, Communist left, (Khomeini even broadened this concept to embrace women's communism!) nor with the American, consumerist, self-indulgent, corrupt, business-oriented, and capitalist right. The two systems are lumped together. Embodiment of the theory of the end of politics.

Thus a *transcendental logic*: God as the solver of contradictions. Yet this Islamic synthesis retains parts of the two spurned systems mentioned above. It borrows from the left a discourse of solidarity with the have-nots, it directs its words to the wretched, it verbally displays a genuine populist determination to do away forever with poverty in the world. And from the bosom of the right it selects small-scale private capitalism and land ownership. The sum of these two borrowed currents of political thought offers an apparent coherence, guaranteed by Allah, begetter of the union. Embodiment of the theory of the end of history.

Moreover, fascism and Islamism commune in a *mystical logic*. At the other extreme from reason in history, from rational linkages of causality or from any constructive dialectic, the ayatollah promulgates the law of the irrational. The triumph of the collective requires the sacrifice of the individual. All individuality must be swallowed up in the totality thus constituted. So that in return for its disappearance, individuality is compensated with a new melting-pot identity — participation in the mystic body of society and therefore in the community, in other words in God. Hence a (falsely) divine future for man. Embodiment of the theory of the end of reason.

The *pantheistic principle* of community entails sublimation of the self for the greater good of the collective political body. The sense of self is diminished, as the individual identifies with a cause and sees himself only as part of something bigger. Martyrdom permits the individual not to perish. Instead, he achieves a transmutation of his being, which survives in the mystic community in a form that is eternal, extrahistoric and transhistoric. Hence Muslim suicide bombers. Embodiment of the theory of existential eschatology.

Similarly, like every kind of fascism, Islamic theocracy rests on a *hypermoral logic*. God commands history, his plan is consistent with reality, his design remains immutable. Allah requires the ethical purification of the believer, hence hatred of the body, the flesh, free sexuality, desires, etc. The realization of moral order as an occasion for hypostasis leads toward the mystic empyrean. This implies condemnation of luxury, homosexuality, gambling, drugs, nightclubs, alcohol, prostitution, cinema, perfume, lotteries, and other vices denounced by the ayatollah. Embodiment of the theory of the ascetic ideal.

Finally, fascism and Islamism imply a *logic of compulsory service*. Nothing and no one may refuse to answer the call, hence total mobilization of every cog in the state machine. A tight rein is kept on all institutions, press, army, journalism, education, the judicial body, police, bureaucrats, intellectuals, artists, scientists, writers, orators (*dixit* the supreme leader), and research workers. Competence in one's field of activity passes into the background. Faith, fervor, religiosity, and zealous religious practice move into the foreground. Embodiment of the theory of the militarization of society.

Everything that usually defines fascism is reproduced in the theory and practice of Islamic government. The masses are directed by an inspired, charismatic leader. Myth, the irrational, the mystical are revamped as the motive forces of history. Law and justice are created by the leader's words. The dominant national ambition is to abolish an old world in order to create a new one—a new man, new values; a vitalist world vision coupled with a bottomless love of death; expansionist warfare experienced as proof of the nation's health; hatred of the Enlightenment (reason, Marxism, science, materialism, books); police terror; abolition of all separation between private and public spheres; construction of a closed society; dilution of the individual in the community; self-realization through the loss of self and salutary sacrifice; celebration of warlike virtues (virility, machismo, brotherhood, comradeship, discipline, misogyny); destruction of all resistance; militarization of politics; suppression of all individual freedom; fundamental hostility to the ideology of human rights; permanent political indoctrination; history couched in the language of negative slogans (anti-Semitic, anti-Marxist, anticapitalist, anti-American, antimodern, anti-Western); the family promoted to the position of first link in the organic whole . . . The above litany more or less constitutes a definition of the essence of fascism, of fascisms of every stripe. Theocracy is still embroidering variations on this theme.

9

Fascism of the fox, fascism of the lion. The twenty-first century has opened on a merciless war. On one side is a *Judeo-*

Christian West, liberal in the economic sense of the term, uncompromisingly capitalist, brutally mercantile, cynically consumerist, producer of false values, without virtue, viscerally nihilistic, strong toward the weak, weak toward the strong, cunning and Machiavellian toward all, spellbound by money and profit, prostrate before the gold that engenders all power, creator of every system designed to dominate the body and the soul. Under this dispensation everyone—in theory—enjoys freedom. In fact, freedom exists for a mere handful, for a very few, while the others, the majority, huddle in poverty, destitution, humiliation.

On the other side, a *Muslim world*, zealous, brutal, intolerant, violent, imperious, conquering. The fascism of the fox against the fascism of the lion, one creating its victims postmodern style with state-of-the-art weapons, the other by resorting to a hyperterrorism of box-cutter knives, hijacked planes, and homemade explosive belts. God is claimed by both camps, each trusting in the trial by ordeal of primitive man. Axis of good against axis of evil, with the front lines perpetually overlapping one another.

Monotheist religions are waging this war, with Jews and Christians on one side and Muslims, postmodern Saracens, on the other. Must we choose a side? Must we opt for the cynicism of one on the pretext of fighting the barbarism of the other? Must we really align ourselves with this or that world vision when we consider both of them to be dead-end streets? Michel Foucault once indulged in Manichaeism and let himself be caught in its trap. He initially welcomed the prospect of a spiritual politics during the Iranian revolution, because it offered an alternative to what he called "planetary systems" (in 1978 nobody yet spoke of globalization). But after that, Foucault observed that the issue of political Islam is vital not only to the present but also to the years ahead. Duly noted.

10

Against "religious" secularism. In this devastated landscape of a Western world at bay, the tactics of some secular figures seem contaminated by the enemy's ideology: many militants in the secular cause look astonishingly like clergy. Worse: like caricatures of clergy. Unfortunately, contemporary freethinking often carries a waft of incense; it sprinkles itself shamelessly with holy water. As clergymen of a church of atheist bigots, the players in this not unimportant movement seem to have missed the postmodern boat.

The freethinkers' struggles have admittedly worked wonders in advancing the cause of modernity. They have given us the deconstruction of Christian fables, the unburdening of consciences, separation of the religious and the judicial. They have given us secularization of education, public-health services, and the army, campaigns against theocracy on behalf of democracy, and—to name their greatest triumph—separation of church and state.

Yet secular catechisms, civil ceremonies (baptisms, communion!), youth congresses, campaigns against the tolling of church bells in villages, dreams of creating a new calendar, iconoclasm, and opposition to the wearing of priestly garb, all smell a little too much like the kindling heaped at the feet of Christian stakes ... De-Christianization does not come about through the manipulation of such trinkets and baubles, but through hard work on the epistemology of a period, through the injection of reason into human consciences. The French Revolution's de-Christianizing phase was swiftly followed by the cult of the Supreme Being and other observances, just as clerically ludicrous and inappropriate.

Let us think in dialectical terms. These excesses can be explained by the bitterness of the struggle ahead, the stubbornness of a Christian enemy still possessing full powers over bodies, souls, and consciences, and his commandeering of all the controls of civil, political, and military society. Freethinkers stigmatize their adversaries by calling them lice and vermin (parasites), spiders and serpents (cunning), swine and goats (filth, stench, lubricity), owls and bats (obscurity, obscurantism), vultures (gluttons for carrion!), and crows (blackness). The clerics hurl back at them apes (Darwin!), pigs (indestructible Epicurean porcines), dogs (the barker copulating in public, so dear to Diogenes) . . . The spectacle becomes more colorful, but the debate deteriorates.

11

Substance and forms of the secular ethic. More disturbingly, militant secularism leans heavily on the Judeo-Christian ethic, which it is often content merely to copy. Immanuel Kant writing *Religion within the Limits of Reason Alone* often serves as a breviary for secular thinkers. The gospel virtues, the message of the Commandments, the testamental recommendations are all merely represented in a new guise. Preservation of the substance, modification of the form . . . This secularization of Judeo-Christian morality often corresponds to an immanent rewriting of a transcendent discourse. What descends from heaven is not erased but reacclimatized for earth. The French priest and the French schoolteacher, self-appointed defender of the secular Republic's values, continue to be at daggers drawn, as they have been for so long — but in the end both fight for an essentially similar world.

Moral handbooks in republican schools preach the excellence of the family, the virtues of work, the need to respect one's parents and honor the old, the rightness of nationalism, patriotic obligations, mistrust of the flesh, the body and passions, the beauty of manual labor, submission to political authority, duty to the poor. What could the village priest object to here? Work, Family, Fatherland: the holy secular Trinity of Christendom ... and of Vichy France.

Secular thought is not de-Christianized thought, but immanent Christian thought. Couched in rational language, it nevertheless preserves the quintessence of the Judeo-Christian ethic. God leaves heaven to come down to earth. He does not die, no one kills him, no one spurns him, he is simply adapted to the terrain of pure immanence. Jesus remains the hero of both visions of the world: he is merely asked to discard his halo and avoid excessively ostentatious gestures.

Hence a relativist definition of secularism: while the epistemology remains Judeo-Christian, secularism acts as if religion no longer impregnates and imbues consciences, bodies, and souls. We speak, think, live, act, imagine, eat, suffer, sleep, and conceive as Judeo-Christians, constructed by two thousand years of formatting by biblical monotheism. At which point, secularism fights to allow everyone to think what he wishes and believe in his own god, provided he does not make it a matter for the community. But publicly, the secularized religion of Christ leads the dance.

This being the case, the secular have no problem asserting the equality of Jew, Christian, and Muslim but also of Buddhist, Shintoist, animist, polytheist, and atheist in the contemporary Western state. Everything can easily be made to seem equal to everything else, once experienced in the depths and intimacy of the individual conscience, since everything outside, at the level of public life, institutions, forms, powers — in other words the essential — remains Judeo-Christian!

Toward a post-Christian secularism. Let us then leave behind us a secularism still too imprinted with what it claims to
oppose. We may sincerely applaud it for what it once was, offer
homage for its past struggles, propose a toast to what we owe it.
But let us push forward in dialectical mode. Today's and tomorrow's battles require new weapons, better forged, more efficient,
weapons suited to present needs. We need yet another effort to
de-Christianize the ethic, politics, and the rest. But also to de-
Christianize secularism, which would benefit immeasurably by
emancipating itself still further from Judeo-Christian metaphysics, and which could truly be of service in the wars ahead.

For by decreeing the equality of all religions and of those
who reject them, as today's regnant brand of secularism recommends, we condone relativism: equality of magical thinking and
rational thought, of fable, myth, and reasoned argument, of thau-
maturgic discourse and scientific thinking, of the Torah and
Descartes's *Discourse on Method*, the New Testament and the
Critique of Pure Reason, the Koran and the *Genealogy of Morality*.
We declare Moses the equal of Descartes, Jesus of Kant, and
Muhammad of Nietzsche.

Equality between the believing Jew — convinced that God
promised his ancestors that they were his chosen people, in token of which he divided the sea, stopped the sun, etc. — and the
philosopher who proceeds according to the hypothetico-deduc-
tive model? Equality between the believer — convinced that his
hero, born of a virgin, crucified under Pontius Pilate, risen on
the third day from the dead, and whiling his life away ever since
sitting at the right hand of the father — and the thinker who de-
constructs the manufacture of belief, the building of a myth, the
creation of a fable? Equality between the Muslim — convinced
that drinking Beaujolais and eating a pork roast disqualifies him

from entering paradise whereas the assassination of an unbeliever throws open its gates for him—and the scrupulous analyst who, on the positivist and empirical principle, demonstrates that monotheistic belief is no more valid than that of the Dogon animist believing that the spirit of his ancestors returns in the shape of a fox? If we say yes to these questions, then let's stop thinking.

This relativism is crushing. In its name and in the name of secularism, all discourse carries equal weight: error and truth, the false and the true, the capricious and the serious. Myth and fable weigh as much as reason. Magic counts for as much as science. Dream for as much as reality. But all discourse does not carry the same weight: the discourse of neurosis, hysteria, and mysticism proceeds from another world than that of the positivist. We can no more tolerate neutrality and benevolence toward every conceivable form of discourse, including that of magical thinking, than we can lump together executioner and victim, good and evil. Must we remain neutral? Can we still afford to? I do not think so.

At this hour when the final battle—already lost—looms for the defense of the Enlightenment's values against magical propositions, we must fight for a post-Christian secularism, that is to say atheistic, militant, and radically opposed to choosing between Western Judeo-Christianity and its Islamic adversary—neither Bible nor Koran. I persist in preferring philosophers to rabbis, priests, imams, ayatollahs, and mullahs. Rather than trust their theological hocus-pocus, I prefer to draw on alternatives to the dominant philosophical historiography: the laughers, materialists, radicals, cynics, hedonists, atheists, sensualists, voluptuaries. They know that there is only one world, and that promotion of an afterlife deprives us of the enjoyment and benefit of the only one there is. A genuinely deadly sin.

Bibliography

ATHEOLOGY

1

Atheist poverty. The bibliography of the atheist question is poverty-stricken. Threadbare in comparison with works devoted to religions: every possible variation on the religious theme boasts multiple subsections — but who has ever seen an "atheism shelf" in a bookstore? And the rare books on the subject are of the poorest quality. As though their authors were in the pay of the god-mongers! Henri Arvon fired the first salvo in 1967 with a work in the *Que sais-je?* (What Do I Know?) series entitled *L'athéisme* (Atheism). Half of this slim volume is devoted to the atheism of Democritus, Epicurus, Lucretius, La Mothe Le Vayer, Gassendi, Pierre Bayle, Thomas Hobbes, John Locke, Hume, and others who never denied the existence of God or gods . . . The same goes for Hegel — an atheist! Max Stirner is disposed of in a chapter focused on Nietzschean atheism, although his only book, *The Ego and Its Own*, dates from the year of Nietzsche's birth: a truly premature Nietzschean! Another deficiency is his failure to mention Freud, who was after all the author of *The Future of an Illusion* (Standard Edition: English translation overseen by Freud himself, by James Strachey, W. W. Norton), which, categorically dismantling religion, takes its place among the great deconstructions of the religious question. A historian of anarchism, Henri Arvon ended his life as a convert to libertarianism — an ultra-conservatism of the kind that delighted Ronald Reagan.

Virtually the same defects are to be found in Georges Minois's monumental *Histoire de l'athéisme* (A History of Atheism), Fayard, 1998, just two of whose 671 pages are devoted to Freud! Apart from the abusive extension of the term "atheist" to include polytheists, deists, unorthodox Christians — Epicurus, Rabelais, and Hobbes sharing the limelight with Sade, Nietzsche, and Sartre! — the introduction in which the author attempts to define atheism is better left unread. The rest of the book merits attention chiefly as a road map directing one to possible further reading material. Generally speaking, a card-index system in need of sorting.

2

God is dead . . . oh, really? To verify the circumstances surrounding his assassination, we of course have Nietzsche and the notorious paragraph 125 — *The Madman* — in *The Gay Science* (translated by Thomas Common, Dover Publications, 2006). Read, too, *Ecce Homo* (translated by Anthony Ludovici, Dover Publications, 2004) and *The Anti-Christ*, in *The Portable Nietzsche* (translated by Walter Kaufmann, Penguin, 1977). To reacquaint ourselves with this question — "God is dead, so everything is permitted" (a proposition worthy of a course in elementary philosophy) — see Dostoyevsky's *The Brothers Karamazov* (translated by Richard Pevear and Larissa Volokhonsky, Farrar, Straus and Giroux, 2002).

In the absence of a good history of atheism (a subject still in search of an author), we might consult two philosophical approaches to the question. First, Jacques-J Natanson's *La mort de Dieu: essai sur l'athéisme moderne* (God's Death: An Essay on Modern Atheism), PUF: Presses Universitaires Françaises, 1975, in which the author combines a lucid and intelligent reading of questions relating to atheism with a blend of information, analysis, and commentary. Eight pages of bibliography. Next, and in the same spirit: Dominique Folscheid, *L'esprit de l'athéisme et son destin* (The Spirit and Fate of Atheism), La Table Ronde, 1991. An exhaustive analysis of Nietzsche and Dostoyevsky.

3

The fruits of antiphilosophy. This idea is specifically addressed in what I think is the only work devoted to the question: Didier Masseau's *Les ennemis des philosophes: l'antiphilosophie au temps des Lumières* (Adversaries of the Philosophers: Anti-Philosophy in the Enlightenment), Albin Michel.

BIBLIOGRAPHY

With the enlightened eighteenth century already well advanced, Jesuits, Jansenists, their apologists, and militant Catholics directed their hatred at philosophers — Rousseau, Voltaire, Diderot — and at philosophy. Historiography has smoothed the rough edges of that century, repainting it as the exclusive playground of the Enlightenment — and forgetting that Christian tradition, vengeful, militant, and contentious, stood at one extreme while at the other stood those I shall call the ultras of philosophy — the atheists (La Mettrie, d'Holbach, Helvetius) — who were criticized and attacked in the name of deism by the upholders of safe Enlightenment values . . . Twenty-seven pages of excellent bibliography.

François Garasse's *Doctrine curieuse* (A Curious Doctrine, shortly to be republished in French by Encre Marine) had paved the way in the previous century. To confirm that Vanini had never been an atheist, but rather a pantheist and a Christian, see Adolphe Delahays's *Oeuvres philosophiques*, (Philosophical Works) published in 1856 (translation by X. Rousselot) and never reissued in French. See also Emile Namer, *La vie et l'oeuvre de J. C. Vanini* (The Life and Work of J. C. Vanini), Vrin, 1980.

As a pendant to antiphilosophy, see the collection of texts published under the direction of Patrick Graille and Mladen Kozul, *Discours antireligieux français du dix-huitième siècle: du curé Meslier au Marquis de Sade* (Anti-Religious French Discourse in the Eighteenth Century, from the Priest Meslier to the Marquis de Sade), L'Harmattan, Les Presses de l'Université de Laval, 2003, an invaluable anthology with equally precious introductory notes. A curative for enemies of philosophy, past and present.

The not-quite-first atheist, Cristovão Ferreira, wrote *La superchérie dévoilée* (The Deception Revealed), originally a Portuguese pamphlet of 1636. This text, some thirty pages long, is laboriously introduced by Jacques Proust, an academic pretentious enough to post his surname on the title page of the work, which he translated in collaboration with a Marianne bearing the same name. The reader thus believes him to be the author, since the very name of Ferreira is nowhere to be seen. What honesty, what impeccable manners! The book's subtitle is *Une réfutation du catholicisme au Japon au XVIIe siècle.* (A Refutation of Catholicism in Japan in the Seventeenth Century). Perhaps a differently worded title might have done something to mask the work's odor of academic sanctity . . . but let's not ask too much. (Published by Chandeigne.) The bibliography of course cites every article ever written by this couple from Hades.

4

High-born bowels and Catholic intestines. We recall the Abbé Meslier's famous plea in favor of hanging and strangling every nobleman with the intestines of priests. Those words are to be found in the three-volume *Oeuvres* (Collected Works) of Jean Meslier (Anthropos, 1970). For those likely to be intimidated by its two thousand pages, see an excellent compendium entitled *Mémoire* (Memoir), Exils, 2000. The indispensable and probably unsurpassable labor of Maurice Dommanget, *Le curé Meslier: athée, communiste et révolutionnaire sous Louis XIV* (Meslier the Priest: Atheist, Communist, and Revolutionary under Louis XIV), Julliard, 1965, encompasses everything we can ever hope to know about this work by an authentic philosopher — inevitably consigned to oblivion because everything about him was guaranteed to offend: his hatred of God, of Christianity, of idealism, of the ascetic ideal, and his championing of freedom, hedonism, and earthly life. Lovers of shortcuts would be well advised to consult Marc Bredel, *Jean Meslier l'enragé: prêtre athée et révolutionnaire sous Louis XIV* (Jean Meslier the Madman: Priest, Atheist, and Revolutionary under Louis XIV), Balland, 1983. Bredel's virtually identical repetition of Dommanget's subtitle is probably a faithful reflection of his debt to the latter.

Another of the excellent Dommanget's works worth reading is his critical intellectual biography *Sylvain Maréchaux, "L'homme sans Dieu": vie et oeuvre du Manifeste des égaux*, (Sylvain Maréchaux, "Man Without God": Life and Work of the Egalitarian Manifesto), as well as his *Dictionnaire des athées* (Atheists' Dictionary), Spartacus, 1950. Here again, an unsurpassed survey of the work of another thinker who has disappeared from contemporary intellectual circulation.

5

The Holbachian clique. Divine d'Holbach! Thanks to the courage and sparkling imagination of Jean-Pierre Jackson — whose editorial flair is obvious in everything he sets his hand to — we possess an edition, still in the making, of his *Oeuvres philosophiques* (Philosophical Works). Three monumental volumes (Alive Publications). They include *Le christianisme dévoilé* (Christianity Unveiled), *La contagion sacrée* (The Holy Contagion), and *Théologie portative* (Portable Theology) in volume 1; *Essai sur les préjugés*

(Essay on Prejudices), *Système de la Nature* (Nature's System), and the incredible *Histoire critique de Jésus-Christ* (Critical History of Jesus Christ) in volume 2, and in volume 3 *Tableau des Saints* (Table of the Saints), *Le bon sens* (Common Sense), *Politique Naturelle* (Natural Politics), and *Ethocratie* (Ethocracy) — all of them absolutely essential teaching material in any curriculum expounding the case for atheism! They pulverize Rousseau's affected deist simperings, the anticlerical plays of Voltaire (stout defender of religion for the masses), and Diderot's shilly-shallying over the God dilemma.

A selection of texts in a hard-to-find volume by René Hubert, *D'Holbach et ses amis* (D'Holbach and His Friends), André Depeuc, publisher, part of an anti-Christian series that also published Gourmont and Jules de Gaultier on Nietzsche. Then, by Pierre Naville, *D'Holbach et la philosophie scientifique au XVIIIe siècle* (D'Holbach and Eighteenth-Century Scientific Philosophy), Gallimard, 1967. The republication of a handful of works by the philosopher in Fayard's excellent Corpus collection brings together a number of contributions on d'Holbach from the review *Corpus*.

6

Planned obsolescence. Feuerbach's absence from the philosophical marketplace is equally scandalous. Apart from the takeover of his legacy and thinking by Louis Althusser, translator from the original German of the *Manifestes philosophiques: textes choisis (1839–1845)* (Philosophical Manifestos: Selected Texts, 1839–1845) for PUF and then for 10/18 in 1960, or that of his epigone Jean-Pierre Osier, to whom we owe *L'essence du christianisme* (The Essence of Christianity), Maspero, 1982, and translated into English by George Elliot (Prometheus Books, 1989), we would seek in vain for anything else. Unless it were the 1864 translation by J. Roy of a volume entitled *La religion* (Religion) and in 1845 *L'essence de la religion* (The Essence of Religion), translated into English by Alexander Loos (Prometheus Books, 2004), *Mort et immortalité* (Death and Immortality), 1830 — and *Pensées diverses* (Random Thoughts) and *Remarques* (Observations), republished by Vrin in 1987. More recently, *Pensées sur la mort et l'immortalité* (Reflections on Death and Immortality), Cerf, translated by Charles Berner, 1991).

Not much on Feuerbach. From Henri Arvon — author of the mediocre *Que sais-je?* text on atheism — we have *Ludwig Feuerbach ou la transformation du sacré* (Ludwig Feuerbach or the Transformation of the Sacred), PUF, 1957, and a selection of texts written by the same author but aiming more specifically at synthesis: *Feuerbach* (PUF, 1964). Alexis Philonenko has published a survey entitled *La jeunesse de Feuerbach (1828–1841): introduction à ses pensées fondamentales* (Feuerbach's Youth, 1828–1841: Introduction to his Basic Thinking), Vrin, 1990. One would like to see the same titanic labor devoted to the philosopher's last thirty years ... Jean Salem steps in briefly with *Une lecture frivole des écritures: "L'Essence du christianisme" de Ludwig Feuerbach* (Irreverent Approach to the Writings: Ludwig Feuerbach's "Essence of Christianity"), Encre Marine, 2003.

7

A Judeo-Christian epistemology. Foucault proposed his notion of episteme in *Les mots et les choses* (*The Order of Things: An Archaeology of Human Sciences*), Routledge, 2001, in 1966. In *Dits et écrits,* volume 2 (French-only anthology), he asserts that "all relational phenomena among the sciences constitute what I call the episteme of a period." Clearly, we can grasp the details of an episteme only in archaeological terms, and on most improbable terrain. Referring to the Christian body in my own *Féeries anatomiques* (Anatomical Sorcery), I proposed an approach to the question of the episteme that takes Western flesh as its starting point. Worth reading on this subject are Nicolas Martin and Antoine Spire in *Dieu aime-t-il les maladies? Les religions monothéistes face à la maladie* (Does God Love Diseases? The Monotheist Religions and Illness), Anne Carrière, 2004, which illustrates the extent to which Judeo-Christian ideology still permeates questions of health, sickness, and, alas, bioethics. A detailed survey of the Christian position on health questions is to be found in the *Health Professionals' Charter* drawn up by the Pontifical Council on health services, and published in 1995 by the Vatican City: horrifying evidence of the extent to which our bioethics mark time — and even march backward — because of the retrograde positions of a Church defended by laymen drunk on holy water.

On the question of law and its Judeo-Christian formatting, I have set out my position in "Proposal for an end to human verdicts" in *L'archipel des comètes* (Archipelago of the Comets), Grasset.

8

A Christian atheism! André Comte-Sponville does not reject my formulation, but prefers "atheist believer." He explains what he means by this in his *A-t-on encore besoin d'une religion?* (Do We Still Need a Religion?) Les Editions de l'Atelier, 2003: "Atheist because I believe in no God; but a believer because I perceive myself as participating in a certain tradition, a certain history, and in those Judeo-Christian (or Greco-Judeo-Christian) values which are ours" (page 58). Likewise Luc Ferry, who — more prudent in every way — rejects the atheist position in favor of the agnostic option. See *L'homme-Dieu* (Man-God), Grasset.

This more explicitly assumed Christian tropism is also to be found in contemporary philosophy, in the thinking of Michel Henry and Giovanni Vattimo. The former approaches Christianity as a phenomenologist in *Incarnation* (Seuil, 2000), *Paroles du Christ* (Christ's Words), Seuil, 2004, and *I Am the Truth: Toward a Philosophy of Christianity*, translated into English by Susan Emanuel (Stanford University Press, 2002). Vattimo's approach is from the standpoint of hermeneutics . . . See his *Espérer croire* (Hoping to Believe), Seuil, 1998, and *Après la chrétienté* (After Christianity), Calmann-Lévy, 2004. Or how to immerse the Bible in the purgative waters of Heidegger's *Being and Time* in order to find a miraculous — in the chemical sense — solution.

9

Enduring scholasticism. Worth reading (although not atheists at all but unashamedly Christian) are Jean-Luc Marion, *Dieu sans l'être* (God Without Being God), PUF, 2002, and René Girard, *Je vois Satan tomber comme l'éclair* (I See Satan Strike Like Lightning), Grasset, 1999. Then, in the Jewish tradition crossbred with Russian, Italian, Spanish, French (but most decidedly not German) philosophy, Vladimir Jankélévitch: fifteen hundred pages in multivolume form: *Le sérieux de l'intention* (Seriousness of Intent), *Les vertus et l'amour* (The Virtues and Love), *L'innocence et la méchanceté* (Innocence and Malice). In the same tradition, but blended here with Heideggerian phenomenology, Emmanuel Levinas, *Autrement qu'être ou au-delà de l'essence* (Other Than Being, or Beyond Essence), Nijhoff, 1974. Whence it emerges that love is preferable to war, courage to cowardice, forgiveness to resentment. Unimpeachable on paper.

MONOTHEISMS

1

The price of the One Book. In theory, each of the three monotheisms presents itself as the one religion of a One book. In fact, these One books are legion. The renowned Pléiade library at Gallimard takes a curious position: it publishes these works in mouse-gray binding, while it issues its ancient texts in green. Why not issue the Bible, the Koran, the Intertestamentary Writings, or the Christian Apocryphal texts in the same colors as Homer, Plato, or Augustine? For they are all exclusively historical writings.

I have used Emile Osty's and Joseph Trinquet's Bible (Seuil). I prefer it to the three-volume Pléiade edition because it facilitates search by incorporating subtitles into the text. On the other hand, its footnotes and cross-reference system are without any real interest. My Koran is the Pléiade version, translated by D. Masson — an Islamophile version as one might expect. Its footnoting also needs revision for much the same reasons.

On biblical historicity: Israël Finkelstein and Neil Asher Silberman, *The Bible Unearthed: Archaeology's New Vision of Ancient Israel and the Origin of its Sacred Texts* (Free Press, 2002). Their work teems with historical information on the myth-manufacturing production line that generated the book. Other basic works: the Pentateuch and the Talmud. There is no genuinely critical and atheistic edition of any of these works!

Also worth reading is the *Catechism of the Catholic Church*. The endurance and longevity of mythologies inherited from a thousand years ago! For those eager to familiarize themselves with the study of angels — a major linchpin of that remote past — see Pseudo-Dionysius the Areopagite's *Complete Works* (English version, long out of print, published by Richwood Publishing, 1976). And a masterly synthesis, *Les anges* (The Angels) by Philippe Faure (Cerf, Fides). On angelic dwelling-places: Soubhi el-Saleh, *La vie future selon le Coran* (Future Life According to the Koran), Vrin.

2

Books on the One book. Bookstores and libraries overflow with religious works. Their abundance is matched only by the rarity of books devoted to atheism! As time passes, these sections continue to proliferate in
bookstores, cheek by jowl with those celebrating the New Age, self-
improvement, astrology, Buddhism, Tarot cards, and other manifestations
of the appeal of the irrational. Take a quick look at Adorno's book on
horoscopes, *From the Stars Down to Earth and Other Essays on the Irrational
Culture* (Routledge, 2001), in which a wealth of analysis serves to facilitate understanding of religious belief.

The question of dictionaries is of real interest. See *Le dictionnaire des
monotheisms* (Dictionary of Monotheisms), issued under the direction of
Jacques Potin and Valentine Zubert (Bayard): three sections, Judaism,
Christianity, Islam, with alphabetical entries, a final index, and another at
the end of each entry that conflates these three phases — enough to provide the reader with the needed minimum on a given subject. The *Dictionnaire de l'Islam: religion et civilisation* (Dictionary of Islam: Religion and
Civilization), Encyclopaedia Universalis, Albin Michel, is remarkable.
And with his *Dictionnaire des symboles musulmans* (Dictionary of Islamic
Symbols), Albin Michel, Malek Chebel has produced what is surely his
best work, or in any event his least partial. Useful footnotes to the suras,
bibliography, and cross-references.

Reading the Talmud is extremely tedious! Timid readers might consult
Adin Steinsaltz, *Introduction au Talmud* (Introduction to the Talmud), Albin
Michel, and Abraham Cohen's *Everyman's Talmud: The Major Teachings of
the Rabbinic Sages* (Schocken, 1995). Excellent historical syntheses in the
former, a thematic approach, rich in quotations, in the latter. But hands-
on knowledge of the text of the Talmud itself is indispensable, naturally
for its ideas and substance, but also in order to grasp the economy of a
logical system, a dialectic, and a way of thinking.

As for Islam, Rohdy Alili's *Qu'est-ce que l'Islam?* (What Is Islam?), La
Découverte, is preferable to Malek Chebel's *Dictionnaire amoureux de
l'Islam* (Loving Dictionary of Islam), Plon, which is both partial and
skimpy: Islam, religion of peace and love (!), tolerant of wine ("There
has never been any question of banning wine outright, simply of dis-
suading true believers from its consumption," page 617), one of many

singular paradoxes in this truly amorous dictionary that avoids such subjects as war, raiding, battles, conquests, and anti-Semitism — all of which more or less defined the life of the Prophet and of Islam for centuries. On the other hand, there is an entry on the Crusades to compensate for the absence of an entry on the Jews ... As for sex, the reader will be gratified to know that "Islam has liberated sexuality and made of it an area of extreme sociability" (page 561). Worth asking women who live under the sharia for their opinion, because Malek Chebel (see the entry for Women) believes that ill-treatment of women is the fault of backward governments and incompetent politicians, never of the text of the Koran itself.

3

The antidote to monotheistic fraud. Read Raoul Vaneigem's *De l'inhumanité de la religion* (On the Inhumanity of Religion), Denoël. But also his preface to *L'art de ne croire en rien* (The Art of Believing in Nothing), followed by the *Livre des trois imposteurs* (Book of Three Frauds), Payot-Rivages. These three frauds were Moses, Jesus, and Muhammad. Also of interest is Jean Soler's important and very wide-ranging book *Aux origines du Dieu unique: l'invention du monothéisme* (On the Origins of the Only God: The Invention of Monotheisms), eds. De Fallois, 2002, which offers some startling conclusions — the Jews, "this mental [as one might speak of 'conceptual' art?] people is a verbal creation" (page 118). In it, the author asserts that the Hebrews went from polytheism to monotheism in order to guarantee their ontological existence on the basis of a One book. But also that their message of love is directed only at their own kind — "God of all mankind or God of the Jews?" (pages 184–186) — not at their neighbor. This last point is developed in *La loi de Moïse*, (The Law of Moses, pages 66–74 and 106–111), same publisher, 2003. A book that also demonstrates (chapter 1) the restrictive interpretation we are required to give to the supposedly universal imperative of "Thou shalt not kill." (My thanks to Jean Soler for the invaluable advice he gave me on looking over my manuscript.)

4

Foreskins, refinements, and libraries. The same Malek Chebel has published his *Histoire de la circoncision des origines à nos jours* (History of

Circumcision from the Origins to the Present Day), Le Nadir, Balland. In his introduction (page 11) he writes: "the information in this book is resolutely accurate and untainted by proselytism." On page 7, he clarifies the nature of this objectivity: "This book is dedicated to the 'surgeons of enlightenment': the circumcisers." And on page 30, still entirely neutral, and in the wake of a number of psychological reflections and considerations (for Malek Chebel also styles himself a psychoanalyst), he asks: "Can one truly consider the ablation of such paper-thin skin as a 'traumatic' or even worse a traumatological act?" Sigmund, where are you when we need you?

On circumcision, the reader will prefer analyses inspired by the utilitarian and pragmatic Anglo-Saxon method (in the best senses of all those terms) of Margaret Somerville's *The Ethical Canary: Science, Society and the Human Spirit* (McGill-Queen's University Press, 2004). Particularly interesting is chapter 8, entitled "Operating on the body of the small boy. The ethical stakes of circumcision" (pages 201–216). These pages changed my mind on this question even before I read them, and then convinced me entirely. See also Moses Maimonides, *Guide for the Perplexed* (Dover Publications, 2000).

To return to the same Malek Chebel: he has given birth to a book with a most beautiful title, *Traité du raffinement* (Treatise on Refinement), Payot, in which he celebrates refinement as a Muslim art, when in fact it proceeds from pre-Islamic Arab culture. The fact that a few princely courts — Baghdad, Cordova, the Maghreb, Egypt — persisted (heedless of Koranic teachings) in their praise of perfume, jewels, precious stones, wine (again!), luxury, gastronomy, and homosexuality does not authorize us to conclude that Islam ever converted to hedonism! We might as well judge the nature of Marxist-Leninism solely on the basis of the daily life of Kremlin hierarchs during the Stalin years.

To gauge the extent of Islam's tolerant hedonism, induce shivers to run down your spine by reading *Jalons sur le chemin de la chasteté* (Landmarks on the Path of Chastity) by Abd Allah b.' Abd al-Rahman al Watban, followed by the work of 'Abd al'Aziz b'.' Abd Allah b. Baz, *Les dangers de la mixité dans le domaine du travail* (The Perils of Mingling the Sexes in the Workplace), al-Hadith Publications. And for Islam's tolerance of books that are neither the Koran nor religious, the reader will be gratified to consult Lucien X. Polastron's *Livres en feu* (Books in Flames), Denoël. There he will learn of the evolution of the Christian relish for autos-da-fé, from the fourth-century origins of the Christian totalitarian state to the (never abolished)

Index of Forbidden Books. The Jews have endured countless book burnings throughout their existence, but have never initiated a single one. There is an admirable synthesis in Anne-Marie Delcambre's *L'Islam des interdits* (The Islam of Prohibitions), Desclée de Brouwer, 2003. We owe the same author and publisher an excellent biography of the Prophet, *Muhammad,* published in 2003.

On the Vatican's relationship to intelligence (and hence to books), see Georges Minois's *L'Eglise et la science: histoire d'un malentendu* (The Church and Science: The Story of a Misunderstanding), Fayard, an extremely factual work, weltering in detail (two volumes where one would have sufficed . . .), totally free of theorizing or conceptualizing. To be read with an eye to Jean Steiman's *Richard Simon: les origines de l'exigèse biblique* (Richard Simon: The Origins of Biblical Exegeis), Editions d'Aujourd'hui. Richard Simon (seventeenth century) inserted intelligence into the reading of so-called holy texts, and in so doing angered Bossuet, the Oratorians, Port-Royal, the Benedictines, the Jesuits, the Jansenists, and the Protestants. All good reasons for making a hero of him. Also read Jean Rocchi, *L'irréductible: Giordano Bruno face à l'Inquisition* (The Diehard: Giordano Bruno Against the Inquisition), with a most bracing foreword by Marc Silbernstein, dynamic inspirer of the (militant-materialist) publisher Syllepse!

CHRISTIANITY

1

Flesh of an ectoplasm. Obviously, there are thousands of stories about Jesus . . . Those that deny his historical existence and reduce this figure to the crystallization of a fiction are, on the other hand, extremely rare. Of course . . . The most famous of these is from the pen of Prosper Alfaric, *A l'école de la raison: étude sur les origines chrétiennes* (The School of Reason: A Study of Christian Origins), Publications de l'Union rationaliste. See in particular pages 97–200, "The problem of Jesus. Did Jesus exist?" The answer: no. Today, Raoul Vaneigem defends this position, making it his own in *La résistance au christianisme: les hérésies des origines au XVIIIe siècle* (Resistance to Christianity: Heresies from the Beginnings to the Eighteenth Century), Fayard. He mentions in particular, on page 104, "the Catholic and Roman fable of a historical Jesus." Unambiguous . . .

Others admittedly believe in his historical existence, but in their lengthy tomes they identify thousands of improbabilities, uncertainties, inconsistencies, and countertruths in the Bible. They assert so many reasons for rejecting certainties that one wonders what prevents them from crowding into the camp of the deniers. Caution? Inability to take responsibility for this major act of iconoclasm? Inability to leave behind them their intellectual training (often they are former seminary students or people with a solid theological background)? For there is the thickness of a cigarette paper between their conclusions and those of the ultras.

Thus Charles Guignebert, *Jésus* (La Renaissance du livre, 1933) and *Le Christ* (same publisher, 1943), to whom I am indebted for several examples I have quoted to stress the excesses of the New Testament — the *titulus*, the language used by Pilate, and so forth. Gérard Mordillat and Jérôme Prieur have made a synthesis of this labor, fleshed out by a few rare recent works, in their *Corpus Christi: enquête sur l'écriture des Evangiles* (Corpus Christi: An Inquiry into the Gospel Writings), five small volumes issued by Mille et Une Nuits in 1997: *Crucifuxion* (Crucifixion), *Procès* (Trial), *Roi des Juifs* (King of the Jews), *Pâques* (Easter), *Résurrection* (Resurrection), and *Christos*. Twelve films distributed by Arte were based on these works by Prieur, *Jésus illustre et inconnu* (Jesus, Illustrious and Unknown), Desclée de Brouwer, 2001, and Mordillat, *Jésus contre Jésus* (Jesus against Jesus), Seuil.

2

God's weakling. It was he who said it . . . Saint Paul . . . in the First Epistle to the Corinthians (15:8). For all the texts on or by Paul, Epistles, Letters, Acts, etc., see *La Bible* (the Bible), translated by Osty, Seuil, 1973. A rich bibliography of course. And not invariably partial . . . Fayard Publications have a reputation for seriousness. This being so, how can we take the work wholly seriously when we read (from the pen of Françoise Baslez) the following detail from the chapter on Paul's conversion on the road to Damascus: "he would never make the slightest allusion to the possibility of blindness" — and then read in the Acts of the Apostles (9:8): "and when his eyes were opened, he saw no man" (and this for three whole days)?

In his television mode (you hear him as you read him), Alain Decaux has committed *Un avorton de Dieu: une vie de Saint Paul* (God's Weakling:

A Life of Saint Paul), Desclée de Brouwer, 2003. The historian does not hide his Catholic loyalties, but he performs an honest task of compilation, particularly on the diseases attributed to the Tarsiot (page 101). Useful because it relieves one of the burden of doing the necessary reading on one's 'own behalf. No criticisms, no reservations, no personal interpretations, but a good introductory narrative.

Alain Badiou, philosopher, mathematician, Lacanian, novelist, and playwright, and also an extreme left-wing militant, confesses in his *Saint Paul: la fondation de l'universalisme* (Saint Paul: The Foundation of Universalism), PUF, 1997, to his interest (which we share) in the religion-founder, the empire-builder. A shame that he considers Paul as standing alone in this role, without incorporating into his argument what Constantine added in order to make the planetary Church a possibility. The ectoplasm needed the hysteric in order to become flesh, but it was the dictator who managed the extension of Jesus's body to the whole empire.

3

Portrait of an era. To comprehend the psychological atmosphere of the Late Empire, its belief in mystery, the miraculous, in images, astrology, its religion, its structural flaws, its taste for the irrational, read E. R. Dodds, *Pagan and Christian in an Age of Anxiety* (Cambridge University Press, 1991). And consult H. I. Marrou, *Décadence romaine ou Antiquité tardive?* (Roman Decadence or the Survival of Antiquity?), Seuil, 1977, which establishes the survival of the ancient world into the early Christian period. It is in this book that we encounter the expression "Totalitarian State of the Late Empire" (page 172). Marrou, a Christian, wrote among other subjects about Augustine, Clement of Alexandria, and the history of the Church. On the world and the workings of paganism under Christian persecution, read Ramsay MacMullen's *Paganism in the Roman Empire* (Yale University Press, 1983), and A. J. Fustigière's *Hermétisme et mystique païenne* (Pagan Alchemy and Mysticism), Aubier-Montaigne, 1967. Gibbon — the English Michelet — wrote with authentic relish about antiquity in his *History of the Decline and Fall of the Roman Empire*.

For downwardly adjusted figures on the number of Christian victims of martyrdom and other persecutions (before they themselves became the persecutors), see Claude Lepelley, *L'Empire romain et le christianisme*

(The Roman Empire and Christianity), Flammarion, 1969. Catholic historiography has substantially inflated these figures for propaganda purposes — motivated in this case, as in others, by apologetic aims.

4

The soldier convert. For a portrait of the tyrant, read Guy Gauthier, *Constantin: le triomphe de la croix* (Constantine: The Cross Triumphant, France-Empire, 1999). He expounds at great length the hypothesis of an astronomical (and therefore rigorously scientific) interpretation of the apparition Constantine saw, and his arguments are convincing. Making no concessions, but free of recrimination, it is a work that takes every position into consideration. Oddly enough, the face of the first emperor converted to Christianity has inspired little writing in France. André Pigagniol's venerable book *L'Empereur Constantin* (The Emperor Constantine), Rieder, 1932 remains a mine of information that has not aged.

A *Que sais-je?* synthesis by Bertrand Lançon, *Constantin* (Constantine), PUF, 1998, is useful. And in the same collection one might profitably read Pierre Maraval's *L'Empereur Justinien* (The Emperor Justinian), 1999, on the continuation of the work of the emperor touched by grace.

5

Christian vandalism. I have long sought proofs of Christian persecution of pagans. Many works remain silent, deny the facts, and even transform the new wielders of power into tolerant, likable, genial figures, book lovers, builders of libraries . . . I say nothing about works (easily the most numerous) that actively promote such commonplace fantasies. To find real traces of persecutions, of autos-da-fé, destruction of temples, statues, sacred groves, and bonfires, I have delved into the following:

First the ancient authors. Julian, that paladin of paganism who resisted (in vain, alas) the Christianization of the empire, wrote *Against the Galileans: An Imprecation Against Christianity.* Celsus, another pagan standard-bearer, published *Against the Christians.* The book itself was destroyed but was immortalized by Origen, who refuted Celsus's arguments and quoted from the book so extensively that its essentials have survived! Louis Rogier's *Celse contre les chrétiens* (Celsus Against the

Christians), Le Labyrinthe, 1997, also addresses the question of Christian vandalism. Porphyry's *Against Christians* went up in flames — we know nothing about the book, except that it was a major loss. And finally, there was Libanius's lamentation addressed to Emperor Theodosius I, *Against the Desecration of Pagan Temples.*

See also Julius Firmicus Maternus's *The Error of Pagan Religions* (XVI-XXIV), and Sozomen, Socrates, and Theodoret, *Histoire ecclésiastique tripartite* (Three-Part Ecclesiastical History), personal translation: Laure Chavel. And Saint John Chrysostom's *Homily on Statues* (1), in Robert Joly, *Origines et évolution de l'intolérance catholique* (Origins and Evolution of Catholic Intolerance), Ed. Université de Bruxelles, 1986. These texts (my thanks to Laure Chavel for her invaluable library work) describe Christian exactions in detail. Yet strangely, historians make no use of their labors in order to show how Christianity was really manufactured — by force, the sword, blood, and terror.

Nor does anyone read the *Codex Theodosianus.* Books XVI and IX, translated by Elisabeth Magnou-Nortier (Cerf, 2002), legitimize all Christian exactions against the pagans: executions, police brutality, creation of a class of citizens not shielded by the law, ban on employment in a judicial capacity, and withdrawal of all protection . . . A blueprint for America's future black codes and Vichy's anti-Semitic laws — or how justice may establish laws that exclude a section of the population — pagans the day before yesterday, American blacks and the Jews only yesterday.

See the passages describing these exactions in Pierre Chuvin's *Chronique des derniers païens: la disparition du paganisme dans l'Empire romain, du règne de Constantin à celui de Justinien* (Belles Lettres-Fayard, 1991), translated into English as *A Chronicle of the Last Pagans,* translated by B. A. Archer (Harvard University Press, 1990). See also Pierre de Labriolle's *La réaction païenne: étude sur la polémique antichrétienne du Ier au Vie siècle* (The Pagan Reaction: Study of Anti-Christian Argument from the First to the Sixth Centuries), Durand Publications, 1954. Read Robin Lane-Fox's *Pagans and Christians* (Penguin, 2006). These works salvage the honor of a profession otherwise unanimous in its silence on Christian vandalism.

6

Patrological mush. With the advent of Christianity, philosophy became the handmaiden of theology, and theology became a discipline of glossing and cross-glossing. Philosophizing now became a labor of commentary on biblical texts and of hairsplitting over details in the creation of a world of pure abstractions and disembodied concepts. When this was not the case, the authors of the Greek and Roman patrology constructed a morality based on the ascetic ideal, obsessed with hatred of the body, of desires, of passions and physical drives, and praise of celibacy, of continence, and of chastity.

C. Mondésert provides a good introduction to this world in his *Pour lire les Pères de l'Eglise dans les sources chrétiennes* (Reading the Church Fathers in Christian Sources), Foi Vivante, 1979, as does Jean-Yves Leloup in *Introduction aux "vrais philosophes." Les Pères grecs: un continent oublié de la pensée occidentale* (Introduction to the "True Philosophers": The Greek Fathers — Forgotten Continent of Western Thought), Albin Michel, 1998. Indeed they do proclaim themselves "true philosophers," but ignorance of their names and their writings is equaled only by their real and effective penetration of daily life over the centuries. We live with a Christian body they themselves manufactured.

THEOCRACY

1

Totalitarianisms, fascisms, and other brutalities. Hannah Arendt's work is of course incontrovertible: see *The Origins of Totalitarianism* (Harvest Books, new edition, 1973). Then there is Emilio Gentile's *Qu'est-ce que le fascisme?* (What Is Facism?), translated by P. E. Dauzat (Folio). The original Italian title is closer to *Fascism: History and Interpretation*, but the formatting of this collection belies the naming of a work that functions less as an introduction than the publisher would have us believe. Perhaps we can now set aside the squabbling of historians — which even emboldens some of them to exclude Vichy from the roster — who are still unable to agree on a definition of the phenomenon.

Less conventional is Jean Grenier's excellent and premonitory book *Essai sur l'esprit d'orthodoxie* (Essay on the Spirit of Orthodoxy), Idées Gallimard, which as far back as 1938 said everything worth knowing on the subject, and which France's New Philosophers picked up forty years later — Nazism, Hiroshima, not to mention May '68 — without ever actually mentioning Grenier's book. An equally indispensable addition to the reading list is Karl Popper's *The Open Society and Its Enemies*, volume 1: *The Spell of Plato*, volume 2: *The High Tide of Prophecy: Hegel, Marx, and the Aftermath* (Routledge, 2002). Here again, France's New Philosophers were quick to jump on the bandwagon.

2

Specific terrors. Yves-Charles Zarka and Cynthia Fleury, *Difficile tolérance* (The Challenge of Tolerance), PUF, 2004. Read it for Cynthia Fleury's convincing analysis which concludes that "Islam possesses no real equivalent of tolerance" and for her highly pertinent demonstration of the Islamic institution of "dhimmitude." However, Zarka's concept of *structure-tolérance* is much less persuasive. Read also Christian Delacampagne's *Islam et Occident: les raisons d'un conflit* (Islam and the West: Grounds for Dispute), PUF, an analysis that assumes the military and political success of the Americans in Iraq. A fine example of the rhetoric of French intellectuals and their predictable conclusions. From the same author come two practical syntheses: *Une histoire du racisme* (A History of Racism), and *Une histoire de l'esclavage* (A History of Slavery), both from Livre de Poche. Terse and telling observations on slavery and the Old Testament, and then on Christianity. More worthwhile is Peter Garnsey's *Ideas of Slavery from Aristotle to Augustine* (Cambridge University Press, 1997). An unsurpassed and indispensable labor on colonialism is Louis Sala-Molins's *Le Code noir ou le calvaire de Canaan* (The Black Code or Canaan's Martyrdom), PUF Quadrige — shattering for the Church, the French monarchy, and for the West as a whole.

A most interesting and dense little work is strategic expert Jean-Paul Charnay's *La Charía et l'Occident* (Sharia and the West), L'Herne. By the same author: *L'Islam et la guerre: de la guerre juste à la révolution sainte* (Islam and War: From Just War to Holy Revolution), Fayard, 1986, and then volume 3 of his *Classiques de la stratégie: principes de stratégie arabe* (Classics of Strategy: Arab Strategic Principles), L'Herne, 1984. The possibility of change in Islam is most cautiously envisaged . . . for a few centuries hence.

To speed this process of change and avoid waiting for ten centuries, Malek Chebel proposes a *Manifeste pour un Islam des Lumières: vingt-sept propositions pour reformer l'Islam* (Manifesto for an Enlightened Islam: Twenty-Seven Proposals for Islamic Reform), Hachette. In a word: if Islam were not Islam it would be much easier to defend! For what else would a feminist Islam *be* — democratic, secular, egalitarian, individualistic, tolerant, acquiescent in the rules of the game, etc. — but the opposite of what it actually, fundamentally *is*? To defend the Western virtues listed above, we have no need of a book and a tradition that have always condemned them. Jettisoning references to the Koran and Hadith seems an infinitely preferable way to bring off Malek Chebel's Enlightenment project!

3

Christian crimes. Georges Minois, *L'Eglise et la guerre: de la Bible à l'ère atomique* (The Church and War: From the Bible to the Atomic Age), Fayard. Rather long, occasionally padded, losing itself in details, short on analysis, factual, even slightly partial in places. Nothing for example on the blessing bestowed by Father George Zabelka on the crew of the *Enola Gay* before it destroyed Hiroshima. I came across that detail in Théodore Monod's *Le chercheur d'absolu* (Seeking the Absolute), Actes Sud, page 89. I learned from the same Théodore Monod (page 93) that the Catholic Church only abandoned use of the Sedia — the royal and papal throne borne on human backs — during the papacy of John XXIII.

On colonialism, read Michael Prior, a priest trained by the Vincentians: *The Bible and Colonialism: A Moral Critique* (Sheffield, 1997). The question of colonialism, slavery, and the trade in African blacks as practiced by Muslims has generated little work. Read Jacques Heers, *Les négriers en terre d'Islam: la première traite des Noirs, VIIe–XVIe siècles* (Slave Traders in Islamic Lands: The First Enslavement of Blacks, Seventh to Sixteenth Centuries), Perrin, 2003. He offers justifications for this rarely mentioned historical episode that fit well with the French talent for self-flagellation and self-denigration. Surely there are better motives for the writing of history?

On Rwanda: Jean-Damiscène Bizimana, *L'Eglise et le génocide au Rwanda: les Pères blancs et le négationnisme* (The Church and the Rwanda Genocide: White Priests and Denial), L'Harmattan, 2001. A pity this publishing house does not take its editorial obligations more seriously: the few factual errors that crop up here and there could be exploited — wrongly — to invalidate the book's unimpeachable theses. Read also the excellent book by Jean Hatzfeld, *Une saison de machettes* (Seuil, 2003), translated into English by Linda Coverdale as *Machete Season:The Killers in Rwanda Speak* (Picador, 2006). It is a masterpiece to be classed alongside the work of Primo Levi or Robert Antelme. Note the chapter entitled "And God in All This?" By the same author: *Dans le nu de la vie: récits des marais rwandais* (Seuil, 2000), translated into English by Gerry Feehily as *Into the Quick of Life: The Rwandan Genocide* — *The Survivors Speak* (Trans-Atlantic, 2005).

The Inquisition has generated a substantial number of books. Among them: Joseph Pérez, *Brève histoire de l'Inquisition en Espagne* (Fayard, 2002), translated into English by Janet Lloyd as *The Spanish Inquisition:A History* (Yale University Press, 2006). Same proliferation for the Crusades: see Albert Dupront's two volumes, *Le mythe de croisade* (The Crusader Myth), Gallimard. On Christian-Muslim relations: John V. Tolan, *Saracens* (Columbia University Press, 2002).

4

Swastika and crucifix. We know of the relationship between the Vatican and National Socialism from the works of Saul Friedlander, *Pius XII and the Third Reich: A Documentation* (Knopf, 1966); and of Daniel Jonah Goldhagen, *Moral Duty:The Role of the Catholic Church in the Holocaust and Its Unfulfilled Duty of Repair* (Vintage, 2003). Unanswerable. Difficult for the Church to respond to this mass of proven facts, opinions, analyses, etc.

Less well known is Hitler's defense of Jesus, of the Christ, of Christianity, of the Church ... A reading of *Mein Kampf* suffices to confirm the führer's fascination with the story of Jesus driving the moneylenders from the Temple, and his admiration for the Church's success in building a European and even a worldwide civilization. The book exists, but who reads this text that everyone talks about but no one has ever opened? (Mariner Books paperback, Houghton Mifflin, translated by Ralph Manheim). Pay special attention to page 307 in volume 1, and to pages 114–120, 307, 454, and 459 in volume 2.

These Hitlerian assertions are confirmed by the chancellor's private remarks. Albert Speer, for example, comments on Hitler's devotion to Christianity and its Church. He also notes the führer's frustration at having no one of high caliber at the head of the Church with whom he might discuss "making the evangelical Church the official Church." See Speer's *Inside the Third Reich* (Simon & Schuster, 1970).

5

Zionism: up front and backstage. Theodor Herzl's Zionist project is of enduring interest to contemporary readers. See *The Jewish State* (originally *Der Judenstaat*, translated by Sylvie D'Avigdor, Dover Publications, 1989). In it we learn that for Herzl, Palestine was not a fixation: he notes that the choice of a homeland could also have fallen on Argentina and that the Jews would have to take what was offered them. The social blueprint was impeccable: work (a seven-hour day), organization, constitution, language (not Hebrew but all languages, with one of them eventually emerging on top), legal system, flag (white with seven gold stars), armed forces (an exclusively professional army quartered in barracks), theocracy (absolutely not: religious leaders would be banned from political activities), tolerance, freedom of belief, of conviction, and of religious denomination. On the acquisition of land, no question of brutal invasion but the auctioning off of property. All this seemed idyllic indeed. Why then the persistent silence over his *Diary*? In particular over Herzl's entry for June 12, 1895: "We must use persuasion in expropriating the land granted to us. We must strive discreetly to send the poorer population into neighboring lands, procuring work for them in transit countries without providing it for them here. The landowners will be on our side ... " Quoted by Michael Prior, op. cit.

6

The philosopher and the Ayatollah. The *Politico-Spiritual Testament* of the Ayatollah Khomeini is a manual for every Islamic government, every Muslim theocracy. Essential reading and material for reflection.

Michel Foucault commented on this Iranian revolution in a series of articles commissioned by the *Corriere della Sera*. These articles have been reprinted in *Dits et écrits* (Comments and Writings), volume 3, 1976–1979. The reader cannot fail to be struck by the pages in which he hails the ayatollah as the spirit of the Iranian people and the return of the spiritual element to politics (which he appears to welcome), the pages in which he refers to the abolition of a tainted regime (about which, on the contrary, he seems lucid and well-informed), and the pages in which he announces the birth of Islamic resistance to globalization — on whose looming implications he conjectures most presciently.

His texts deserve better than his polemics: blind Foucault/heroic Foucault; Foucault the ayatollah's henchman/Foucault the infallible. That a man like Foucault (who that same year was working at the Collège de France on the birth of biopower and who could excel in textual analysis) could at the same time be so wrong in the analysis of facts — that is something for historians of philosophy to consider! We will read with fresh eyes his famous text entitled "Les 'reportages' d'idées" (The Transference of Ideas) pages 706–707.

7

A post-Christian secularism. For an account of those pioneering moments of secularism in history, read Jacqueline Lalouette, *La libre-pensée en France, 1848–1940* (Free Thinking in France, 1848–1940), Albin Michel. A survey by a historian who brings to light a substantial number of facts on the subject. Reading this book encourages us to ponder the kind of secularism that may prove more effective in confronting the challenges of the twenty-first century — challenges that are no longer the purely domestic ones involved in the fight for separation of church and state. The work still has to be done — and it is now of planetary concern.

Whence the interest of postmodern (and therefore post-Christian) secular thinking. Among a timely range of works on the subject, see the labor of synthesis by Henri Pena-Ruiz, *Qu-est-ce que la laïcité?* (What is Secularism?), Folio. Since he advocates a definition of benevolent neutrality in the terms of France's Third Republic, yet simultaneously defends the notion that the concept of secularism is also part and parcel of republican values (page 97), it is hard to see how he can defend these values at the same time as he defends monotheism — which substantially contradicts them. His well-founded analysis of the sects he debars from secular tolerance (page 98) and of the "charlatans who promise happiness on the cheap and try to subject men to an almost infantile quest for readymade recipes and solutions" (a definition that strikes me as applicable to every religion without exception) could profitably be expanded. Which would contribute enormously to the definition of a post-Christian secularism!